SECRETS OF THE
SOMMELIERS

CELLAR, DOMAINE DUJAC

SECRETS OF THE
SOMMELIERS

HOW TO THINK AND DRINK LIKE
THE WORLD'S TOP WINE PROFESSIONALS

RAJAT PARR AND **JORDAN MACKAY**

FOREWORD BY DREW NIEPORENT

PHOTOGRAPHS BY ED ANDERSON

TEN SPEED PRESS

BERKELEY

CONTENTS

Wine and sommeliers have been a big part of my life since I opened Montrachet, my first restaurant, in 1985. In those days, you seldom found restaurants that focused on wine, and ones that employed full-time sommeliers were even less common. But a growing group of us knew that more important than just good wine or good food was the combination of the two.

Then as now, good food is essential to a successful restaurant, and I was lucky enough and smart enough to hire a young David Bouley as chef. But by naming my first restaurant after the greatest white wine in the world, I was also declaring that wine was going to be a huge part of what we did. So Daniel Johnnes, who joined the staff as a waiter with both an interest and an expertise in wine, quickly became a crucial part of Montrachet.

At the beginning, our resources for purchasing wine were limited, so we assembled a carefully chosen selection of sixty American and French wines. Because the food at Montrachet was affordable (the opening menus were sixteen dollars and twenty-seven dollars), and the environment was casual, people were comfortable splurging a little on wine. As the restaurant's popularity grew, the wine program under Daniel became equally celebrated. He was passionate, he spoke French, he knew food, he was developing relationships with winemakers in France. He was, in short, becoming a sommelier, and a model one at that. Over the past twenty-five years, Daniel has become one of the world's most important wine personalities, and he has helped define the role of sommelier for a generation.

It has been my job to recognize potentially great sommeliers and give them a platform, and I have been blessed with a knack for identifying that talent. Twenty years ago, I hired David Gordon, fresh out of Cornell Hotel School, who crafted and remains the guiding spirit behind the world-class wine list at the Tribeca Grill. Soon after, I had the opportunity to work with Larry Stone, who, in addition to his wine responsibilities, was my partner (with Robert De Niro, Francis Ford Coppola, and Robin Williams) at San Francisco's Rubicon.

Larry also has an extraordinarily keen eye for young talent. At Rubicon, he brought in dozens of aspiring wine professionals who now illuminate the San Francisco wine scene. Perhaps the most talented of these sommeliers was Rajat Parr. He absorbed Larry's wisdom like a sponge, spending countless hours expanding his knowledge. (Interestingly, a young Michael Mina—now Rajat's partner and employer—also worked at the Tribeca Grill. If I were a truly gifted talent scout, I would have made him my partner, and would be considerably richer today for the decision.) What has driven all of these people is passion. And in the wine world, if you do not have passion, you will be left behind.

One skill that is indispensable in a successful sommelier is the ability to make wine accessible. When I am in a restaurant, I want the wine experience to be informative. Wine is all about the story: where it comes from and who made it, what makes it different from other wines, why it tastes the way it does, and, most important, why it is the right wine at that time. Sommeliers have to be informed, and they have to be able to translate that knowledge with passion and conviction to customers. Rajat does that brilliantly, and now with this book, he is able to impart his remarkable wisdom to others. It has been a pleasure to watch him grow and evolve over his career, and his expertise, coupled with Jordan Mackay's writing and Ed Anderson's photography, makes this book an incredible read.

In the following pages, the rarefied art of the sommelier is made accessible, and it is done with great passion. Those are two of the qualities I look out for in any sommelier I hire, and it is only fitting that they are the two defining qualities of this book.

Drew Nieporent

MYRIAD RESTAURANT GROUP (CORTON, TRIBECA GRILL, NOBU, CENTRICO, CRUSH WINE & SPIRITS)

Being a sommelier is not my job. It's my life. From the moment I wake up each day, there is never a time when I am not thinking about wine (unless I am playing squash or watching my beloved Lakers play). Tasting wine, talking about wine, thinking about food and cooking, making reservations for guests, poring over sales figures—I enjoy every minute of it.

As someone who is fully wrapped up in what he does, I have two major impulses. I want to share my passion for wine with as many people as I can, and I want to relate to other sommeliers who share my drive and learn from them. This book has allowed me to indulge both desires. Here I have expressed my thoughts and tastes as honestly and as straightforwardly as I can. In working on the book, I have also had the good fortune to have spent amazing time with many of my most revered colleagues. Hopefully, the result is as valuable to the reader as it has been to me.

I realize that the rarity, cost, and inaccessibility of some of the wines discussed in the following pages will make it difficult, if not impossible, for many people to taste them. It is not necessary to taste these bottles to have a fierce passion for wine and to build confidence in your own palate, however. If anything, my tastes have become simpler and humbler as I have grown older. Wine is a journey, and we each have our path. My journey is ongoing, and my hope is that our paths will cross. No doubt it will be in the presence of wine.

R. P.

I first met some of the people featured in this book almost ten years ago, while writing a magazine article about sommeliers in San Francisco. At the time, I barely knew what the word meant, nor did I foresee how central to my life sommeliers would become. In the course of one week of interviews, I encountered Rajat Parr, Larry Stone, and Christie Dufault. A few years later, I was marrying Christie on a hilltop in Sonoma, Larry was officiating at the ceremony, and Rajat was sabering a magnum of Bollinger RD 1995 to kick off the celebration.

Being granted entry to the sommelier world has been a curious and wonderful turn in my life. I have learned a lot about wine, of course, but I have also had the opportunity to observe a group of people who are as driven and passionate about their profession as any I have ever encountered. Theirs is an intriguing and rarefied subculture into which this book is a window.

Rajat and I decided that most of the book should be in the third person, so that he could be both character and source. As such, he can be observed as a sommelier in the context of his world, and at the same time provide insight through the main body of the text. The one deviation is the appendix, where Rajat shares his thoughts on the wines that mean the most to him. In the spirit in which Rajat and his colleagues practice their art, it is a highly selective document, rather than one that surveys the entire wine world with equal attention.

J.M.

MANUEL PEYRONDET, NAMED MEILLEUR SOMMELIER DE FRANCE 2008, AT LE BRISTOL, PARIS

CHAPTER ONE

WHAT IS A SOMMELIER?

Several years ago, on a cool November evening, a couple—a young man and his wife—dropped into Michael Mina, one of San Francisco's top fine-dining restaurants. Tucked in the crook of the man's right arm, underneath his folded coat, was a half-drunk bottle of wine in a brown paper bag.

The guests were aware that showing up at a high-end restaurant with an open wine bottle simply isn't done. But they were regulars, known by the staff to be serious wine drinkers, and their action wasn't questioned. They had purchased the bagged bottle at a restaurant where they had just eaten dinner, and because they thought the wine was particularly good, they wanted Rajat Parr, Michael Mina's wine director, to taste it. His pronouncement on its quality would confirm or deny their own less-confident conclusions.

It was a busy night as usual at Michael Mina. The well-dressed clientele clustered around the bar, and waiters going to and from the kitchen picked their way through the crowd. Pouncing on some chairs freed by an exiting party, the couple sat down and waited for Rajat to notice them.

"We have something for you to taste," the man said, flashing the package at Rajat when he eventually headed their way. Rajat understood immediately: in the sommelier world, a bottle in a brown bag is the universal signal that the wine is to be tasted blind. Recognizing the challenge, Rajat reflexively raised his hands in a defensive gesture.

"Oh, I don't know," he said, shaking his head. "I've got a cold. Been congested for a couple of days." He was wearing a beautifully cut, dark gray suit that made his bulk seem elegant and distinguished. While a sharply cut suit is the favored attire for today's fine-dining sommelier, Rajat does not have the bearing that most people associate with a celebrated wine star. His large, round head is bald, his skin light brown, almost sallow. When compelled to sustain mindless chitchat, his face can seem dark and expressionless, his mind elsewhere. He sometimes mumbles, creating the impression that he lacks confidence in what he is saying.

But when the subject turns to wine, Rajat's mien undergoes a transformation. At the mention of a seemingly innocuous word like Pinot, one can almost hear the whoosh of a pilot light being ignited inside that bald head. His face becomes suddenly animated, and he begins to gesture with his hands. As the conversation gathers momentum, his head rocks gently forward and back, as if he is having a vision. When he makes a point, he raises his right hand, fingers slowly separating, and his body rises a couple of inches off the ground. And then, poised to deliver his conclusion on the wine, his once-opaque eyes widen and begin to radiate. Finally, Rajat, lifting his eyebrows, exclaims something encapsulating, such as, "And that, my friends, is why they call it *Grand Cru*!"

Yet, on this night, he didn't want to taste the wine, didn't feel up to the test. But the couple cajoled, and ultimately Rajat couldn't resist the challenge. He grabbed a wineglass from behind the bar, and the man poured a couple of ruby ounces into it. Rajat swirled the wine around in the Burgundy bowl, tilting it into the incandescent light of the bar for a better look.

2

He sniffed a couple of times, holding the glass at different angles under his nose. His eyes closed and then reopened.

"I'm not sure," he said, almost to himself. "Volnay perhaps. Premier Cru." He had yet to take a sip. He then reared his head back and tipped the glass toward his mouth, taking in a good-sized gulp. After a swish and a swallow, he was silent as the taste of the wine sat on his tongue, slowly dissipating. Then he gently rolled his head from side to side as if he were receiving a stream of information from above and coiling it like a rope in his brain.

"So what is it?" the man asked.

"Hmm," Rajat said, almost stalling. "I'll say Volnay Premier Cru 1998."

"That's all?" the man prodded, beginning to nod his head. "You're not going to tell me who made the wine?"

"I'm sick."

The man peeled off the brown bag, revealing the wine: 1998 Volnay Premier Cru. "Lafarge," his wife said. "Clos des Chênes," citing the producer and the exact vineyard.

"Ach," Rajat cried, suddenly animated. "I was going to say Lafarge!" Not that it was necessary. The couple was more than impressed. Through congested nasal passages and with a dulled palate, Rajat had identified the grape variety, the country of origin, and the region precisely to a village of only eight hundred people in eastern France, as well as the wine's designation (Premier Cru) and the year in which it was made—a volume of information divined by the briefest interaction between nose, mouth, and wine. Had he been more on his game, he might have mentioned the name of the thirty-eight-acre plot where the grapes were grown—Clos des Chênes—and the producer, Frédéric Lafarge, whose hands worked that soil.

Since that night, the couple has gotten to know Rajat much better and has seen him perform such feats with regularity. Hundreds of people have. Indeed, Rajat is celebrated for his unerring blind tasting, much as a math prodigy might be revered for the ability to calculate the square roots of large integers on demand.

To be able to blind taste with such precision is a rare talent, a skill that many gifted people practice intensively, yet never master. How great tasters recognize vintages, vineyards, and vintners in a glass of fermented grape juice is a mystery. When Rajat tastes a wine, it is as if he is reading code that others cannot decipher, hearing sounds that other ears don't pick up.

Although blind tasting at the level Rajat and his peers practice it cannot be fully taught, it is a skill that can be developed. Young wine directors and future sommeliers around the world practice blind tasting every night in their restaurants and in their off-hours. Of course, it is largely a parlor trick and serves no practical function in a restaurant. However, a good blind taster demonstrates the palate sensitivity and wine fluency one expects to find in an effective buyer and seller of wine. And, as a parlor trick, nailing a wine as Rajat did that night is one of the more impressive things a sommelier can do—a talent that brings acclaim and prestige to both the individual and the restaurant that employs him or her.

THE SOMMELIER THROUGHOUT TIME

The question Rajat is asked most often is, how do I become a sommelier? But the second most asked is, what is a sommelier? Despite the growing status of the profession, many people outside of wine circles have never heard the term.

The history of the word *sommelier* as it applies to wine is murky. Although it is generally agreed that some form of wine service dates back to Greek or Roman times, the role of wine server was not formalized until the Middle Ages. According to *A Historical Perspective of the Art of the Sommelier,* an article by British master sommelier David M. Johnson, the word *sommelier* evolved from the French *sommier,* which itself evolved from various terms referring to cargo, the animals transporting said cargo, and the people in charge of those animals. As Johnson explains, *sommelier* was used to identify people in charge of specific classes of items, such as weapons and food. The term eventually came to mean a servant in charge of the wine.

The restaurant as we know it in the West first appeared in the late eighteenth century, and with it arrived a form of wine service, a custom that until then had been enjoyed only by the highborn. With the growth of the merchant class in the nineteenth century, the business of restaurants began to take off and with it the importance of wine service.

In France, the job of sommelier was not initially vested with the sheen of glamour it enjoys today. As wine writer Michael Steinberger, author of *Au Revoir to All That*, a book about fine-dining culture in France, wrote in *Slate*, "Many French sommeliers came to the job not by choice but by conscription, and the position has usually been a life sentence. In France, the sommelier was often someone who entered the restaurant trade as a barely pubescent teen with dreams of becoming a chef (and no prospect of attending university). Then, deemed unworthy of a place at the stove, our man (and it was always a man) got shunted off to the wine cellar, where he was condemned to spend the rest of his working days in the shadow of the egomaniacal prick who beat him out in the kitchen." Consequently, the reputation of French sommeliers for surliness and hauteur has a basis in reality: "Condescension and humorlessness have long been defining features of French wine service," Steinberger writes.

Judging by early mentions of the occupation in the *New York Times*, Americans in Paris found sommeliers neither trustworthy nor necessary. An 1887 item complaining about the bill at Bignon's, a well-known Parisian restaurant, noted that, among a litany of other criticisms, "one could desire . . . above all the limitation of the privilege which the sommelier enjoys of recommending certain wines on which, it is to be presumed, he gets a commission." A 1921 rant titled "A Bas Le Sommelier!"(Down with the Sommelier!) in the same newspaper cried, "The wage earners in question are those strange employees, infesting the better class restaurants of Paris, who are known as 'sommeliers.' . . . He is the incarnation of a pernicious principle. . . . It became perfectly clear to me that my duty, as a patriotic American, was to try

4

to put the 'sommelier' out of business before he spreads, octopus-like, to Broadway. A bas le sommelier!"

Of course, such harsh opinions eventually softened. In the decades following World War II, sommeliers slowly began to appear in the United States in a few high-end French restaurants. And by the late 1970s and the 1980s, they were making their way into less rarified, not-exclusively-French dining rooms. Today, as it has for centuries, the sommelier's core function remains the management of the wine cellar. But as the expertise of the sommelier has become more highly valued by the media and the public alike, the profile of the position has been elevated, especially in restaurants with ambitious wine programs. These newly respected professionals now make regular appearances on high-visibility tasting panels, such as Eric Asimov's *New York Times* panel, and on popular television shows, including Andrea Immer Robinson's *Simply Wine* on the Fine Living channel. And they are often featured in magazines like *Wine & Spirits* and *Food & Wine*. In 2008, they even got their own publication, *Sommelier Journal*.

FOUR PATHS

The elevation of the sommelier position in America remains in sharp contrast to its standing in France. "In the United States, you can run down a list of restaurants renowned not just for their wine program but also for the people running their wine program," says Michael Steinberger. "I can't think of a case in France where that's happened to the extent that it does here. Sommeliers there are not and never have been the main attractions at their restaurants."

Why has this elevation occurred in the United States? Is it simply a by-product of our celebrity-obsessed food culture? Perhaps. But it's also evidence of the efforts of a handful of groundbreaking sommeliers who worked to make sure wine was not overlooked during the country's now forty-year-old gastronomical revolution. As Steinberger put it in his *Slate* piece, these "pioneering figures . . . were all college-educated and came to wine out of passion, not because they were frog-marched into the bottle room. They saw their role as mainly pedagogical, an outlook perfectly tailored to a time when Americans were developing an interest in wine. They made wine service educational, and they made it fun. They also brought an entrepreneurial spirit to the work; rather than let the role of sommelier define them, they defined it."

The following brief histories relate the career paths of four of America's pioneering sommeliers, all of whom have had a significant impact on raising the profile of the profession. The foundation of Larry Stone's career was a knowledge of wine so encyclopedic that he seemed to have been born with it. Kevin Zraly's climb grew out of a compulsion to teach, to empower people through knowledge of wine. In the case of Daniel Johnnes, it was a love of two things—restaurants and French wine—that drove him down the path to become an important ambassador of both. Fred Dame's motivational and organizational skills led to a more formal establishment of the profession that has ultimately brought thousands into its embrace. Stone, the wine genius; Zraly, the wine teacher; Johnnes, the inspirer; and Dame, the administrator and motivator: together they mentored a generation.

LARRY STONE

"In Seattle, where I grew up in the 1950s and 1960s, there were two positions for sommeliers," recalls Larry Stone. "One was at the Olympic Hotel. They had a guy there who didn't know much about wine, really, but was very striking and very dramatic. He wore a red jacket and a turban, and they used to ring a big Chinese gong when he came out into the dining room with a bottle of wine, because the sommelier was called so rarely. The wine list was small, and he was famous because he would just recommend something like the Lafite or the Mouton or the Dom Pérignon."

Stone was a wine prodigy, having learned about it from books and from tasting with his parents at an early age. But because he possessed a celebrated intellect that encompassed far more than wine, he was headed toward a career in academia. Wine was only a passion and a hobby. Then, towards the end of his graduate school years—they totaled a remarkable eleven—a friend encouraged him to apply for an assistant sommelier position at what was then Seattle's top wine destination, the Red Cabbage.

During the job interview, the manager, a sommelier himself, asked Stone some basic wine questions, which he answered easily. His performance was enough to convince the manager to hire him, but the owner of the Red Cabbage was not sold. Two days later, Stone was asked to return for a second interview, which the imperious owner decided to conduct himself. Determined to stump Stone, the owner sat at a table with a copy of Alexis Lichine's seven-hundred-page encyclopedia of wine before him. Instead of working from a script of prepared questions, he flipped randomly through the book, paused to read, and then asked Stone a question from the entry. Some were easy, such as what level of growth in Bordeaux is Château Doisy-Daëne (second growth of Sauternes), or what is the major red variety used in the Hungarian wine Egri Bikavér (Kadarka). As Stone dispatched each question without hesitation, the owner became flustered. Finally, he asked the most obscure question he could find, "What is Gumpoldskirchen?"

Stone had the answer, and calmly explained what he knew about the Austrian village, its wines, and famous wine culture. At that, the restaurant owner closed the encyclopedia with a loud thump, sighed, and looked up at Stone. "Alright," he said, "I don't know where you

LARRY STONE

come from. Frankly, I took the last two days to have you checked out, even had an investigator look into whether you have any sort of record. He said he couldn't find anything on you. But, I gotta say, you left ten years off your résumé, so I had a feeling that you might have a record or you've done something wrong. You know a lot and are obviously suited for this job. So, if you have done something, please come clean now, because I can forgive a lot of things."

Stone said that he had been in graduate school for over a decade, a pursuit that failed to impress the owner. What did win him over was Stone's two-year stint as a dishwasher in a student café. On the strength of having worked a restaurant's most humble position, Stone was hired as an assistant sommelier.

Stone made his name at the Red Cabbage. As a teaching assistant in graduate school, he earned a paltry $3,600 a year. In his first year as a sommelier, he made $27,000. His salary was not huge, but tips from the wealthy people he turned on to good wine made a big difference. "We had fishermen coming into the restaurant off the boats from Alaska and ordering La Tâche or Lafite, because they were making more money than anyone in the workforce, more than Boeing engineers," he remembers. "They came in wearing jeans and muddy shoes and would say, 'Get us the best wine you've got.' And I'd say, okay, how about a Montrachet? Then, it was $120."

In 1984, Stone was recruited away by the Four Seasons Hotel. That was the year that his life would begin to change dramatically. One day, his boss called him into the office and told him that the next day he would be competing in a French wine competition held in the hotel. Stone explained that French wine wasn't his strength; his real expertise was in German, Austrian, and American wines. His boss wasn't sympathetic. "Well, you're competing tomorrow," he said.

Stone went home to study and then won the competition the next day, beating out the most knowledgeable people in the Seattle wine scene. This was the regional feeder contest for an international competition held every two years in Paris, at which the Best Sommelier in French Wines was named. The next year at the national competition, Stone was suffering from bronchitis and came in fourth. But he won nationally the following year, and in 1988 beat everyone to become the world's Best Sommelier in French Wines.

Stone's career from then on is well known. In 1989, he moved to Chicago to open up a Four Seasons, but was recruited away by Charlie Trotter, whose restaurant during Stone's tenure became America's most prestigious destination for food and wine. He was succeeded there by the great Joseph Spellman, another master sommelier. In 1994, Stone teamed up with Francis Ford Coppola to open Rubicon, a celebrated wine destination in San Francisco that became Stone's home base for years. It was here that he brought along an incredible slew of wine talent, including Rajat Parr. Today, Stone is the general manager of Coppola's Rubicon Estate winery in Napa.

8

Kevin Zraly, author of *Windows on the World Complete Wine Course,* the best-selling wine book in American history, is also known as the greatest wine teacher in America. His passion for both teaching and wine were forged at an early age. In 1970, when he was in his late teens, Zraly began working at the Depuy Canal House in upstate New York, which was unexpectedly reviewed by Craig Claiborne in the *New York Times.* Even more unexpectedly, it was a four-star review. With only four employees, the restaurant was overwhelmed by the resulting deluge, and young Zraly, forced into duty at the bar, had to educate himself about beer, spirits, and wine. On Mondays, he would travel to New York City to take the Grossman Beverage Program. On Tuesdays, he would take the same information back and teach it to a class of thirty-five adults. He was twenty years old.

It was during his days at Canal House that Zraly began seriously indulging his interest in wine. One restaurant customer with a particularly deep cellar introduced Zraly to some of the great wines of the world. "I was tasting Bordeaux from the 1800s," he said. "The greatest vintages—1921, '45, '59. It was amazing. I was a history major and I thought to myself, 'By god, this is history! And I can live it through wine.'"

Wine became the driving force in Zraly's life. "I didn't care about college, though I did graduate," he said. "My parents asked me to, that was the deal. 'If you want to do the wine thing,' they said, 'you've got to finish college.'" But between his sophomore and junior years he took a semester off and hitchhiked to California, where he checked out pretty much every winery that existed in 1973. After graduation, outfitted with a Eurail Pass, he spent a year in Europe, sleeping in hostels and visiting major regions from Bordeaux to Burgundy to Tuscany. "Did some of my girlfriends think I was nuts studying wine instead of being out having a great time with them?" he asked. "Yes, but that's what I had to do."

In 1976, Zraly was hired by Joe Baum, creator of the Four Seasons empire, to be the cellar master at a new restaurant, Windows on the World, in the World Trade Center. Baum was looking for a "young American," indicating a new direction in the field of restaurant wine. "I wasn't called a sommelier," recalls Zraly. "I was the cellar master. Joe Baum did not want the stuffy, red-cheeked sommelier who spoke French and intimidated people. I got the job and my job was cellar master." Zraly's list was famous for its diversity, a mix of both the traditional greats from France and Italy and obscure labels from places like Chile, Argentina, Yugoslavia, and South Africa.

"It was a lonely profession," says Zraly of being a sommelier in Manhattan at age twenty-six. "In New York, there were a few sommeliers, but they were much older, retired waiters. And they were exclusively in French restaurants. There was not one young person."

Unable to find a community of sommeliers, Zraly created his own. He was not given an assistant to help manage America's most famous and perhaps largest wine program, so

DANIEL JOHNNES

he taught everyone he could about wine, from waiters and busboys to cocktail waitresses and dishwashers. He continued as the titular wine director of Windows on the World until September 11, 2001. Despite that tragic loss, Zraly has not given up his calling. Begun over thirty years ago, his eight-week course, the Windows on the World Wine School, has graduated more than twenty thousand students and is still going strong (it's now taught at the Marriott in Times Square). Otherwise, he stays busy lecturing on wine around the world, including, in 1997, to a young prodigy at the Culinary Institute of America named Rajat Parr.

DANIEL JOHNNES

The seed that would become the sommelier was planted on Johnnes's first trip to France in 1974, with his family. He was nineteen and the seed would lie dormant for a number of years, until he started working as a busboy at the Landmark Tavern on 46th Street and 11th Avenue in Manhattan. It wasn't wine that first excited Johnnes's passions, but restaurants themselves. "The Landmark was a beer hall, but I fell in love with the energy inside a restaurant—the interaction between staff and customer, the conviviality and the team spirit," he says.

Between 1974 and 1981, Johnnes spent a great deal of time in France, going to school and also living with a family in Provence, only six miles from Châteauneuf-du-Pape, a region whose wines had not yet been widely discovered by outsiders. "I don't think Kermit Lynch had been there yet," recalls Johnnes, "and it was well before Peter Mayle wrote his book." During this period, Johnnes worked in a vineyard for the first time, and saw his first truffle.

In 1982, Johnnes returned to France to apprentice in the kitchen of Guy Savoy in Paris. Although not an experienced cook, he benefited from his time there, which he followed up with stints in a top Parisian bakery and in a professional kitchen in southwest France.

After two years of working for French chefs, Johnnes, missing the front-of-the-house energy that charges restaurant service, returned to the United States. An ad for a back waiter job in New York would change his life. The restaurant was Le Regence in the new Hôtel Plaza Athénée. The headwaiter was Drew Nieporent (his next and longest-lasting employer). The chef was Daniel Boulud (with whom he currently works).

Nieporent soon left to open what would be the first restaurant, Montrachet, of an empire that would grow to include Nobu, the Tribeca Grill, and more. Johnnes offered to help him get Montrachet off the ground. Since his return, Johnnes had been steadily fortifying the basic wine knowledge he gained in France with other jobs, including moonlighting at the wine merchant Acker Merrall & Condit under a man named Jerry Jacobson, whom he has called the "original Burgundy freak." Jacobson would be the first to take Johnnes to Burgundy, igniting a passion that in many ways defines Johnnes's career. However, in 1984, Jacobson would sell Johnnes his "epiphany" wine, and it wasn't a Burgundy.

11

"I said to Jerry," Johnnes recalls, "I gotta bring a nice wine to my mom's for Thanksgiving, and I don't want to spend more than thirty dollars—at the time, that was a pretty expensive bottle. So he sold me a bottle of Guigal Côte-Rôtie La Mouline 1976"—a bottle that today would cost at least a thousand dollars. "I had no idea. We drank it with the meal, and I was completely blown away. 'Nice turkey wine,' I thought. Everyone has one of those epiphanies that really pushes them into wine, and this was the trigger for me."

Montrachet ended up getting a great review and exploded. The first of a new breed of restaurants for New York, it featured excellent French food (from young chef David Bouley), good wine, and fine service, but in a fairly casual atmosphere. Noting its three stars in the *New York Times*, guests began to arrive with higher and higher expectations. Johnnes offered to take over management of the wine program. To better serve an ever-growing clientele, he expanded his wine knowledge through books and tasting groups and continued to visit French wine regions when possible. In short, he became a sommelier. Today, as corporate wine director for Daniel Boulud, Johnnes is still in the restaurant business, though he also has his own wines, an import company, and La Paulée, a popular annual wine event dedicated to the best wines of Burgundy (see page 150).

FRED DAME

Fred Dame grew up around grapes—his parents were grape growers for the raisin business in California—but he didn't grow up drinking wine. Instead, it was a trip to Europe when he was eighteen that ignited his interest in great wine and food. On his return to the United States, he entered law school but worked summers at the Sardine Factory, a restaurant on California's central coast that was slowly becoming a stronghold of wine in the West. He quickly found that his priorities had shifted. "I went to law school," Dame remembers, "but it wasn't fascinating. Food and wine were fascinating." Dame took a leave of absence from school to work full-time for the Sardine Factory, where he took over the wine program and in short order made the restaurant one of the best-known wine destinations on the West Coast.

In 1984—the same year Johnnes was starting at Montrachet and Stone was competing in his first Best Sommelier of French Wines competition—Fred Dame read a newspaper article about the Court of Master Sommeliers, a professional trade group in England with an accreditation program. Intrigued, he wrote the organization a letter to ask if he could join. He was brushed off. Dame sent a second letter, asking again if he could enter the accreditation program. The grudging response assented, but stipulated that he would not be allowed to take any of the introductory exams, that he would be thrown right in at the hardest level, the master sommelier exam.

"There's two ways they must have looked at me," said Dame. "One was, 'The pass rate is so low that this clown will never pass anyway.' The other was, 'If this guy is so motivated, let's give him a shot and see what he's made of, see if he's worth investing in.'"

The master sommelier exam is famously difficult. Even today the pass rate is about 6 percent. It consists of three parts. One is an oral quiz in which the candidate must answer one hundred questions, often brutally arcane in nature, such as, what are the subregions of Valtellina Superiore? or, what are the third growths of Margaux? The second part is a service exam that takes place in a simulated restaurant environment. Candidates are asked to display everything from fundamentals, such as opening and decanting wines, to more rarefied skills, like offering pairing suggestions and cocktail recipes. The third component is a blind tasting of six wines in twenty-five minutes in front of a panel of judges. But the candidate is not simply required to identify the wines. He or she must also offer a detailed explanation of how each conclusion was reached.

Dame crammed for a few months, went to England, and was first in the exam, passing all three parts of the test on his first try with the highest total score, a feat known as winning the Krug Cup. The person he beat out for the cup was Claudia Harris, then England's top-rated sommelier and the first woman to pass the exam. Dame still laughs about how the event was reported in an article in a British paper. "The headline blasted 'First Female Master Sommelier,'" he recalls, "and the last line said something to the effect that, oh, yes, Fred Dame won the Krug Cup."

The passage of Fred Dame proved a major turning point for the English Court of Master Sommeliers. It had ushered in a person whose missionary zeal would eventually give the court reach and popularity that it might never have enjoyed without him. The third American to pass the test, Dame returned home to great acclaim. But after two years of basking in the glow of his new title, he decided that there had to be more to life than restaurant wine consulting and being feted as a top sommelier. Over the years, Dame had become friends with Zraly, Stone, and other sommeliers, all of them proof that being a sommelier was a viable profession in the United States. But he increasingly saw that they were all operating in isolation—that they were in a profession without a center or a set of standards. The English had that set of standards, so he petitioned the English Court of Master Sommeliers to let him institute its program in America.

Dame convinced the National Restaurant Association to fund the nascent program for two years, and then wrangled the few serious American sommeliers he knew to come out to California to take the test. Some English master sommeliers flew over to help administer the first exams. One person passed that first year, Madeline Triffon (currently the wine director at the Unique Restaurant Corporation in Detroit). The next year two passed. "Pretty soon, the crème de la crème was through," Dame says, citing celebrated names like Evan Goldstein,

Larry Stone, Roger Dagorn, and Nunzio Alioto. "None of us was rich, but we were self-sufficient."

Today, testing is combined with teaching and tasting at four levels of certification: Introductory, Certified, Advanced, and Master. As of early 2010, the twenty-fifth year of the American chapter of the Court of Master Sommeliers, there are one hundred masters in the United States, and the growth has been spectacular. Ten years ago, Dame estimated, there were five hundred people going through the various levels of the program annually. Today, the number is five thousand. Tellingly, the demographic of the lower-level classes has shifted. Five years ago, the age range was primarily thirty to forty years old; today, it is twenty-one to thirty. "Every time I see a new master pass, I get the same rush I got the day I passed," Dame says. "When you see the quality of student that is produced today, it is astounding, way beyond what I ever dreamed."

THE SOMMELIER TODAY

As Dame suggested, the quality of the American sommelier today is the highest it has ever been. Thanks to the efforts of Stone, Zraly, Johnnes, and Dame; their colleagues; and the restaurateurs who saw their value, the profession of sommelier is now something that a surly French cellar master at Bignon's in 1887 would not even recognize.

So, what is a sommelier today? "A sommelier is a translator," says Robert Bohr, former wine director of CRU, a New York City restaurant known for its expansive cellar, and now a consultant. "We absorb all sorts of wine knowledge—through tasting, through reading, through meeting with winemakers and importers, through talking to one another and to chefs—and then we are expected to render any morsel of that information to a guest at a moment's notice."

On top of that, adds Aldo Sohm, of New York's Le Bernardin, "we are expected to provide a positive wine experience. If a restaurant is ambitious enough to even have a wine cellar and employ a sommelier, we must pair the wine and serve it perfectly, and the customer must be happy. When you take it all together, it's a big job." Indeed, the best way to understand what a sommelier does is to see how he or she might spend a day.

Managing a wine cellar, whether modest or vast, is a daunting task on its own. Few people realize that the workday of most sommeliers begins at one or two in the afternoon and typically doesn't end until at least midnight.

Afternoons are for cellar work, the unsexy backstage stuff that allows the show to go on. Before anything else, wines must be procured. Sourcing wine for a restaurant list involves a rigorous selection process, with considerations of price and availability coming into play as

14

DAVID LYNCH AT QUINCE, SAN FRANCISCO

PAUL GRIECO

much as a question like, what tastes great with the lamb? The number of wines available to a sommelier is intimidating, and behind each wine is a producer or salesperson desperate to get that bottle on the restaurant's list.

To narrow the field, most sommeliers set aside a few hours a week for tasting new wines, during which sales reps can make appointments to bring by special bottles from their portfolios. Obtaining a one-on-one appointment with most top buyers is not easy, let alone making the sale. Rajat's method for buying wine in this situation is to taste a rep's wines blind. "As I taste them," he says, "I come up with a price I think each wine is worth. Then I look at the price list. If my number is close to the wholesale cost of the wine, it's a buyable wine for me."

A good wine list is a living document. To keep it fluid, sommeliers must always be tasting, bringing in new wines for their list and keeping tabs on those they already own. The latter "is not just for inventory's sake," Robert Bohr says. "It's also to remind myself of what I have. It's important that I retaste the bottles on my own list to track their evolution."

With tasting and purchasing comes the laborious work of receiving newly ordered wines from delivery trucks. If the sommelier is lucky, he has an assistant or two to help with this task. Given that many restaurant wine cellars are below ground and down a flight of stairs, receiving cases and cases of wine is a physically demanding job. After reception, bottles must be recorded in inventory and put away individually on the shelves.

Beyond the ongoing job of managing the cellar, a sommelier's day is further harried with the obligations of the restaurant as a whole. Manager meetings. Service meetings. Menu meetings with the chef. Meetings with the reservationists about who is coming in: various regulars, serious wine collectors, important winemakers and chefs, frequent big spenders on wines (good restaurants know who dines with them).

Sometimes—perhaps once a day, week, or month—the sommelier holds staff trainings in which wines are tasted with the servers, who are asked to know and competently describe, pair, and sell many of the wines off the list. From 1996 to 1998, Robert Bohr worked at Danny Meyer's Gramercy Tavern as a waiter captain and bartender while attending New York University. He remembers the importance of staff tastings, which were conducted by then–beverage director Paul Grieco (today co-owner of New York's Hearth and Terroir). "It was really an education in wine. If you were curious, you could learn anything, because we tasted wine twice a day, mostly blind, and it was all about deduction," Bohr recalls. "Paul was really good at teaching people and opening everything. It was the first time I tasted Quintarelli, the first time I tasted Harlan Estate, Sassicaia. What he would open for the staff was unbelievable. But Gramercy had no sommeliers. The staff was selling those wines and needed to know them."

Rajat conducts staff tastings once a month, opening as many as ten bottles at a time. Usually, the wines will demonstrate the range of a particular region—say, the Loire Valley or Italy's Piedmont. Rajat will explain the grapes, climates, and soils and then offer specifics about how the wines will work with certain dishes on the menu.

17

Finally, there is the daily lineup, the brief group meeting with servers, managers, chefs, and other sommeliers to discuss every detail pertinent to that night's restaurant service. Here, the chef may discuss and occasionally offer tastes of the night's special dishes. The general manager might profile important guests, even going into detail about their careers. The sommeliers might talk about new wines by the glass.

Then the doors open and it's showtime. For busy sommeliers, what happens between six o'clock and midnight is an exhausting theatrical and physical exhibition of wine service that involves dozens of personalized tableside performances, long and occasionally exasperating conversations, precise demonstrations of wine knowledge, nuanced suggestions of wine pairing, athletic dashes to the cellar to fetch bottles, and the calm uncorking and decanting of delicate old bottles—all the while looking graceful and relaxed.

Waiters often complain about the sommeliers' apparent life of luxury, spending every evening simply selling, opening, and often tasting fine wine. But looks can be deceiving. "On some nights, it seems like every single table wants to talk to me," says Heather Branch, most recently the wine director of Manhattan's restaurant Eighty One. "And it's never just a simple interaction like, 'I'll have the steak and my wife will have the fish.' When they call for me, they not only want to ask questions about wine, but they also want to tell me about their wine experiences, whether it's something pretentious like offering their detailed opinion of the latest vintage in Bordeaux and all the cult Cabernet they have in their cellar, or something modest like describing the wine they drank in Paris on their anniversary. In the meantime, you have five parties waiting to see you, and they need wine on their tables now."

Despite its rigors, service is also the heart of the job, the way sommeliers most impact the culture at large. Knowing wine is not enough; skill in presenting it and selling it is equally important. "Good service takes time. It really comes down to time spent at the table," says Christie Dufault, a sommelier at San Francisco's RN74 and former wine director of San Francisco's Gary Danko and Quince. "You've got to observe the guest. You've got to read each table individually, listen to what they mean, not just what they say. Often, for instance, guests will ask for a sweet wine when they instead mean something with good fruit."

The art of the job is to be present and calm enough to deliver that kind of interaction with each table, while still running at a hectic pace. "Service can be tense," adds Branch. "Sometimes you can't find the exact bottle a customer is looking for. You know that his duck has been fired and you're frantically searching for his Burgundy, which is not where it's supposed to be."

Beyond the dining room, the sommelier is the restaurant's ambassador to the wine community. This aspect of the position cannot be taken lightly. The high-profile sommeliers, the ones you might know or have read about in magazines, are generally the ones who get out and participate in the larger wine culture.

18

These days, there are many avenues for sommeliers to reach potential clients. Of course, having great wines is itself an attraction, particularly older and hard-to-find bottles. Such bottles, if well publicized, will bring in high-dollar customers by themselves. Inviting winemakers to host dinners, which makes a restaurant the middle ground between customers and producers, also attracts diners. So, too, does opening special wines for important guests to taste, a gesture that makes everyone feel part of the game. "If I have a winemaker like Stéphane Ogier of Côte-Rôtie in the restaurant one night," Rajat says, "I'll open a bottle of great California Syrah for him to taste. He learns, I learn. It's fun." Volunteering at wine events is another way to connect with customers. Many sommeliers donate their time to work such events as Daniel Johnnes's La Paulée and World of Pinot Noir precisely to reach potential clients. Travel, in general, is also important, whether it is going out to colleagues' restaurants and sitting at the bar or passing out your card at a tasting in Paris. And, increasingly, sommeliers are using social media to reach out. For instance, Rajat, Robert Bohr, Laura Maniec (B.R. Guest Restaurants), and Hristo Zisovski (Jean Georges) are all active Twitter users, tweeting several times daily about wines they are serving, wine or restaurant news of the day, or what they themselves are eating and drinking.

BECOMING A SOMMELIER

Much like their forebears, few of today's top U.S. sommeliers came into the restaurant business planning to do what they are currently doing. But a common factor binds them now: a passion for wine that almost defies description. Both their professional lives and their personal lives are centered around wine. Their friends are wine drinkers. They base meals not around what's in the refrigerator, but around what they want to drink that night. They routinely talk with one another about wine and read wine magazines in their spare time. They travel to wine-growing regions on their vacations and spend their own hard-earned money collecting the very bottles that they open and serve every night.

Thus, the first step to becoming a sommelier is to identify your passion for wine. It need not be a lifelong passion, but it must be driving. In Rajat's case, he had hardly heard the word *wine* until he was in college in 1991, at the age of eighteen. His roots, as with many sommeliers, were in food.

Growing up in Calcutta, Rajat recalls, "Our family life was organized around food. Both grandmothers and my mother were amazing cooks. I had every meal with my parents until I was eighteen, and I tried everything that was put in front of me. We were constantly talking about what we should eat today, tomorrow, next week." His family ate vegetables, fruits, fish, and—rarely—meat. From the age of ten, Rajat was in the kitchen, watching and learning, and by the time he was twelve, he was cooking breakfast for his family. In those days, Chinese and other East Asian cuisines were not uncommon in Calcutta, and Rajat was introduced to flavors that he still weaves into his cooking today. In the few American food magazines that he could get his hands on, he saw photographs of nouvelle cuisine and longed to taste it.

Rajat was likewise attracted to the restaurant industry. His cousin in Delhi owned two restaurants. Even as a teen, Rajat was fascinated by the restaurant business. "For five or six years, I spent vacations in my cousin's office, listening to him deal with purveyors and chefs." At the same time, Rajat learned about the Culinary Institute of America (CIA) from his cache of American food magazines. In his midteens, he began formulating a plan to go there. But when he was eighteen, his mother, unwilling to let her son leave the country, convinced him to attend a hotel school (one of only two in India at the time) in the southern town of Manipal, over thirteen hundred miles—a fifty-hour train ride—away.

At the school, which was run by the Sheraton Corporation, Rajat remembers, "no one was really into food," except for himself and two fellow students, Ash and Harris. The three friends passed the time by constantly planning meals and snacks. Rajat worked in the school kitchen, which was attached to an operating hotel, for over two years, often from dawn to close, taking breaks to attend class before returning to work.

Rajat's first taste of wine came on his school vacation in the summer of 1993, during a visit to family in England. When an uncle who collected wine shared a humble glass of Mouton Cadet with the young chef, Rajat's reaction was not revelation but curiosity. Tastes of more wines on the trip—Riesling, Bordeaux, even Dom Pérignon—led to murmurings of a new interest. "Growing up, grapes were my favorite food," recalls Rajat. "And when I was first exposed to wine, I was amazed at the thought that different kinds of grapes could yield so many different tastes. I couldn't get that out of my mind."

After three years at the hotel school, Rajat was accepted into the CIA in New York. While he didn't regret his time in southern India—"to get the most out of the CIA, you should know how to cook before you go"—he was thrilled to have his dream realized. Rajat arrived at the Hyde Park campus in the fall of 1994, at age twenty-two. Many new experiences lay before him, including winter. But among the first things Rajat did was join the wine club. "I can't say that I had a great thirst for drinking wine at that time," he reflects, "but something inside me knew it was important."

At the CIA, Rajat's classes began at six or seven in the morning. Afterward, he sat in on wine lectures. And at the end of the day, he took an hour-long bus ride to Poughkeepsie, where he worked the dinner shift at an Indian restaurant. "I didn't drink alcohol for the first couple of years," he recalls. "I had no money and ate mostly popcorn and ramen." On weekends, he took the train down to Manhattan to stay with Ash, his friend from hotel school. There, Rajat and Ash, obsessed with restaurants and food, would walk hundreds of blocks, stopping to read every restaurant's menu, feeding their imaginations if not their bellies. "Everything I would learn about food and wine during the week, I would see put into action on those menus," Rajat recalls. "My sense of food was beginning to come into focus."

After a grueling but eye-opening six-month internship at the Raffles Hotel in Singapore, where he was introduced to famous chefs like Jean-Louis Palladin, Alain Ducasse, and Roy Yamaguchi, Rajat returned to Hyde Park for his final year. Now Rajat's fascination with wine was reaching full bloom. He was finally eligible to take the wine course, which he did twice, simultaneously—the same seminar, in both the morning and the afternoon sessions. Outside of class, he was driven to go deeper. To buy a few cases of wine, he sold a new laptop his uncle had given him. "I'd open the bottles, taste them, make notes, and then give them away to my friends," he recalls. To this day, despite his obvious affinity for wine, Rajat is not a big drinker.

Rajat won the *Wine Spectator* scholarship that year, and several of his mentors and teachers at the CIA recommended he acquire some front-of-the-house experience while continuing to develop his palate. At graduation, he sent résumés to sixty Manhattan restaurants for front-of-the-house positions with an emphasis on wine. Three or four offers came back—all line-cook positions. Rajat was referred to Daniel Johnnes, wine director of Montrachet, then one of the hottest restaurants in Manhattan. Johnnes had nothing to offer except for a single piece of advice: "Call Larry Stone in San Francisco. He might have something for you."

Coincidentally, Rajat had just run across Stone's name and picture in a *Wine Spectator* feature on the top restaurants in San Francisco. By phone, Rajat made an appointment to interview at Rubicon, borrowed two thousand dollars from Ash, packed all his things, and flew to the West Coast. He went straight from the airport to Rubicon, suitcase in hand. Stone was not there, but the manager interviewed Rajat and offered him a position running food. He started the next day.

It was a month before Rajat finally met the great Larry Stone. When he did, Stone paid him little attention. After two months, Rajat was promoted to bartender and began stocking wine in the cellar. He was also invited to participate in staff tastings. Noting Rajat's ability in blind tasting and his devotion to the work, Stone quickly promoted him to assistant sommelier–manager.

During his apprenticeship under Stone, Rajat exhibited the all-consuming passion and drive that are essential to becoming an elite sommelier. "For three years," Rajat recalls, "I did nothing other than read and taste. On Sundays, when the restaurant was closed, I would drive to wine country to look at the vines. I was obsessed. I used to read a wine book and write a paper about it for myself. I wrote profiles of famous domains like DRC, Vega-Sicilia, Lafite."

21

In 1997, after a year at Rubicon, Rajat signed on to work the harvest at Calera, Josh Jensen's famous Pinot Noir estate in Hollister, California. He worked for three months at the winery, driving back to the city to work at Rubicon on weekend nights. And after two more years of tasting, traveling, and learning from Stone, Rajat left Rubicon to become the opening wine director of a new restaurant, the Fifth Floor, in San Francisco. It was the height of the dot-com boom and one of the best periods in the last twenty years to be selling fine wines.

In just two years, Rajat created a wine list that won *Wine Spectator*'s coveted Grand Award and turned the ultrahot Fifth Floor into the most fashionable wine cellar on the West Coast. But a year later, Rajat was lured away by entrepreneurial chef Michael Mina to be the corporate wine director for what was to be an ambitious group of restaurants around the country. Rajat began his work for Mina by opening Seablue in Las Vegas, but returned to his beloved San Francisco to launch Mina's eponymous flagship restaurant in 2004 (where he would earn another Grand Award). In subsequent years, he traveled around the country, from Washington, D.C. to Los Angeles with many stops in between, creating lists for restaurants in the Mina Group. In 2009, Rajat opened the Mina Group's RN74 in San Francisco, a casual wine bar and restaurant designed from his own vision. He can be found there almost nightly.

Rajat's story is unique in its distance traveled, both culturally and geographically, but not unique in its depiction of the transformative power of wine. Consider the tale of Richard Betts, a master sommelier and former wine director of Aspen's The Little Nell. Betts met Bobby Stuckey—whose career arc took him from teenage busboy in Arizona to wine director of the French Laundry to owner of Boulder's acclaimed Frasca—in Brix, a restaurant in Flagstaff. Betts, who came in often, was in graduate school and Stuckey was the headwaiter. One day, Betts expressed to Stuckey that he didn't want to go back to law school, explaining that a glass of wine had changed his life: as he sniffed a glass of Chianti raised to celebrate his law-school acceptance, the aroma brought back potent sense memories of a recent trip to Italy. So powerful were these smell-induced recollections that Betts realized his true passions were food and wine. Stuckey encouraged Betts to follow his dream, much as Stuckey was doing himself. Betts was soon working in a kitchen and recommending wines from behind the stove. His path would later find him succeeding Stuckey as wine director of The Little Nell. Today, Betts owns a wine label and imports wine and spirits for Castle Brands.

Debbie Zachareas was another graduate-school dropout. Her revelation came at a moment eerily similar to Betts's. An essay question on an application to a psychology program in San Francisco asked, in five hundred words or less, to describe where you see yourself in five to ten years. To her surprise, Zachareas found herself writing one sentence: "I see myself making enough money to buy great wine." And with that she got up and put all her essays and applications into the trash. "I said to myself, 'You've got to follow your heart.'" The next day, she went around San Francisco applying for wine jobs. She landed one stocking shelves at the

Ashbury Market, though later she would work for Larry Stone at Rubicon, and eventually, in 2000, open Bacar, then San Francisco's most ambitious wine bar. Today, she's co-owns and runs the highly successful Ferry Plaza Wine Merchant & Wine Bar and the Oxbow Wine Merchant, of San Francisco and Napa, respectively.

A LEGACY OF PEOPLE

Stories along the lines of Betts's and Zachareas's are not uncommon among sommeliers. One way or another, they all start with a sip of a wine—a sip that triggers something deep and meaningful that compels the individual to change the direction of his or her life toward an unrestrained pursuit of wine knowledge. Not many liquids have that kind of power.

But in pursuing their passions, what the second and third generations of American sommeliers have found that the first generation did not have were mentors and community. So, perhaps the most important creation of pioneers like Stone, Johnnes, Zraly, and Dame (and others such as Joshua Wesson, Joseph Spellman, and Steve Olson) was not a tasting protocol or a serving methodology, but the tight, interlocking sommelier community that exists in the United States today. As Rajat, fighting off the tears, said of Larry Stone at a dinner honoring the great master, "My parents live far away. . . . He taught me everything I know."

Almost any sommelier under forty in the United States could say something similar about one of these men. The American Court of Master Sommeliers, largely a testament to the work of Fred Dame (and, he would insist on adding, all the educators who have worked alongside him), is many things: a title, a test, a path. Yet the one aspect of the organization that often goes unmentioned is the importance of the community it has fostered and the system of mentorship it offers.

At Rubicon, Larry Stone constructed an environment that likewise drew young wine minds into the fold and minted many new sommeliers. Montrachet—and all of Drew Nieporent's restaurants—under Johnnes fulfilled much the same role on the East Coast. And Zraly, in addition to the sommeliers he mentored at Windows on the World, has reached an astounding number of people. Today, several of Rajat's protégés have gone on to become wine directors and restaurant owners.

The legacy of these sommeliers is not wine itself, but rather the network of people they mentored and trained. And their careers illuminate the path anyone can take to become a sommelier—work in a restaurant, love wine, devote yourself to studying it, tasting it, and comprehending it. And, foremost, find a mentor, because any true understanding of wine can never be approached in isolation.

DOMINIQUE LAFON, DOMAINE DES COMTES LAFON, MEURSAULT

CHAPTER TWO

TASTING WINE

It was just after midnight one late October evening at Coi, the Michelin two-star restaurant in San Francisco. Under the blinking lights from the strip club across the street (given Coi's elegance and sophistication, its location in a sketchy corner of North Beach is somewhat incongruous), the last guests were saying their good-byes to the maître d' and putting on their coats. Yet, as they were getting into their valet-parked cars, other individuals, dressed in suits and ties, were walking into the restaurant.

These latecomers weren't hungry diners trying to get a last bite before the end of the night. They were sommeliers. Each one carried a shoulder bag, stuffed full and tightly zipped. Most of them had been at work since at least two the previous afternoon, but their night was not over. They had come to taste.

Each new arrival was greeted by Paul Einbund, Coi's wine director (now at restaurant Frances). Impeccably dressed in a mahogany brown suit and sporting a goatee and thick-rimmed glasses, Einbund is known not only for his love of esoteric wines but also for his outrageous sense of humor. He handed each sommelier a glass of Egly-Ouriet, a small-grower Champagne popular among sommeliers for its richness, purity, and intensity.

"Put your wines over there," Einbund instructed. "There are bags for the bottles and a fridge if you need to keep them cold." As the last sommeliers arrived, the others recounted their nights: the number of covers their restaurants had done, the big bottles they had opened, the wines they had tasted. The group included Rajat, along with his two sommeliers at restaurant Michael Mina, Tony Cha and Noah Dranow; Alan Murray, an Australian and master sommelier from Masa's; and Cezar Kusik from Rubicon.

Then, the first wine, a white, was poured from a bagged bottle. Silence descended over the room as each sommelier tilted and swirled his glass in the restaurant's amber light. Pointing the bowls to their noses at various angles, they examined the complex aromas emanating from the wine as a jeweler might eye a diamond. Slurping and sloshing commenced as the wine was tasted, chewed, and generally deconstructed by each palate. Otherwise, still silence—an indication that the bottle was a fine one, worthy of savoring. Unlike at a formal professional tasting, no one was spitting; rather, the wine was swallowed thirstily by the gulp. After all, it was Saturday night, the beginning of the weekend for most of the group. They were there to taste wine, but also to drink it.

"Okay. What do you think about this wine?" Rajat said to Kusik, assuming the role of moderator. Kusik, a thick-necked, muscular, bald former nightclub bouncer from Poland who might be intimidating if he weren't so quick to laugh, answered in his guttural bass voice: "Well, it's a deep yellow, golden color. A nose of pear, earth, smoke, and lemon. Lots of acid and intensity. It's a high-quality wine. Vintage 2002 Puligny-Montrachet. Maybe Leflaive."

During Kusik's evaluation, Rajat nodded but his face was completely expressionless, offering no encouragement, no hint as to whether he agreed with the conclusion. This kind of poker-faced seriousness and intensity can make blind tasting an intimidating sport even for professionals, as if their reputations are on the line with every wine. (That said, even a group of experienced tasters will often come up with a fairly wide range of conclusions about the same wine.)

Rajat moved on to the next sommelier, who agreed with Kusik that the wine was a white Burgundy, but thought it was from Meursault rather than Puligny, and a different vintage. Around the circle the tasting went, wine after wine. The lineup was strong, full of epic wines from classic regions: two Chablis, two white Burgundies, three red Burgundies, a Rhône red, a Savennières. A couple of the wines were outliers—a Vermentino from Sardinia, an old Napa Cab. Later in the evening, Jean-Laurent Vacheron, one of the top winemakers of the Loire Valley, dropped by and joined in the tasting. At one point, Kusik rushed out of the restaurant to stop a fight between two people on their way home from the clubs. Meanwhile, heated discussions broke out inside Coi as to the superiority of various producers and vintages. By the end of the evening, with the hour pushing three and taxis hailed, the sommeliers had tasted and drunk several thousand dollars worth of wine. A typical late-night sommelier Saturday.

San Francisco's late-night sommelier tastings are an acknowledged tradition now, having already garnered a story in *Food & Wine* in 2002. They began around 1997, the beginning of the dot-com boom, when epic wines were flowing in San Francisco restaurants like beer flows in Munich. Those original tastings were held Saturday nights at Rubicon, where Larry Stone, Alan Murray, and Rajat all worked at the time. Other original members of the tasting group were Peter Birmingham (then at Elizabeth Daniel, now a wine consultant in Los Angeles), William Sherer (then at Aqua, now at Aureole in Las Vegas), and Andrew Green (beverage director for San Francisco's Bacchus Management Group, whose restaurants include Spruce and the Village Pub).

The late-night group would taste the classic wines of the world together, each sommelier bringing a fine wine on which to blind taste the others. Hours into the night, hunger inevitably set in, and the sommeliers would raid Rubicon's kitchen for leftover *rillettes*, pasta, whatever they could scrounge. Memorably, Peter Birmingham once made scrambled eggs with truffles at three in the morning. When the Fifth Floor opened in 1999, with Rajat as its wine director, the gatherings moved there.

Regular, late-night tastings among sommeliers from different venues were unheard of in the restaurant world and became indicative of San Francisco's uniquely collegial sommelier community. The anchor of the group was Larry Stone, the master and mentor, who happily devoted his predawn hours to blind tasting with his young charges. "Nothing's more important than tasting with people who are better than you, who know more than you," says Alan Murray, who had not yet earned his master sommelier diploma in those early days. "It's crucial to improving your own skills and staying sharp. Everyone there had an exquisite palate and a lot of knowledge. But there's only one Larry. All those nights tasting with him were priceless."

In his book *On Wine*, longtime *Gourmet* wine editor Gerald Asher writes, "I never ask a guest to identify a wine. It can too easily wreck friendship and cause indignation." Sommeliers, then, must be thick-skinned and have either great humility or great skill. For in their world, blind tasting is a core discipline, a fitness, and an art. No sommeliers worth their corkscrew turn down an invitation to taste wine blind, nor do they let an incorrect guess humiliate them.

The abiding ethic is that something can be learned from any wine, good or bad. Just as professional tennis players continue to practice their forehands, or PGA tour members have swing coaches, sommeliers must keep their palates in shape.

THE FUNDAMENTALS OF WINE TASTING

Tasting wine is a skill that can be developed. This applies to everyone, whether or not he or she grew up in a family of wine drinkers or came to wine relatively late in life. Rajat, who had barely heard of wine, let alone tasted it, until his early twenties, is a great example. His prowess is a combination of smelling and tasting practices developed over his whole life. Those same fundamentals must be put into play by anyone who hopes to master tasting.

When tasting a wine blind, don't forget to spend some time looking at it. Visual analysis can offer hints about what to later examine with the nose and mouth. For instance, color can indicate oxidation (and therefore age). The color of white wine darkens with age, whereas red wines become lighter. If this color change occurs prematurely, it is likely that the wine is oxidized. Furthermore, as discussed below, color can offer clues to a wine's identity. Syrah has a purplish hue, for example, and a hint of green in a white wine can indicate youth or a cool-climate origin. And, finally, appearance can hint at the wine making itself. A slight cloudiness shows that the wine was unfiltered and unfined, while crystal clarity suggests that it may have undergone some filtration or fining.

THE NOSE

Although tasting sounds like a singular act, it is really several actions rolled into one. What we perceive as flavor is a combination of taste and smell, and according to some researchers, smell accounts for up to 90 percent of the sensory information sent to our brains. Olfaction and memory are also closely related. Not only can smell trigger memory, but the mind also has a profound ability to remember and catalog scents. Learning to smell and to recall scents are the two most critical skills for anyone interested in becoming a great blind taster.

30

CHRISTIE DUFAULT

Learning to smell for Rajat began with smelling *everything*. "I grew up in Calcutta. I was exposed to all these spices, exotic flavors, and scents. It was my second nature to taste everything. Today when I go to the market, I make a point of smelling things: fruits, herbs, vegetables. It's good for your sense memory to be reminded of even the most basic scents, like the scent of a lemon."

Long before he tasted his first wine, Rajat had developed a vast vocabulary of flavors and smells. His experience with foods grew when he came to New York to attend the CIA. His first class was titled Product Knowledge, which the course catalog describes as "an introduction to the identification and use of vegetables, fruits, herbs, nuts, grains, dry goods, prepared goods, dairy products, and spices in various forms. . . . Students will also learn to evaluate products for taste, texture, smell, appearance, and other quality attributes."

Although Rajat had the product knowledge of someone who had grown up eating and cooking in India, many Western foods were new to him. Identifying unfamiliar herbs, for instance, proved particularly challenging. "I used my nose to tell them apart," he said. "They all looked similar enough to me to make it difficult to identify them quickly. But when I held them up to my nose and took in their aromas, the answers snapped into place." Beyond understanding the way a Key lime looks and smells and how it is subtly different from a Persian variety, Rajat learned to dig deeper into what makes a Key lime a Key lime. "The flesh smells different from the skin," he says. "The pith smells different from the zest. How do the zest and pith smell when taken together?"

But because fresh fruits, vegetables, and herbs are all raw, they are no more than an introduction to the world of smell. "All sommeliers must know how to cook," proclaims Rajat. Cooking opens up new doors to the senses. One of the reasons we cook, he says, is to make ingredients more complex and interesting to our noses, tongues, and minds, and therefore more appetizing. This complexity is echoed in wine. "A good wine taster will know the distinct aromas of ingredients in all their forms. If you don't know the difference between raw, underripe, ripe, and overripe pineapple, you're missing something. You must also know how grilled, candied, or caramelized pineapple smells. This coffee I'm drinking? Smelling it, I can tell that the beans were overroasted. It has a burnt, slightly bitter aroma that coffee shouldn't have. How do you learn these nuances? By smelling them over and over again."

Rajat's advice is confirmed by research in Avery Gilbert's *What the Nose Knows: The Science of Scent in Everyday Life*. Gilbert writes that "constant honing of perceptual skills may actually change how an expert's brain responds to scent." When testing both sommeliers and nonexperts in wine tasting, sommeliers showed significant activity in areas of the brain associated with cognitive processing, and nonexperts showed brain response in zones associated with emotional response. "Practice in making deliberate judgments about what one smells," Gilbert concludes, "leads to changes in brain function and makes a person into a better smeller."

Blind tasting a wine is mostly about the nose, yet the mouth plays a role, too. Indeed, Rajat says, "a great wine will make you want to taste it after you smell it. It will cause you to salivate until you can't resist putting the wine in your mouth." But even if you think you can identify the wine just by smelling it, you need to test it with your tongue, as well.

Receptors on the tongue are able to pick up only five tastes: sweet, sour, bitter, salty, and umami. They are all important to wine tasting (though some people dispute the presence of umami), but they are much simpler than the world of scent. The mouth also picks up such sensations as acidity and astringency. These sensations are not complex, personal, or associated with emotional memory in the way smell is. Instead, they are physical, producing an impact on the tongue and throat that pretty much every person feels identically. Yet this impact is still highly valuable to the blind taster.

In wine, sweet and sour are inextricably bound together in an eternal dance. Sweetness comes from sugar, sourness from acidity. They must play against each other harmoniously in order for the wine to appear balanced. A wine containing a fair amount of sugar can seem dry if the acidity is high enough—brut Champagne is a good example—whereas a wine containing too little acidity can seem flat and cloying, even if there isn't any or much residual sugar.

"Acidity is the electric spark that ignites a wine," Rajat says. In blind tasting, acidity levels are fundamental to indicating the grape variety, country or village of origin, and vintage. "Take a vintage like 1996," he continues. "In northern France, you see very high ripeness with very high acidity. The wines have tons of fruit, but they have mouthwatering acidity, too. You don't often see these elements together in such an exaggerated way. In that sense, 1996 is a pretty easy vintage to spot."

Acidity levels are also related to climate. In general, cool-climate grapes such as German Riesling or Chardonnay from Chablis have high acidity and low sugar, which yield sharper, more angular, brighter wines. Warm-climate grapes—Shiraz from Australia, Merlot from Napa—often have low acid and high sugar, resulting in naturally softer, rounder, sweet-tasting wines. Winemakers respond to natural deficiencies in their grapes with manipulation. In cool regions, where the grapes have trouble attaining ripeness and sugar, it's common for winemakers to add sugar to the fermenting wine to bring up the final alcohol level, a process known as chaptalization. In warmer regions, winemakers often add acid to wines to perk them up and give them structure, which is known as acidification. Despite both these practices, wines from extremely cool or warm regions are still recognizable in a blind tasting. The manipulation, if artfully handled, is rarely enough to distort the basic character of the wine.

Rajat's advice for understanding acidity is to learn to recognize its various forms as they pertain to the sensation of wine. This is done through tasting. To understand malic acid, he suggests tasting an apple and focusing on the tingling it produces on the tongue. The same kind of acidity is found in Riesling and Chenin Blanc, both of which often show an applelike character. Malic acid is less present in wines from warmer climates than from cooler ones. The other acid to know is lactic, which is found in milk and yogurt and is sometimes detectable in wine. Much milder than malic acid, it is created in a bacterial conversion called malolactic fermentation. The effect is a reduction and softening of the harshness of malic acid, often creating aromas reminiscent of milk, cream, or even butter in the process. Most red wines undergo malolactic fermentation, but only some white wines do, most notably Chardonnay, which is famous for its creamy notes. Often the sharper, tarter white wines, like Sauvignon Blanc and Riesling, have less lactic acid.

Tannins, the constellation of phenolic compounds found in grape skins, stems, and seeds and in the wood of barrels, are the second important contributor to a wine's mouthfeel. Since white wines are rarely fermented on their skins, tannin is a more critical factor in red wine, serving a handful of vital functions. The level and quality of a wine's tannins can have a profound effect on how it tastes. Light tannins are typically gentle and flowing on the palate; heavier ones often have a grainy or coarse texture. Some can be so aggressive that they make the mouth pucker. Tannins can almost be perceived to have a flavor profile: some may seem sweet and others bitter. They also prevent oxidation, thereby extending a wine's longevity.

The kind and amount of tannins in a wine can reveal where it is from and the nature of its vintage. Some regions or even specific vineyards naturally produce more or different kinds of tannin. "Compare a Gevrey-Chambertin with a Volnay," Rajat says. "Both are from Burgundy, but one has relatively coarse, massive tannins, and the other generally has smoother, more gentle tannins." Likewise, he notes that hotter vintages often produce wines with more tannin. "In warm years, red grapes develop thicker skins to protect themselves from the heat and light. The extra tannin from the skins can result in wines with a massive tannic profile."

Rajat, a habitual tea drinker, suggests brewing a few cups of tea to gain a rudimentary understand of the impact of tannins on the mouthfeel and flavor of a beverage. "Get a green tea or a black tea," he counsels, "and brew cups that have steeped for thirty seconds, one minute, three minutes, and five minutes. You can easily taste the differences in astringency." The job of the winemaker, he asserts, is to get that extraction right by soaking the "tea bag" of grape skins in the fermenting grape juice for the proper amount of time and at the right temperature. To do this, "The winemaker has to know what kind of tannin he or she has—is it sweet, rough, bitter?—and extract accordingly."

Taken together, tannin and acid work to contribute to what is known as a wine's structure. Structure, which is sensed in the mouth, on the tongue, and in the back of the throat, is the architecture of a wine, its layout, the means by which its characteristics are organized. Sommeliers may refer to some wines as relying on acid for their structure (obviously, white wines, but also many reds). These are wines whose taut line of acidity dominates the taster's impression of it. Other characteristics, like its fruit, its viscosity, seem to be organized around the central beam of acidity. Wines lacking acid structure will seem formless and flabby. Other wines (almost always red) will have structures defined by their tannins. This could be evident in, say, a light but dense coating of fine tannin that you sense across your mouth and tongue, such as is common in the Pinot Noirs of Domaine Dujac in Burgundy. Or, the structure might be dominated by a mass of thick, astringent tannin that assails the back of the tongue, such as you might find in a young Bordeaux. But acid and tannin must work in harmony. If they don't, the wine may seem obtuse. Too much acidity in a tannic wine can make those tannins seem bitter and harsh, whereas too little acidity will make the tannins seem flat and overbearing.

HOW TO JUDGE A WINE

One question that comes up frequently is, how does one evaluate a wine? Let's say you have been smelling fruits, flowers, and vegetables religiously since you were a small child and have a well-developed vocabulary of scents, and that you have honed your palate into a highly sensitive detector of acidity and tannin. Even with these life experiences, the question remains, how do you know a wine is good?

We come by our standards for judging wine the same way we do for assessing music or film. First, we absorb what our parents, friends, teachers, and other authorities have to say. And then, when those standards have been sufficiently internalized, we notice that we have begun to develop the confidence to judge wines not only by the classic criteria, but also by our own idiosyncratic sensibilities.

Some terms for evaluating wines are universal. Balance, for Rajat, is a key to quality. What is balance? "It's almost easier to define in the negative," he says. "Good balance is when nothing sticks out in an ugly way, when nothing is out of place. You don't taste too much or too little acidity, too much tannin, or too much alcohol. Balance is hard to define with words, but obvious when you encounter it in a wine."

Finish, another much ballyhooed wine term, is also essential, but it is not as crucial as balance for Rajat. "The finish doesn't always have to be the so-called long finish," he says. "More important is how the wine finishes. Is it clean? Is it not bitter? Does it leave you wanting to take another sip? That's what's important to me."

Intensity and purity are two other common terms. Paul Einbund, of restaurant Frances in San Francisco, acknowledges their importance, but always in the context of balance. "Intensity can be great," he says. "But wines can also be too intense. There needs to be balance. It's the same with purity. I like a wine that shows a purity of fruit or mineral or acid. At the same time, the purity should fit within the overall profile of the wine. I don't need fruit purity if it's completely obscured by new oak. Likewise, purity can often be a euphemism for simplicity."

AMBOLLE
MUSIGNY
1ER CRU
BEAUX BRUNS
FRANCE
RÔTIE
sique
DOMAINE
VOLNAY
TAVANNE
1er CRU

But the successful evaluation of wines goes beyond these traditional factors. Self-expression always plays a role. That is what sets great sommeliers and other tastemakers apart. Ultimately, the decision about what is good is a personal one. Sometimes certain flaws can actually become assets, when viewed in the correct light. A blemish can be what makes a wine distinctive. "Everyone has to have his or her own tastes and be true to them," notes Robert Bohr of New York's CRU. "The best sommeliers, the best tasters of wine are the ones who will go out on a limb for a wine they like. That's called confidence, and it is one of the final pieces to becoming a great wine taster."

Rajat's last bit of advice for the advancing blind taster is simple: "Be curious. Never assume." So many people, he says, take one whiff of a wine and have immediately decided what it is without being certain. It is a way to get yourself into trouble. "Taste what's in your glass, not what's in your mind."

CLASSIC WINES FROM CLASSIC REGIONS AND BENCHMARK WINES

Wine-tasting training, Rajat holds, must begin and end with the classics: "If you want to be a good taster, you must have reference points. You must know the Old World wine regions backward and forward. Most great wine being made elsewhere in the world—from Napa to New Zealand—gets its style and its identity from the wines that came before it. This is why we focus on regions—Bordeaux, Burgundy, Champagne, Tuscany—whose wine styles are as consistent and relevant today as they were twenty or forty years ago or even longer."

Insisting on benchmark wines is especially important in blind tastings. "People try to trick one another by putting obscure ringer wines into a blind tasting," explains Rajat. "If you want to get a sense of how Pinot Noir should taste, don't start with a Pinot from Argentina. It might be a good wine, but when you are trying to learn, it's not helpful. To understand the essence of Pinot Noir, begin with Burgundy. If you want to know what Merlot should taste like, try wines from Pomerol."

Within the sommelier community, deviation from these principles is not welcome, especially during a time of instruction, as this brief story illustrates: In 2004, a newcomer had been invited to participate in one of the Saturday-afternoon tasting tutorials that Larry Stone hosted for his staff at Rubicon. Eight or nine servers and one or two ex-Rubicon sommeliers who had moved on to other restaurants typically gathered weekly. Each attendee was required to bring a wine wrapped in a paper bag to taste blind with the group. On this Saturday, the guest had the mistaken impression that the goal was to stump fellow tasters with an esoteric wine, rather than to train their palates with classic wines from classic regions. He brought a

Tempranillo from California's Mendocino County, a bottle released by a second-tier producer from unhallowed soil in a new region, and made with a grape that had no significant track record in the state. In short, it was about as random as a wine can be. When the Tempranillo was poured, the wine came tumbling out of the bottle, black as ink. Stone asked one of the servers to take stock. "A dark wine, suggesting youth," he began. "On the nose there are dirty, reduced notes. I detect a little blackberry fruit, but mostly smoke and rot." Stone's brow furrowed, and he began shaking his head. "This wine is terribly flawed. What is it?" he barked, demanding that it be revealed before anyone even took a guess. When he saw what it was, he dismissed it curtly. "Next wine." Later, the newcomer was told politely but firmly that if he wanted to attend another session, he had to bring better wine.

Which wines qualify within the sommelier tasting protocol as "classic wines from classic regions"? There is no exact list, and occasionally disagreement arises about which wines are fair game in a blind tasting, whether for a casual get-together or for the blind tasting segment of the master sommelier exam. Inarguable, however, is that the category centers around Old World regions with lengthy track records, with identities founded on a long-term consistency of both grape(s) and style. Most French wines fit the bill, as they issue from the most rigid, refined, and systematic approach to wine production in regions like Burgundy, the Loire, Champagne, the Rhône, Bordeaux, and to a lesser extent the Savoie and Jura (wines from the latter two regions are somewhat esoteric, yet they are highly distinctive and representative of well-defined regional wine-making traditions). German Rieslings from the Mosel, Rheingau, Pfalz, and Rheinhessen make the list, as do Austrian Riesling and Grüner Veltliner. In Italy, classic status has traditionally been limited to the wines from Piedmont, Tuscany, and Veneto; that is, it might be rare to find other wines from Italy's vast plethora of grapes and zones in blind tastings. However, as Italy continues to improve the consistency and quality of wine from its less-heralded regions, many of those places—Friuli, Alto Adige, Marche, Umbria, Campania, Sardinia, Sicily—increasingly make the cut.

Determining if a wine is classic is more difficult when it comes to Spain. Undeniably an Old World country, Spain has experienced a wine revolution in the last two decades. Entire regions and their old vineyards that had been effectively dormant and internationally unknown a generation ago were revived. However, the wines of these reborn regions have been largely made in the image of New World wines and the so-called international style. They are ripe, highly extracted, and extravagantly oaked, and therefore show insufficient varietal and regional character to be instructive in a blind tasting. Spanish wines that qualify as classic are old school Rioja (for example, Muga and López de Heredia), sherry, and Albariño. Wine regions that don't qualify include Toro, La Mancha, and Ribera del Duero. "Most sommeliers," adds Rajat, "are on the fence about whether Bierzo or Priorat can be considered classic at this point." Portugal is in the midst of a surge in the production of dry red table wines, but still its only classic wines would be its ports and its vinho verde, the crisp, dry white.

Some New World wines, while lacking perhaps the tradition and track record of Old World classics, are nevertheless established and well defined enough to carry the mantle of "classic wines from classic regions." New Zealand Sauvignon Blanc is so unique, so popular around the world, and so distinctive that it is considered acceptable in blind tastings. For the same reasons, Australian Shiraz is considered fair game. In the United States, Napa Valley Cabernet Sauvignon and Oregon Pinot Noir are also granted the exalted "classic" status and can reasonably be included in blind lineups. But that's all there is in the New World, and it's easy to understand why. No baseline exists for something like Chardonnay in the New World as it does in the Burgundian communes of Puligny, Chassagne, and Meursault. Sure, a California-style Chardonnay has traditionally been seen as tropical, buttery, and oaky. But Chardonnay can just as easily be made in that style in Washington State, Oregon, Argentina, South Africa, or Australia. "It is not enough that a wine comes from a place," Rajat says. "It has to *be* of that place and no other."

According to Rajat, the key to memorizing and comprehending wine styles from classic regions is to establish a single benchmark wine that represents a region or style. This becomes the definitive wine, the textbook version of what a wine in a good vintage and from a particular location should taste like. Sommeliers and winemakers call this typicity—how a wine should taste. Typicity can be understood at various levels of magnification, in terms of varietal, location, and vintage. Take, for example, a good red Burgundy from the Grand Cru vineyard of Bonnes Mares. "It obviously must be made of Pinot Noir," says Rajat. "Does it taste like Pinot Noir? That's the first level of typicity. Then, does it taste like Pinot Noir from Burgundy? Does it taste like Pinot Noir from the village of Chambolle-Musigny? And, finally, does it taste like Pinot Noir from the Chambolle-Musigny vineyard of Bonnes Mares? For me, that wine is Domaine Roumier Bonnes Mares. When I think of Bonnes Mares, I think of that wine—and I think of Bonnes Mares from other producers for how they are different from Roumier's." Naturally, the more you zoom in on the map, the greater knowledge of an area is required to distinguish between, say, contiguous vineyards in Burgundy. But top sommeliers have to know what these wines taste like young, middle-aged, and old.

How do you establish these benchmark wines? "You learn from others, from listening and tasting," Rajat says. "That's the importance of community. You can train your palate to recognize flavors and aromas, but you can't learn how to be a top-notch wine taster in a vacuum. Finding a mentor—or a number of mentors—to help you lock in the sense of how a particular classic wine should taste is step one in becoming a good taster and a good sommelier." That's the role played by the late-night sommelier gatherings and, in the past, by Larry Stone's afternoon tastings with his staff.

At Rubicon, Stone was fanatical about the tasting of benchmark wines, even during service hours. When Rajat first worked as a waiter there, he always had to be ready to taste. On a busy night, with every table full and an hour wait, Stone would come by holding a wineglass with only an ounce in it. "Tell me what it is," he would say, thrusting it up to the nose of a waiter, who would have to give an answer on the spot. He would do this many times a night. "It was speed tasting, but you could get good at it," Rajat remembers. "You learn to go with your first impression, to make quick decisions. And the repetition is crucial. Do this every night ten times and you begin to get the hang of it."

THE IMPORTANCE OF TASTING NOTES

All good tasters take notes as they taste, especially at the beginning of their careers, when they are learning. This is imperative for two reasons. First, taking notes helps to focus the mind. In many situations, you will not be tasting alone. Other people will be with you, probably tasting the same thing, and they will be talking. Writing your own observations helps you focus on the wine and not on what's going on around you, ensuring that you form clear impressions.

The other reason to take notes is to log reference points. This is true at all levels, for both the beginning wine taster and the expert. If you are new to tasting, say, French or Italian wines, the names of the producers, vineyards, regions, and even grapes are often unfamiliar. The ritual of writing down the details of the wine will begin to embed in your memory these strange names and words. Also, a tasting note is a snapshot of a wine at a moment in time. Wines are living, changing things. A great wine will evolve much as a person will, growing from a youthful state and whatever that may comprise (vitality, dumbness, simplicity) to maturity (perhaps completeness, complexity, tiredness). Along its path, the wine will go through many phases and, particularly for the sommelier, it is important to know in which state the wine currently resides to better understand its likely trajectory. And this kind of information is most useful when it comes from your own notes.

A tasting note should be neither an encyclopedic entry nor a gushing burst of lyric prose. Its most important function is to identify the features that are most striking about the wine and anything else that might be salient to its present and future. Often the more succinct the note, the more useful it is. Jancis Robinson's wine notes are a model of incisive brevity. Here is one of her typical entries:

- -

Dr Bürklin-Wolf Riesling trocken 2008 Pfalz 16.5 Drink 2010-13
Wonderful spine and purity. Bone dry and very dense. Biodynamic viticulture.
Even slightly austere, and only just ready to drink. 12%

- -

She notes its structure (spine), texture and concentration (very dense), and its appeal (even slightly austere). In addition, there is a note on its likely future and a score (16.5). Even if

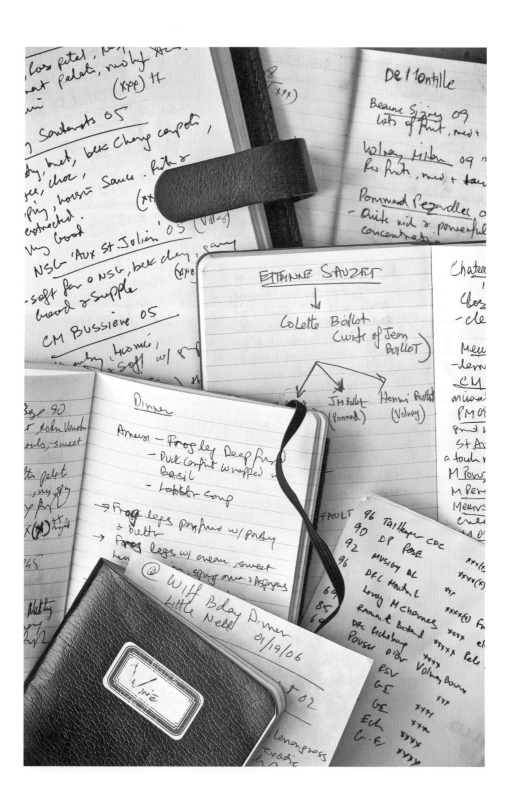

RAJAT'S TASTING NOTEBOOKS

you're not a professional wine critic like Robinson, you may want to develop a personal scoring system (stars, a point scale from 1 to 100 or 1 to 20) to remind yourself how well you liked the wine. Rajat's informal scoring system is a little more exuberant. Average wines rarely merit a comment. "Brilliant" is his exclamation for a high-scoring wine. Even better-faring wines are punctuated by a gleeful declaration of "genius!" And at the pinnacle, reserved for the greatest wines of the world: "iconic!"

A VARIETAL GUIDE TO BLIND TASTING

Good tasters—whether sommeliers or not—must have a detailed mental database of all the classic grape varieties, including where they are grown and how they tend to taste and smell in each place. If a given wine is tasted blind, the variety (or varieties in the case of a blend) is usually the first clue to deciphering its identity. If it is not tasted blind, the expression of variety will become the foundation of your analysis of the wine. Occasionally, the provenance of a wine may express itself more loudly than grape variety. For example, some wines scream Italian, regardless of the grape used to make them, and limestone-based soils occasionally express themselves more adamantly than the variety grown in them. But great wines express both grape and place.

When you are evaluating a wine, however, it's not enough to register that the grape variety is expressed. You must also consider how it is expressed. Take a glass of Cabernet Sauvignon. Is it fruit-forward and juicy, or is it more earthy and savory? Or is it something in between? Whether you are tasting the wine blind or not, the simple question of how the grape is expressed allows you to deduce things about the vineyard or the vintage, details that are often missing from the label. If the expression of the Cabernet is ripe and fruity, why? The answer may be that it was a great, warm vintage, or that the vineyard has wonderful exposure to the evening sun. If the expression is dense and supple, you might think the soil was rich in clay. Understanding a variety includes possessing a sense of how it is expressed in different soils and climates. That familiarity will be the foundation of your analysis as you layer on considerations of vintage and style of vinification.

What follows are dossiers of common grapes from the classic wine regions and what you can expect to see, taste, and smell in each of them. These are rough sketches using common descriptors and features, and in using them you must remember two things: First, our senses of taste and smell are deeply personal; even the most classic examples of a wine will be sensed differently by different people. Second, grapes can express themselves in nontraditional ways. Not all Syrahs are peppery. Not all Sauvignon Blancs are grassy. As Rajat says, "Smell the wine that's in the glass, not the wine that's in your head."

42

Often considered merely a blending partner for Cabernet Sauvignon, Cabernet Franc is the parent (along with Sauvignon Blanc) of the more famous Cabernet Sauvignon. And while it is often blended in small amounts with Cabernet Sauvignon on Bordeaux's left bank, on the right bank it features much more prominently, showing up in many blends along with Merlot.

Cabernet Franc yields a lighter wine than Cabernet Sauvignon and is notable for its herbaceous flavors, which are a turnoff to some drinkers. But Cabernet Franc is the dominant red grape of the Loire region, starring in red wines and rosés from the appellations Anjou, Bourgueil, Chinon, and Saumur-Champigny. The Loire's traditional reputation for thin, green Cab Franc was well earned. But a drier, warmer climate has emerged there in the last twenty years. That shift has been complemented with better wine growing, resulting in riper, more delicious wines. They are lighter than the Cab Francs of Bordeaux, but offer a compelling mix of fruit and savory flavors and moderate tannins for early to midterm drinking (although some of the more serious versions can age for decades). In Bordeaux, Cabernet Franc, lacking in tannin and structure, is usually blended with Cabernet Sauvignon and Merlot to produce wines of the epic stature for which that region is known.

In a blind tasting, Cabernet Franc should be fairly easy to determine because of its herbaceous side. "If it's a Chinon or Loire Cab Franc," says sommelier Heather Branch, "my two indicators are always green bell pepper and strawberry jam." Rajat also looks to the wine's texture. "Cab Franc likes cooler weather than Cabernet Sauvignon, so it makes wines with fewer and lighter tannins. Look for a more elegant, lighter body, unless the wine is grown in the heat of Napa. There, the tannins can get spiky and harsh."

ICONIC: Château Cheval Blanc Saint-Émilion (Bordeaux, France). The greatest expression of Cabernet Franc (though usually blended with 40 percent Merlot), notable for possessing more sweetness and density than Cabernet Sauvignon–based wines from Bordeaux. As it ages, its aromas morph into porcini, coffee, and chocolate. In contrast, its left-bank counterparts typically acquire scents of cedar, lead pencil, and dried cassis.

CLASSIC: Clos Rougeard Saumur-Champigny "Le Bourg" (Loire, France). The other side of the coin from Cheval Blanc. Rich and concentrated with fruit intensity, but silkier in texture, oak, and tannin. Made from eighty-year-old vines and aged in new oak, this is the reference point for Cabernet Franc's potential in the Loire. Will improve with long aging.

VALUE: Philippe Alliet Chinon (Loire, France). Pure, exhilarating Cabernet Franc that is a great partner to many foods. Ripe and juicy with red fruits and a whiff of violets, the wine is balanced and smooth but vibrates with great energy.

Easy to identify in a blind tasting, Cabernet Sauvignon is one of the planet's great red grapes. Highly expressive, the wine typically declares its inherent qualities as a grape with vehemence, though it remains evocative of where it is from. What can make it challenging to isolate in a blind tasting is its ability to make creditable wines in many diverse locations and climates. When the grape is perfectly ripe, classic Cabernet descriptors include such fruit flavors as cassis (black currant) and black cherry. When it is overripe, jammy notes of plum and blackberry prevail. Additionally, herbaceous hints of bell pepper, tomato, and tobacco leaves often come through at lesser degrees of ripeness. Cabernets are usually made with a high percentage (60 to 100 percent) of new oak.

Cabernet's two most famous regions are Bordeaux and Napa Valley, and it grows very differently in each of them. Bordeaux's climate is moderate and maritime and often struggles to ripen Cabernet Sauvignon, which is usually blended with lesser amounts of Merlot and Cabernet Franc to produce medium-bodied, complex, tannic wines that can develop great complexity with long storage. In Napa's hot, sunny climate, Cabernet makes a full-bodied wine several degrees higher in alcohol than in Bordeaux and typically with riper fruit flavors. Nevertheless, both styles will almost always be intense and well concentrated, with a long, lingering finish. Because of the lower level of ripeness in cooler climes like Bordeaux, young Cabernets can often have brutal tannins. Warmer sites can still result in highly tannic wines, but long ripening in warm weather usually yields softer, more velvety tannins. Cabernet Sauvignon also makes good wines in Australia, South Africa, Chile, Argentina, Washington State, and Italy.

In a blind tasting, the taster will often be asked to name the commune of Bordeaux from which the wine comes. To do so is challenging, but each Bordeaux commune has a general profile on which to base deductions. Bordeaux's left bank and right bank (of the Garonne River) have different geologies. Subsoils on the left bank are dominated by ancient alluvial gravels. The right bank features a limestone plateau, the erosion of which has given birth to clay-based soils on its descending slopes. The left bank's gravels are perfect for Cabernet Sauvignon, and its commune of Pauillac is considered quintessential Bordeaux: muscular, powerful, and dense with black currant. Saint-Estèphe makes robust and solid long-agers. Margaux is the famous "iron fist in the velvet glove," where power meets finesse and beauty. Saint-Julien is reliably stout, but more elegant than Pauillac, and often delivers a signature touch of cedar and lead pencil. Graves is known for its mineral, gravelly texture.

Because the grape is high in tannins, the wines often require aging (except for those in the soft-tannin, superripe New World style, which are more or less made to drink right away). Very old Bordeaux can become wonderfully musty and complex, evocative of mushrooms and the forest floor, meat, and leather. It can be easily confused with older Burgundy or Syrah.

"Sometimes it can be difficult to tell a Cabernet from a ripe Merlot or Cabernet Franc, especially in the New World," says Rob Renteria, wine director of Napa's Martini House. "To determine Cabernet, I look first at the structure. Where is that flavor being carried? Cabernet Sauvignon usually delivers its flavor smack in the middle of the palate and carries long and deep to the back palate on the tannins. Merlot and Cab Franc do not as reliably and insistently deliver their core flavors that way."

Rajat agrees, adding that warmer-climate New World Cabernet Sauvignons and blends can usually be distinguished by their emphasis on smooth, pillowy texture. "Most New World Cabs have a mouthfeel built on the suppleness of alcohol and rounded tannin. Bordeaux is still at its heart a wine with acidity and with tannins that soften with time, not heat."

ICONIC: Château Latour Paulliac (Bordeaux, France). In a tasting of top vintages from 1864 to 2000, Rajat noted one major characteristic of Cabernet Sauvignon embodied by Latour: consistency. "There was no weak patch, always the high tones, all the wines are profound." Beyond Cabernet's steadiness, Latour has a signature minerality to go with a purity of cassis fruit and violets. Aromas of tobacco arise within a few years of release.

CLASSIC: Tenuta San Guido Bolgheri Sassicaia "Sassicaia" (Tuscany, Italy). Since it is from neither Bordeaux nor Napa—the world's two most famous outposts of Cabernet Sauvignon— some might quibble with calling Sassicaia classic. In Tuscany's maritime climate, which is similar to but drier than Bordeaux's and suitably cooler than Napa's, the Cabernet grows in relatively neutral sandy soil. Those conditions arguably make Sassicaia the perfect waypoint between Bordeaux and the New World and therefore the most perfect expression. Rajat is prone to thinking so, as the lithe, aromatic, and pure form of cassis in Sassicaia makes it one of his favorite Cabernets (though the wine usually includes 25 percent Cabernet Franc).

VALUE: Mount Eden Vineyards "Saratoga Cuvée" (Santa Cruz Mountains, California). This Cabernet Sauvignon–dominated blend features wonderful Old World complexity in the form of underbrush, earth, tobacco, and dried herbs, but it is layered on a firm bed of New World fruit, featuring black cherry and plum. Its tannins are silky and ripe.

CHARDONNAY

If not for Riesling—which most sommeliers consider king—Chardonnay might be considered the greatest white wine grape. It makes many of the world's most collectible and expensive wines. But this excellence is somewhat paradoxical, since Chardonnay is a fairly bland grape with little inherent flavor. Respected for its prized trait of transparency, it is also known as "the winemaker's grape," as its inherent blandness puts the producer's skill in growing it and making it on display. Of course, having a good site is paramount to making epic Chardonnay-based wine. When grown on ordinary soils, the grape will yield ordinary wine; but when the grape comes from the limestone-rich earth of Burgundy, it has the potential to turn into something extraordinary. Good Chardonnays have also been produced on well-draining sandy soils in California and chalky soils in New Zealand, but to date, nothing in the world has been able to compete with the Chardonnay grown on the calcareous slopes of the Côte de Beaune, Chablis, and Champagne.

Because of Chardonnay's neutral character, recognizing it in a blind tasting requires deciphering the clues. It doesn't announce itself with high-toned or floral aromatics. Rather, it may show creamy hints of lees and malolactic fermentation, and toasty aromas of oak. Limestone comes through as a pleasant but gripping minerality coupled with the ripe characters of lemon curd, pear, and melon and balanced-to-high acidity. Degrees of these features traditionally vary depending on where the Chardonnay comes from in Burgundy.

In the case of Chablis, says Eugenio Jardim of San Francisco's Jardinière, "I look for little or no influence of oak—fresh wines, searingly high in acid, tons of minerality, hints of sea foam, and oyster shell." Jardim views Chassagne-Montrachet as "richer, more dense, a combination of power and elegance with stewed apple and lemon curd." Meursault, for him, has an imprint of masculinity. "They're powerful, assertive, with a grainy, earthy minerality. Look for that sense of nuttiness and sometimes a hint of smoke, as well as for pears and apples." And, if he is divining a wine he thinks is from Puligny-Montrachet, Jardim looks for feminine qualities in contrast to Meursault's masculinity. "Pulignys still have power, but it's a little more matriarchal," he says. "There are notes of white flowers and rose petals sometimes, and an acidity that's incredibly ethereal and pure. These are often the most finely etched whites of Burgundy."

Chardonnay outside of Burgundy is less obvious, as it rarely has the limestone-driven minerality to define it. Without this, and given the hotter climates in which they are commonly grown, Chardonnays from different New World countries are sometimes interchangeable. Nonmineral wines with tropical flavors like pineapple, mango, papaya, or coconut suggest warmer climates like California, Australia, or Argentina.

ICONIC: Jean-François Coche-Dury Corton-Charlemagne (Burgundy, France). Iconic Chardonnay in its rich, nutty, creamy glory. Round and sun-kissed, the wine amazingly retains a taut mineral and acid core.

VINEYARDS, MEURSAULT

CLASSIC: Domaine Roulot Meursault Les Tessons (Burgundy, France). This wine's pear and melon flavors are prototypical and are usually complemented by high-toned herbs. A light minerality decorates the texture, which is so graceful and flowing as to resemble (and this is no insult) water.

VALUE: Domaine de la Cadette Bourgogne Blanc (Burgundy, France). A simple but pleasurable expression of the citrus, green pear, and high-acid side of Chardonnay. Well rounded, with refreshing acidity.

CHENIN BLANC

Chenin Blanc is an eccentric grape, well loved by sommeliers and connoisseurs but obscure to most wine drinkers. It is grown in quantity in only two places in the world: the Loire Valley, its place of origin; and South Africa. And even in the vast Loire Valley, Chenin Blanc is not the dominant variety, but isgrown mostly in the middle regions, north of Muscadet (where Melon de Bourgogne is the grape) and south of Sancerre (where Sauvignon Blanc dominates). Despite its small planting zone, it makes a dizzying variety of wine styles: dry (*sec*), sweet (*moelleux*), and sparkling, with variations in each category.

The aromas of Chenin-based wine are both distinctive and difficult to articulate, with the most common descriptors relying on such esoteric smells as lanolin (an oil in sheep's wool), damp hay, beeswax, honey, and honeysuckle or other nectarous flowers. It is the combination of these aromas, rather than any one of them, that gives the wine away.

In the mouth, Chenin Blanc wines are known for a ripping-high acidity in the dry and sparkling styles and a syrupy, delicious viscosity in the sweet styles. The wines, whether dry from Savennières or sweet from Quarts de Chaume, age wonderfully and become even more deeply and intensely themselves with time in bottle.

Even though its aromas are unique, Chenin from the Loire "is not as obvious as you'd think in a blind tasting," says Justin Hall, a sommelier at San Francisco's RN74. "When it's superlean and racy, as in 2007 and 2008, the palate and the nose don't give you much. When it has that neutrality, I often identify it through the process of elimination, determining first that it's not Albariño, not Riesling. When it has oxidative qualities, it can be confused with white Burgundy."

"For me, the biggest note for Chenin is chamomile," says Rob Renteria. "If I can pick up chamomile tea in the wine, that always points me toward Loire Chenin Blanc."

ICONIC: Domaine Huet Vouvray Clos du Bourg Sec (Loire, France). Powerful, structured Chenin with bracing acid and deep concentration. Closed when young but flowers after twenty years, emitting a world of aromas from meadow flowers to hay to ripe peaches and pears.

- -

CLASSIC: Domaine des Baumard Savennières Clos du Papillon (Loire, France). Textbook aromas of mineral, quince, and lanolin always animate this wine. It has richness and viscosity, but is kept firmly in line with a brisk whoosh of acidity.

- -

VALUE: Domaine Jo Pithon Anjou Les Bergères (Loire, France). Outstanding combination of tangy green and decadent tropical fruits. The acid is high and eminently refreshing.

GAMAY

- -

The gateway drug into the world of fine red wine, Gamay comes from the Beaujolais region, an hour south of the bottom of Burgundy's Côte d'Or. In its best iterations, the grape makes a light- to medium-bodied wine that incorporates many of the flavors and characteristics of Burgundian Pinot Noir, but without the same complexity and tannin structure. (It also makes the notorious Beaujolais Nouveau, an often bright, fruity, cloyingly simple wine that is shipped only five or six weeks after the grapes have been picked.) Good Gamay is Burgundy Lite, you might say—in cost as well: a top Cru Beaujolais is cheaper than even the cheapest examples of high-quality Burgundy.

Gamay is recognizable for its overt fruitiness resulting from carbonic maceration, a whole-grape fermentation technique that emphasizes pure fruit and lightness. The most consequential wines of Beaujolais are the Crus: the highest classification for vineyards in the region, based around seven villages and three additional sites. Cru Beaujolais is serious red wine, mixing its fruitiness with a refreshing earthiness, buttressed by good acidity and a bit of soft tannin. Flavors run from plum and blackberry to cherry and cranberry. Most Beaujolais is not age-worthy, but some of the Crus—most famously, Moulin-à-Vent—can make long-lived wines. Because of its light, refreshing qualities, Beaujolais is often served slightly chilled.

In a blind tasting, "Beaujolais is the easiest to get if you often drink the wine," points out Eric Railsback, a sommelier at San Francisco's RN74. "If you don't drink it, it can be the hardest, because it tastes like nothing else."

- -

ICONIC: Marcel Lapierre Morgon "Cuvée Lapierre" (Beaujolais, France). Made only in ripe vintages and from very old vines, this Morgon shows amazing depth, density, and complexity. Violets and blueberries highlight the flavors. With its dense slurry of tannins, it is a wine that can soften in the bottle for thirty or more years.

- -

CLASSIC: Jean Foillard Morgon Côte du Py (Beaujolais, France). Beaujolais at its dark, deep best. Light in form, dense in composition. Blackberries and bramble give it rangy but purely fruited aromas. The refined tannins offer a chewy grace.

VALUE: Domaine Trénel Chiroubles (Beaujolais, France). A thinner, buoyant, juicier version of Gamay. Its candied cranberry and plum fruits come off as pretty, playful, and winning, while its light structure makes it a quaffer.

GRENACHE

Grenache is the dominant grape of France's southern Rhône. Its best versions—such as the famed Château Rayas—are incredible, long-lived, vibrant, and complex wines. While Grenache is rarely found alone in the wines of the southern Rhône—its usual blending partners are Carignan, Mourvèdre, and Syrah—it is nevertheless the preeminent grape in the wines of Châteauneuf-du-Pape, Gigondas, and Vacqueyras. Grenache shares a few traits with Pinot Noir: both grapes are thin skinned and relatively generous in sugar production, and tend to make light-colored, reddish wines. Where they differ is that Pinot likes cool, even foggy weather, and Grenache thrives in hot sun. Consequently, Pinot makes lighter, lower-alcohol wines, and Grenache can produce ripe, jammy, candied-fruit flavors and alcohol levels of 15 percent and above. But when Grenache is kept in check, it can make some of the most alluring reds in the world, as well as some of the greatest rosés (in the southern Rhône, Provence, and the Spanish region of Navarre).

In a blind tasting, Grenache is a possibility if the wine in question is both light in color and high in alcohol, an otherwise unusual combination. Grenache also has relatively low acidity. Wines made from Grenache typically show red fruit (cherry, strawberry) to Syrah's usual blackberry and blueberry, and they smell like white pepper to Syrah's black pepper. "Whether the bottle is from France or Australia, I almost always get something that's a little burnt or charred in Grenache," says Justin Hall. "White pepper, garigue, and Brett," adds Railsback. There are exceptions: modern-style Grenache, which is found in Priorat and which is increasingly fashionable in Châteauneuf-du-Pape, is more extracted and thus darker, heavier, and glossed with new oak.

However, a classic old Châteauneuf, with burnished cherry fruit, earthiness, and light color, can easily remind a taster of an aged Burgundy. "It's one of the most beautiful and versatile wines in existence," says Heather Branch. Even in a place as hot and dry as Australia, she continues, "Grenache can make big, powerful wines like those of Clarendon Hills that still have elegance, purity of cherry fruit, and silky tannins. It's a miraculous grape, on par with

Pinot Noir for me—and sometimes even more versatile with food than Pinot, because it can stand up to bigger meats yet still perform wonderfully with game and fowl."

ICONIC: Château Rayas Châteauneuf-du-Pape (Rhône, France). Uncommonly graceful texture and density meet red-fruit brightness. Rayas is made from 100 percent Grenache grown in sandy soil. The wine develops iconic complexity over time.

CLASSIC: Domaine Gramenon Côtes du Rhône "La Sagesse" (Rhône, France). As pure as Grenache gets, aged in old *barriques* with little sulfur. From the northern, cooler end of the southern Rhône, so the expression is darker, with classic white and black pepper, wild berries, elegance, and spice.

VALUE: Bodegas Borsao Campo de Borja "Tres Picos" (Aragón, Spain). Offers red fruit, earth, and spice from forty-year-old vines grown at twenty-one hundred feet. Vinified in stainless steel, giving the wine tautness and linearity.

MERLOT

"I'll never forget one of my first blind tasting experiences at Rubicon, back when I was still a food runner," Rajat recalls. "I tasted the wine, a red, and called it as 1994 Lewis Merlot from Napa. Turned out I nailed it. Forever, its features became engrained in my mind as the essence of Merlot: plummy, juicy, and soft, with pillowy tannins and a hint of smoke."

Not all Merlots will be like a ripe, plump one from Napa, but Raj's description hits on one of Merlot's classic shapes: soft and plummy. The riddle of the grape is this: at its best, it can make some of the greatest reds on the planet, but it is rarely at its best. Even in its favored clay and limestone soils in the Bordeaux commune of Pomerol, Merlot is seldom found on its own, needing the structure and backbone of Cabernet Sauvignon or Cabernet Franc. When it finds an ideal spot, however, Merlot is delicious, combining a sensual, velvety texture with aromas of blackberry, plum, violets, and sometimes some gaminess. Superior Merlot has also been produced in Tuscany, where Bordelais varieties seem to thrive.

In the warm climates and rich soils of the New World, Merlot often makes flabby, formless wines. Their undemanding drinkability may be why the variety became so popular in the U.S. in the late 1980s and early '90s, when Americans were beginning to drink more wine.

In blind tastings, look for "blue fruit, a plummy depth of color," remarks Heather Branch. "I also think of full-bodied viscosity, whether from Bordeaux or California." Texturally, adds Rob Renteria, Merlot is "deep, round, and soft, with an acidic profile a little

51

higher than Cabernet. The tannins are round, not spiky. If Merlot were a designer suit it would be Armani—smooth, sloping, drapes well. Cabernet is more angular—Hugo Boss."

- -

ICONIC: Château Pétrus Pomerol (Bordeaux, France). Merlot at its complex, smoky, mineral best. Structure meets suppleness in a magical way.

- -

CLASSIC: Château Le Gay Pomerol (Bordeaux, France). A great Merlot for the price; qualities of blueberry, graphite, violet, and spice in a lithe, flowing package.

- -

VALUE: Seven Hills Winery Merlot (Walla Walla Valley, Washington). Ripe, plump, and juicy, with blueberry and plum notes. Although soft, the wine still finds definition with a touch of acid and well-rounded tannins.

NEBBIOLO

- -

Nebbiolo produces some of the planet's greatest red wines and is similar to Pinot Noir in that it only makes great wine in a small bandwidth of climate and soil. The lone classic Nebbiolo at this time comes from one small part of Italy: Piedmont, the home of Barolo and Barbaresco.

Because its fruit characteristics tend toward bright, ripe, sometimes tart cherry, old Nebbiolo in a blind tasting is often confused with old Burgundy or even aged Brunello di Montalcino. Nebbiolo also shows aromatic hints of roses, tar, violets, and earth, but its main giveaway to the blind taster is in the mouth: no other red grape has the same preponderance of acid and tannin. In classic Nebbiolo, both are present to such a degree that young wines are difficult to drink. Top Barolos need a minimum of a decade in the bottle, and Barbaresco, a more delicate wine but still quite burly, may come around in a few years less than that. Both wines, when vinified by top producers in good vintages, can improve over a long time—thirty to forty years minimum. The more lowly Piedmontese designations of Langhe and Gattinara offer softer, lighter versions of Nebbiolo, and other good examples come from the treacherously steep slopes of Valtellina, northeast of Piedmont in Lombardy, near the Swiss border.

Piedmont Nebbiolo has been marked by two schools of production. The traditionalists make wine that is notable for its purity of fruit and *terroir* expression and for its hard, tannic structure that can require long aging to soften (Giacomo Conterno and Bruno Giacosa are examples). The so-called modern school uses new oak barrels and contemporary fermentation techniques to make softer, earlier-drinking wines with a hint of woody toast (Roberto Voerzio and Paolo Scavino are practitioners). But today, more than ever, most producers occupy a middle ground between the styles, so the distinction is less relevant.

54

Picking out Nebbiolo in a blind tasting can turn on a couple of factors. "Look for hints of orange in the color," recommends Hristo Zisovski of New York's Jean Georges. "Nebbiolo can go from red-orange in its youth to orange-amber with age." Zisovski also finds it helpful to contrast with Sangiovese. "Nebbiolo is very aromatic, more aromatic than Sangiovese—more floral, obviously with tar, cherries. But it's the tannins that are the separation. You taste Nebbiolo and your mouth gets dry from the tannins. Drink Sangiovese and your mouth gushes and salivates from the acidity."

ICONIC: Giacomo Conterno Barolo Monfortino (Piedmont, Italy). Legendary perfume of cherry, tar, roses, and truffles—a symphony of delicious complexity. Dense and structured for the long haul, the wine is silky and gentle when finally mature. Nebbiolo at its finest.

CLASSIC: Bruno Giacosa Barbaresco (Piedmont, Italy). Lighter and more graceful than a first-rate Barolo, but with all the same complexity, emphasizing a tart-cherry and mineral, earthy beauty. Youthful tannins can be sharp and piercing.

VALUE: Vietti Langhe Nebbiolo "Perbacco" (Piedmont, Italy). A simple but gloriously balanced and delectable Nebbiolo, dominated by the pure taste of tart cherry. Flavor is concentrated on the midpalate, but falls off in the finish.

PINOT NOIR

Many sommeliers consider Pinot Noir the greatest red grape. At its best, it can make the most transparent, the most sensual, and the most ethereal red wines in the world. And even when average, Pinot can still yield simple, fruity wines that are a pleasure to drink. Burgundy is the home of Pinot Noir. It reaches its peak and most varied expressions there in the Côte d'Or, with the dark, powerful wines of Gevrey-Chambertin, the delicate perfume of Chambolle-Musigny, and the sweet generosity of Volnay. Pinot Noir also makes fine wine in the Loire, especially as Sancerre Rouge. In the New World, good Pinot comes from Oregon, California, and New Zealand. These wines rarely reach the sublime fineness of perfume, mineral texture, and detail of Burgundian Pinot, but sometimes they do—and they continue to get better. A grape of good acidity and moderate-to-light tannin, Pinot Noir is generally consumed within its first five to ten years, though some versions can age for decades.

The color of Pinot is the first giveaway in a blind tasting, as it is a lighter and brighter red than many other wines. Aromas can vary, but they are typically in the cherry family, with additional notes of raspberry, rhubarb, beet, earth, and/or spice rounding out the nose. In

SHARING WINE AT LA PAULÉE

the mouth, Pinot is famous for its silky texture and a lively acidity that makes it bright, fresh, and expressive. But Pinot is not always the delicate, pretty wine some claim it is. Young and middle-aged Burgundy Pinots are austere and hard with tannins and sharp with acid.

Burgundy can generally be deduced by its earthiness, minerality, and punchy acidity. "In wines from the northern Côte d'Or like Gevrey-Chambertin," says Rajat, "look for structure and darker fruits. As you move south toward Chambolle and Vosne-Romanée, red fruits like cherries and raspberries begin to dominate. Morey, Nuits, and Beaune wines are typically earthy."

Oregon Pinot usually shares the earthiness of its Burgundian counterpart, but it is often fruitier, higher in alcohol, and looser in structure. California Pinot Noir can be fruitier yet, and higher in alcohol, especially from warmer areas like Carneros and the Russian River Valley. Cooler areas of California—the Sonoma Coast, Anderson Valley, Santa Barbara County—can produce Pinot Noir of admirable structure, acid, and balance.

- -

ICONIC: Domaine de la Romanée-Conti Romanée-Conti, Vosne-Romanée (Burgundy, France). Ethereal finesse offered in a wine with the concentration and density to last decades. Contains a world in its nose.

- -

CLASSIC: Jacques-Frédéric Mugnier Chambolle-Musigny (Burgundy, France). The pale, reddish pink side of Pinot suggests the cherries and raspberries found on the nose, which is further garnished with hints of stones and flowers. Beautifully pure and limpid.

- -

VALUE: Domaine de Montille Bourgogne Rouge (Burgundy, France). A high-toned nose of red fruit and soft earth precedes sappy concentration and good length. A simple but perfect quaffer.

RIESLING

- -

"If there is one goal of sommeliers," Rajat says, "it's to make Riesling more famous." What makes it great are the same things that make any noble grape exceptional: its ability to communicate *terroir* and to evolve with age.

Because of its sensitivity to *terroir*, Riesling tastes noticeably different depending on where it is grown. Riesling can also make a dizzying number of styles of wine, from light, dry wines ideal for an aperitif to some of the richest, most intense, and longest-lived sweet wines in the world.

The hallmarks of youthful, dry Rieslings include aromas from the tarter members of the citrus family—lemon, lime, citrus peel, grapefruit. Sweeter, riper styles tend toward oranges, apricots, tropical fruits like pineapple, and peaches. As Riesling ages, its most famous trait is the aroma of petroleum or, as some say, diesel, a key indicator in a blind tasting. Riesling does not need to be very old to conjure crude oil, however. Sometimes it rears its head only two or three years after bottling.

In the mouth, Riesling's calling card is acidity, which is juicy, zesty, and refreshing. Its sense of balance comes from the interaction of the remarkably high acid with the residual sugar that is often left in the wine to soften the impact of the acidity. It is the same principle that governs the making of lemonade. Keep in mind that as Riesling ages, its sweetness recedes and its acid remains the same. Therefore, old Riesling, even if it begins its life as a sweet wine, will taste drier over time.

The other signature of Riesling is minerality, which shows up as that beautiful textural sensation found in glacial water. Whether the grapes are grown on the slate hillsides of the Mosel in Germany, the limestone marls of Alsace, or the granite cliffs of Austria's Wachau, minerality is a constant in Riesling.

Sommeliers generally consider "classic" Riesling to come from three countries: Germany, Austria, and France. German Riesling tends to be light-bodied, high acid, low in alcohol, and off-dry (though more producers are pushing their wines to drier levels). Wines from the Mosel and its tributaries are the lightest and most citrus. Those from warmer regions like the Rheingau and the Pfalz may express tropical fruit along with citrus and have a rounder, richer body.

Alsace is the only region in France known for Riesling. More southerly than Germany's best Riesling regions, it produces a style that is reliably bigger. It used to be that most Alsatian Riesling was fermented dry, but modern styles vary broadly from bone-dry to sweet, depending on the producer and vintage. To complicate matters, labels seldom reveal the style of wine. Nevertheless, Alsace's characteristic profile is dry, with wines notable for their less overtly citrus character compared to German wines and for their more floral aromas combined with a certain steeliness.

Austrian Rieslings from the granite and mica slopes of the Wachau are noteworthy for almost always being dry. Although they can easily be confused with Alsatian Rieslings, at their best, Austrian versions combine the body and power of Alsace with the minerality, transparency, and vibrancy of German examples. As in Alsace, Austrian Rieslings from a ripe vintage can be rich—verging on cloying—and high in alcohol. In blind tasting dry Riesling, Justin Hall notes, "There is often something more green in Alsatian bottles, a touch of resin. Alsatian Rieslings also tend to be rounder with more obvious alcohol than Austrian. It's not necessarily higher alcohol. It is just not carried as well. Austrian Rieslings are tight, well-tuned race cars."

ICONIC: J. J. Prüm Wehlener Sonnenuhr (Mosel, Germany). The perfect example of the balance of off-dry Riesling. Fruit characteristics center around lime zest, apricots, and grapes, underlaid by a slatey minerality. Irresistible and gentle when young, gathering force with age.

- -

CLASSIC: Prager Achleiten Smaragd (Wachau, Austria). This wine tastes as if it were grown out of pure rock, a great example of Riesling's transparency. There's fruit—citrus, apples, pears—but it's the rock sensation that dominates. You don't feel as if you are tasting the grape, but rather through it and down to the soil.

- -

VALUE: Dönnhoff (Nahe, Germany). Helmut Dönnhoff's basic estate wine is an amazing value that brings together the two pleasures of Riesling: the sensual and the intellectual. Aromas run from white flowers to grapefruit and orange, while a gentle stoniness is persistent from the tip of the tongue to the back of the throat.

SANGIOVESE

- -

Duking it out with Nebbiolo for title of Italy's most regal red grape, Sangiovese is grown all over the country but reaches its apex in Tuscany, where it is the backbone of Chianti and Brunello di Montalcino.

Tuscan Sangiovese (the version most likely to show up in a sommelier blind tasting) is recognizable for its dominant flavor of tart cherry, which is often complemented by a bouquet of herbs and a sprinkling of dust. "The only primary fruit I get in Sangiovese is cherry," confirms Hristo Zisovski. "It's always tart cherry, never overripened. And it often comes on a cloud of volatile acidity. You can sometimes recognize it by a pinching of nose, a burning of eyes when you smell it." Eric Railsback of RN74 also looks for the classic texture of Sangiovese, which he describes as "coarse in a finely ground way—almost like broken SweeTarts."

In the mouth, the alluring cherry is made tense by strident acidity. Traditionally made Chiantis balance the acidity with a solid level of ripeness, lightly prickly tannins, and integrated oak. "In a classically made Chianti aged in a large wooden cask," adds Zisovski, "you get wet wood more than new wood." On the other hand, Sangiovese made in the modern style will have a darker fruit—pushing from red cherry to black—a richer texture, and lots of toasty, vanilla-laden oak. For most sommeliers, the more traditional style is the benchmark.

These wines, especially high-end Chianti and Brunello, can age well. After eight to ten years, their ruby color begins to take on an orange tone around the rim, and earthy notes creep into the aromas as the cherry scent begins to fade. "I often find some eucalyptus and soy sauce in older Tuscan wines," says Zisovski.

- -

ICONIC: Case Basse Soldera Brunello di Montalcino Riserva (Tuscany, Italy). Complex, dense, and moody, but with an undeniably joyful spark of tart cherry, mineral, and spring flowers. Mind-blowing with age, as it develops a magical complexity.

CLASSIC: Montevertine "Le Pergole Torte" (Tuscany, Italy). The perfect Tuscan Sangiovese—dusty cherry, stones, and herbs in a rich and structured but lovely flow. As elegant as Sangiovese comes.

VALUE: Fattoria di Fèlsina Chianti Classico Riserva (Tuscany, Italy). Light and bright, marrying flavors of cherry and earth. Appetizing acidity makes this wine ideal with food.

SAUVIGNON BLANC

Like its offspring, Cabernet Sauvignon, this white grape does well in a variety of climates and terrains. But it is considered prototypical in only three locations: the Loire Valley and Bordeaux regions of France and the Marlborough region of New Zealand. Because of its unique aromatics, Sauvignon Blanc is relatively easy to identify in a blind tasting.

If the color green were an aroma, that's what Sauvignon Blanc would smell like. In the cool northern stretches of the Loire, this "green" aspect is expressed as grassiness, mixed with green apple, tomato leaf, and gooseberry. In New Zealand, the aromas are more garishly green notes of asparagus and green pepper mixed with punchy gooseberry and tropical hints of passion fruit, grapefruit, and guava. In Bordeaux, Sauvignon Blanc is almost always blended with the plumper Sémillon, but it remains recognizable by its grassy note that overlays tropical fruits, even though the wines are often slathered with new oak.

Sauvignon Blanc is fairly apparent in most blind tastings, but determining the precise provenance can be harder. For example, in the Loire, the Sancerre region has three types of soil that produce three very different styles of wine. The Chavignol side has chalky, steep hillsides made of Kimmeridgian marl known as *terres blanches*. They produce high-toned wines with assertive minerality and richness that still speak with finesse. Next comes a rougher, stony soil called *caillottes* that produces a lighter wine with fewer high notes—more mezzo-soprano to the soprano of the *terres blanches*. Finally, the lower, flint-topped clay and limestone mix, known as *silex*, yields wines that are famous for a smoky minerality, richness, and girth.

"Sauvignon Blanc blind is usually quite obvious," says Bernie Sun, wine director for Jean-Georges Vongerichten's restaurant empire, "but some of the less-expressive Loire Sauvignons can occasionally be confused with Chenin Blanc or even Chablis, which grow on the exact same kind of Kimmeridgian chalk. It's an occasion where the soil speaks louder than the variety, so you have to be on the lookout for that."

Another blind tasting sign of Sauvignon Blanc is the aroma of—there's no polite way to put it—cat pee. This telltale tip-off is caused by compounds called pyrazines (also responsible for green pepper scents), and it shows up most often in the Sauvignon Blancs of New Zealand and the northern Italian regions of Friuli and Alto Adige, though it can appear in Sauvignon Blanc from anywhere.

ICONIC: Edmond Vatan Sancerre Clos la Néore (Loire, France). The greatest example from the Chavignol side. Wildly complex with savory notes, as well as fruits from melon to citrus, a deep mineral density, and a long herb-dominated finish.

CLASSIC: Domaine Vacheron Sancerre (Loire, France). Joyful, bright, and highly perfumed. A Sauvignon animated by tension between a sharp streak of minerality and a mouth-filling richness.

VALUE: Philippe Portier Quincy (Loire, France). Highly aromatic with flowers and pear and green apple skins. In the mouth, grassy notes with some bitter grapefruit predominate. The acidity here is literally mouthwatering.

SYRAH

The red grape of France's northern Rhône, Syrah has blossomed around the world, making popular wines in Australia, South Africa, California, and Washington State. No matter where it is grown, it has a reputation for making burly, tannic wines, big in stature and body. They also tend to be dark: blackish purple with hints of blue.

The flavor and aromatic profiles of a Syrah depend on the climate in which it is grown. The cooler climes of the northern Rhône produce wines that taste of black and white pepper, wild blackberry, and violets and whose aromas suggest meat, game, or leather. In its most famous New World growing areas of Washington State, California, and Australia, Syrah is often much riper, with jammy blackberry and blueberry flavors and notes of leather and game, high alcohol, and a thick, dense body. However, the New World—particularly cool coastal California—is showing it can also produce wonderful Rhône-style Syrah.

In a blind tasting, it is not enough to identify the northern Rhône as a Syrah's place of origin. Tasters should also be able to guess a wine's specific appellation: Côte-Rôtie, Hermitage, Cornas, Crozes-Hermitage, or Saint-Joseph. Once he has determined that the wine is a northern Rhône Syrah, Rajat breaks it down by village. Côte-Rôtie, he says, tends to make the lightest, finest wines of the region. "I look for a slightly lighter body, higher acidity, and a perfume that goes from white pepper to beef jerky to just-ripe blackberries. Alcohol

BOTTLES IN THE CELLAR OF JEAN-LOUIS CHAVE, HERMITAGE

levels are relatively low—between 12½ and 13½ percent—indicating a medium-bodied wine." Hermitage makes a denser, darker wine, he observes. "It's got more beef teriyaki, darker black fruits, and often smells of asphalt or Band-Aids. There will be more alcohol and thus a bigger body. Tannins will be more intense." Cornas may have even more jagged tannins than Hermitage, Rajat says, and will sometimes have a more fruity, less savory expression. "I think of Cornas as being more rustic, but as having the most fruit purity. The blackberry fruit here is riper, tending sometimes to black cherry and cassis." Crozes-Hermitage and Saint-Joseph are much larger and less well-defined appellations, and thus harder to identify, according to Rajat. "Some good Syrahs are found in those appellations," he adds, "but I guess them only if the wine is less profound, concentrated, tannic, or ripe than my sense of a Côte-Rôtie."

Australian Shiraz is Syrah in a very different form. Ripened to extreme jamminess and with alcohol reaching 15 or 16 percent, it's strikingly different from its French cousin. "I find aromas of plum, blackberry or cherry pie, pepper, and leather in Shiraz," says Laura Maniec, director of wine and spirits for New York's B.R. Guest Restaurants. "There's often a fair bit of new American oak, too, resulting in vanilla and sometimes even dill aromas." Sommeliers in the United States, she adds, tend not to list much Australian Shiraz, as its high alcohol, low acid, and jammy fruits "don't tend to be food friendly." However, she notes, there are exceptions, and wines like Penfolds Grange are considered world-class collectibles that can age well for decades.

ICONIC: Domaine Jamet Côte-Rôtie Côte Brune (Rhône, France). Dazzling complexity brings a slew of references: smoke, meat, wild blackberry, flowers, tar, earth. Medium-bodied, with intense flavors carried deep into a long finish.

CLASSIC: Thierry Allemand Cornas Reynard (Rhône, France). A less savory, more deeply fruited vision of Syrah, with gorgeous blackberry and violet perfume. Thick with sweet, chewy tannins, the wine is juicy, joyous, and carnal.

VALUE: Domaine Combier Crozes-Hermitage (Rhône, France). A light, smooth style of Syrah. Fruit and pepper dominate the nose, with hints of meat. The palate is savory and earthy, structured with firm acidity and medium tannin.

A PRIZED JEROBOAM AT LA PAULÉE

CHAPTER THREE

BUYING AND STORING WINE

In January 2003, Rajat, who had just left the Fifth Floor in San Francisco to become the wine director for chef Michael Mina's fledgling restaurant group, took up the first assignment of his new position: Las Vegas. The Mina Group already had one restaurant in the city, Nobhill in the MGM Grand, and was scheduled to open a second one, Seablue, in November. Rajat's mission was twofold: revamp the wine list at Nobhill and create the program for Seablue. But a task expected to require just a few months turned into an entire year. And what was supposed to be the routine creation of a new wine list turned into an ordeal of the kind that few sommeliers ever have to endure.

Rajat arrived in Las Vegas with no professional experience in the city. Coming from the open-minded and enthusiastic wine-drinking culture of the Bay Area, he was determined to create a San Francisco–style wine list for Seablue: a worldly inventory full of diverse, even obscure wines that would challenge diners as well as please them.

Las Vegas was in the midst of a well-documented food revolution that began in the mid-1990s with the arrival of star chefs like Wolfgang Puck, Emeril Lagasse, and Tom Colicchio. In true Vegas fashion, the stakes climbed higher in the early 2000s with the arrival of a trio of Michelin-starred French chefs: Alain Ducasse, Guy Savoy, and Joël Robuchon. The brutal, seedy Vegas depicted in movies like *Casino* was becoming softer. What was once just a place for men to lose their money at the tables was now a destination where their wives could spend their money at the spas and shops and at dining tables overseen by chefs who had previously only worked in New York, Paris, San Francisco, and Los Angeles.

But the wine culture lagged behind the food culture. Serious dining calls for great service and great wine; by most accounts, the Las Vegas wine scene had been surprisingly moribund for decades, especially considering the amount of money that circulated. Steven Geddes, a master sommelier who worked in the city most of his career, recalls that wine programs of the 1970s and 1980s were notable only for their lack of ambition. "Most hotels," he says, "had off vintages of the first growths, *négociant* Burgundies . . . fifty to sixty selections. There were two or three sommeliers in town, and they were old school."

During the same era, the distribution industry evolved to be controlled by some powerful, deeply entrenched companies that dictated terms to their clients and thrived on stifling competition. To be fair, these companies performed the services required of them and helped the town grow in many ways. Nothing they did was illegal, but they undoubtedly played business hardball. Spirits and beer were the profit center, and wine was peripheral at best. "In the past," Steven Geddes explains, "the high rollers wanted their Dom Pérignon and their Lafite, and it didn't go too much beyond that. Distribution was locked into place, and it was simple and easily controlled."

With the arrival of the star chefs and a serious dining culture, sommelier positions began to emerge in greater numbers, and the wine began to flow. In 1997, Barrie Larvin, a Las

66

Vegas sommelier, made headlines and forged the city's reputation for wine excess (he once bragged, "We go through a case of first growths every weekend") by going on a high-profile auction spree, snapping up, among other purchases, Andrew Lloyd Webber's famous cellar for four hundred thousand dollars and a bottle of 1800 Madeira once owned by Thomas Jefferson for twenty thousand dollars.

Even though rare, ever-more-expensive bottles were available to the elite clientele who patronized the burgeoning fine-dining scene, little precedent existed for a list like the one Rajat envisioned—less-celebrated, more idiosyncratic choices like Rieslings from Germany, Moschofileros from Greece, Vermentinos from Sardinia—to accompany Mina's fish-centric menu. Las Vegas was a label-drinking culture, and was not ready to have the more thorough and curious relationship to wine Rajat wanted to cultivate. Plus, finding the wines he needed to build his list wasn't as easy as Rajat had thought it would be.

A wine list is a form of expression. Sommeliers new to Las Vegas arrived with a lot to say, but the city's antiquated wine distribution system did not give them the words to say it. They required a lexicon of small, unheralded producers and of diverse countries and grapes. The big distributors couldn't supply them with what they needed, nor did they seem interested in expanding the vocabulary. The roster of familiar wines was easily manageable, highly profitable, and had worked seamlessly for years. "Sommeliers coming in from New York and California didn't want to have to buy from one or two big companies," Geddes adds. "They didn't want to have their brands dictated to them, but they didn't realize that's how things worked here. Vegas adapted to culinary change quite easily, but wine was a dinosaur industry."

The methods used by the big distributors to maintain control were simple. A list of available wines was presented to the sommeliers, but it contained no prices or quantities. If a sommelier wanted to order a wine, the salesman would promise to get back to him or her with the price and availability. Lacking that knowledge made it difficult for sommeliers to plan a wine list or make a budget. On the rare occasions when some of the unique wines that Rajat and his colleagues sought were obtainable, it could take weeks or even months after the order was placed for the wines to arrive. The system worked well for the wine sellers, who could foist whatever brands they wanted onto the sommeliers. Wines that were less profitable or took more time or effort to source and deliver were put on the back burner.

There were stories of more ruthless tactics, of ultimatums made to casino management that offending wine buyers be fired or demoted. Leverage to make such demands came from the big suppliers' control of spirits and beer. Any threat to the supply of those casino staples, or to withholding millions of dollars in advertising, was enough to get sommeliers who didn't play along a one-way ticket out of town. Most sommeliers, content to bank their salaries in a state without an income tax and enjoy the perks of a town that knows hospitality, were unwilling to challenge the status quo.

One young sommelier named Ken Fredrickson did. The sharp-eyed, dark-haired Fredrickson, who would become one of Rajat's closest friends, had gone to hospitality school at University of Nevada, Las Vegas, and then earned a master sommelier degree while developing restaurants and consulting in Wyoming and Colorado. Fredrickson saw the Las Vegas restaurant boom in the late 1990s and early 2000s as an opportunity to bring in and sell wine that wasn't available in the market—gems from California (Copain, Radio-Coteau), Oregon (J.K. Carriere), and Washington (Cayuse) that had never sniffed the Nevada border. Beyond the West Coast, the rights to great import portfolios like Terry Theise's (wonderful grower Champagnes, German Rieslings, and Austrian wines) were languishing in the dusty ledgers of the big boys, not promoted, ordered, or sold. So, in 2002, with the investment of a few backers, Fredrickson started Nevada Wine Agents (NWA) with the primary intent to give the new generation of sommeliers the lexicon they needed to make their wine lists as intriguing and opulent as the cuisines of the great chefs who were changing the way people ate in the city.

Rajat and Ken found each other just as NWA was getting off the ground. They shared an apartment for much of that year, and Fredrickson's company became Rajat's go-to distributor for getting him the wines he wanted. "When Nevada Wine Agents opened," Rajat remembers, "it drew a line in the sand between the old and the new. On one side of the line were people who didn't care how a wine tasted and how it went with the food. Their only concern was how it sold, and they had no interest in finding the next great producer. Then you had the people like me who would do anything to have a certain wine on their list." Rajat was not the only sommelier helping foment this quiet revolution. At one point, Fredrickson recalls, a single restaurant—the wine-themed Aureole, with a program run by the visionary Andrew Bradbury—accounted for more than a quarter of his business.

The big distributors immediately pegged Fredrickson as a threat, and he lived a hair-raising life for a while. With Nevada Wine Agents challenging the system, customers were forced to choose sides, and Fredrickson quickly learned who his friends were. A number of restaurants and hotels refused to do business with him. Believing that no wine list could be considered contemporary without at least a couple of his offerings, he was astounded. "I tried as hard as I could to break through, but they wouldn't do business with me," he recalls. "I even offered one sommelier some Châteauneuf-du-Pape Clos du Caillou—a 100-point Parker wine!—and he wouldn't take it. I had some dark days. There were times that I didn't think we were going to make it."

Confident in his extensive network, his credibility as a master sommelier, his excellent, cutting-edge portfolio, and the company's unique commitment to service and education, Fredrickson persisted. Try as it might to run Fredrickson out of business, Big Distribution had to face the facts: Vegas was changing, the growth of the restaurant scene was ineluctable, and wine was a big part of it. "For a long time, we didn't sell a single bottle of wine to the Bellagio," Fredrickson recalled. "Then management changed and suddenly we had our largest order ever."

Frederickson's decision to take on the big distributors changed his life and the town's wine culture. In 2005, he merged NWA with a large, well-endowed distributor that wanted to expand its liquor-dominated portfolio into fine wine. A few years later, he moved to Chicago to take a greater executive position. Rajat left town shortly after Seablue opened, his work done. Anchored by wines from the NWA portfolio, the Seablue list was named one of the ten best of 2003 by *Food & Wine*. The wine-buyers' revolution that Rajat had walked in on and for a time contributed to would continue in Las Vegas, and today the city is one of the most exciting wine destinations in the world, with more master sommeliers per capita than any other city.

The lesson for aspiring sommeliers is clear: a wine list is a unique form of expression and must not be taken for granted. "Shopping for wine must go beyond buying only what's offered in some distributor's book," Rajat says. "You have to know what you want and find out how to get it. If the wine isn't offered in the state, figure out how to bring it in. . . . For me, it doesn't matter who brings it in—I just want the wine."

BUYING SECRETS

Few wine-buying tales are as dramatic as what happened in Las Vegas when Rajat was there, but that episode serves to illustrate how crucial being able to shop in an open and free market is to a sommelier's ability to do the best job. To get wines not carried by the government-run shops in control states like Pennsylvania and Utah, sommeliers have to petition the state to import them. Furthermore, once the authorities do respond and bring in the wines—which can take months—the wines are usually more expensive than they would be in other states. Obviously, this can create havoc for a wine buyer trying to please clients with specific tastes. Good sommeliers spend long hours figuring out how to source specific wines.

By extension, the techniques and strategies of the professional wine buyer can be applied to buying wine at all levels, from a glitzy restaurant in a Las Vegas casino to a small café seeking an interesting wine card to a home enthusiast who just wants shelves stocked with a diverse array of great bottles.

Of course, there are no surefire tricks to being a successful wine buyer. And how do you even judge success? A wine collection should only be judged on the intent behind its creation. For example, an investment cellar will be lined with expensive wines that the buyer hopes will grow in value. Some of them will be for drinking, but many more of them are sealed in their wooden boxes, never to be opened or tasted. Or, a specialist's cellar will differ from a generalist's. The former might stock wines from only two or three regions or producers, but would display incredible depth and variety within those categories. The latter might be crammed with wines from all over, some young, some old, some expensive, some cheap.

69

Owning a wine cellar of any type is immensely satisfying, but shopping for it can be intimidating and overwhelming. Not only are there tens of thousands of labels, but there are also countless places to shop for them and maddeningly varying prices. The way to become a successful wine buyer—whether for a restaurant cellar or a home cellar—is to take control of the process. That advice may sound a bit like self-help mumbo jumbo, but it isn't. Any attempt to buy wine at more than a bottle-by-bottle pace without taking preparatory steps is foolish.

Assuming control of the process is really nothing more than arming yourself with information. Three kinds of wisdom are critical to being a good shopper: information about your own palate and preferences, including, in the case of a restaurant cellar, the context in which the wines will be served; information about the specific wines you have determined you are interested in; and information about the marketplace. Chapters Two and Six will help you develop the first two areas of knowledge, and this chapter explores the third.

Understanding your own palate is a matter of tasting lots of different wines and having confidence in your taste. It can be helpful to find critics or friends with palates you trust, but the final opinion must be your own. "I don't believe in points or critics," says Rajat, noting his predisposition to dislike salespeople who try to woo him by telling him the scores of wines that he is tasting. "I understand critics have to score wines to sell subscriptions, but I don't see the value of attaching a number to something that is inherently more complex than that. The question is not just how good a wine is, but what does it say—how will it be with meat or with fish, how does it represent the vintage or vineyard. A number cannot express those things."

To cut a path through the crushing number of wines in the marketplace, Paul Einbund, wine director of San Francisco's Frances, starts with a rubric. "The way I purchase wines for my wine lists is to start with flavor and then figure out the rest," he says. "I look at it like an artist's palette. The flavors are the colors, the wines are the paint, and the chef's cooking is the canvas." When composing a new list, Einbund creates a spreadsheet. "I make columns for all the bases I need the wines to cover: the food, the venue, the clientele, and so on. The rows list the flavors and weights that the wines should have, from crisp, mineral whites to heavily extracted reds with black fruits." And then he starts to taste, going to as many tastings as possible and requesting all the reps he wants to work with to bring him a lot of wine. As he tastes, he begins to fill in his matrix. It is a systematic, rational approach that can work well for the business or the home.

With this in mind, it's time to start shopping. At each tier of the wine production and distribution network, strategies exist that a successful wine buyer—whether sommelier or savvy home shopper—can apply. What follows are some fundamental philosophies regarding the approach to wine producers, wine importers, and wine sales. In addition, you will find a few situational tips that, when applicable, can lead to discovering terrific bottles at great prices—and buying the best wine at the lowest cost is always the name of the game.

Sommeliers buy wine based on producer, explains Rajat. Or, as wine consultant Robert Bohr puts it, "I'm a producer whore, not a vintage whore."

Wine magazines, says Rajat, constantly declare vintages "the best ever" or "the greatest of the century," as if to suggest that other vintages have lesser appeal. But sommeliers don't think like that. "We don't pick and choose from vintage or vineyard. We find producers who we like and trust, and then we stick by them through thick and thin. I've been buying many of the same wines every year since I started buying wines." Among those, he says, are Au Bon Climat and Qupé from California, Roumier and Tollot-Beaut in Burgundy, and Jacques Selosse in Champagne.

Shopping by producer is not an act of blind loyalty. There are good reasons for it, both practical and aesthetic. On the practical side, a wine buyer who purchases the same wines annually is appreciated by those who produce and import them. Small producers in particular are grateful for the stability. And there is often reciprocity on the winery's part. Loyal sommeliers and private customers alike may be treated to special bottlings, library offerings, or the opportunity to develop a personal relationship with the producer, which can be among the most rewarding aspects of selling and drinking wine.

Rajat has experienced the benefits of reciprocity with the wines of Domaine Roulot, which are in much greater demand today than they were when he started buying and promoting them in his restaurants. Over the years, Rajat and Jean-Marc Roulot have become great friends. "When distributors know that you are friends with the owners and winemakers," Rajat says, "they take good care of you. With Roulot, they always make sure that I have exactly what I want. It pays off."

Einbund has benefited from similar reciprocity. He has been pouring the Madeiras imported by the Rare Wine Company for all of the fourteen years he has been a sommelier, and because of his fanaticism for the wine, the forty-seven-seat Frances sells more Madeira than most restaurants three or four times its size. So when it came time to source wines for a special Madeira dinner, Einbund's loyalty was returned. "The Rare Wine Company hooked me up with all sorts of treasures going back to the 1700s," he recalls.

Loyalty is a two-way street, of course. In great vintage years or when a particular wine receives a glowing review and suddenly the entire world is willing to pay ridiculously inflated prices for it, most producers make sure that the customers who buy every year get their usual allocation. To breach this unspoken agreement is seen as a serious betrayal. "The worst," says Rajat, "was with the 2005 Burgundies, a highly rated vintage. There were producers whose wines I'd been buying in mass quantities for years, and suddenly, I couldn't get any of it. The importers and distributors must have sold it off in places where they have higher margins.

MÉTAYAGE

One way to find great deals in France, and especially in Burgundy, is to discover *métayage* agreements. *Métayage* is basically sharecropping, an arrangement by which the *vigneron*, as opposed to the vineyard owner, manages the land and makes the wine in exchange for a percentage of the finished wine. The terms of the agreement—the length of its duration, the division of the fruit—differ from contract to contract.

The result is two bottlings of the same wine under different labels: the vineyard owner's and the *vigneron*'s. In cases in which the *vigneron* is famous, a portion of the same wine that he may sell at a high price might be sold by the vineyard owner (who usually has no fame as a producer) at a much lower price. In this scenario, *métayage* agreements are never advertised, because one wine is clearly a much better deal than the other. Sometimes the *métayage* contracts become known, however. Indeed, sometimes they become quite famous.

A Burgundian example of this phenomenon (which happens in other regions, but most famously in Burgundy) is the Ruchottes-Chambertin made by the great Christophe Roumier. The vineyard is owned by a businessman named Bonnefond, and Roumier bottles the same wine for Bonnefond's label as goes into his own Ruchottes. The Bonnefond frequently sells for one hundred dollars less a bottle than the Roumier. Another famous example is the Griotte-Chambertin of Domaine des Chézeaux, a wine made under a *métayage* agreement with the celebrated Domaine Ponsot, whose Griotte commands a much higher price. The proprietor of Burgundy's wonderful L'Hôtel de Beaune, Johan Björklund, has his own label, Domaine et Sélection, for which his Meursault is made by the unparalleled Jean-François Coche of Domaine Coche-Dury. A *métayage* agreement between Jean Tardy and Domaine Méo-Camuzet expired in 2007; prior to that vintage, the Clos de Vougeot and Vosne-Romanée Premier Cru from Domaine Tardy were the same wines as the higher-priced versions from Méo-Camuzet.

These agreements are being struck and ending all the time and, consequently, are difficult to track. Certainly, they are not heavily publicized by the participating parties. But when you learn of them—which you do by talking to winemakers, importers, and anyone with firsthand knowledge—the information can be worth its weight in Grand Cru wine.

74

And now all I can say to those distributors is, 'Don't call me when you're desperate to sell off that weak vintage.'" Inveighing against his distributors for the 2005 betrayal brought Rajat assurances that the same would not happen again. He's expecting better when vintage 2009, which will be even more hyped than 2005, hits American shores.

Extending loyalty to buying a producer's so-called lesser vintages (Rajat prefers the term *difficult*) can yield aesthetic rewards. "Vintage of the century" years almost always deliver massive, fruit-forward, tannic reds and powerful, opulent whites. Although these monolithic wines are epic and may last for decades, you need to make room in your cellar and on your table for vintages that are lighter, higher acid, and less concentrated. Such wines are often drinkable younger, so while you wait ages for your iconic purchases to approach readiness, you can drink up their youthful counterparts. They are also usually much less expensive.

Quite often, these lighter, brighter, more acidic vintages work better—or at least differently—at the table. Maybe a heavier vintage of a certain red is good with meat, but a lighter vintage works better with poultry or even fish. "You can buy 2004 Rhône reds," says Raj, "at half the price of 2005 and 2007. The 2004s don't have the power, structure, or intensity, but they are velvety and silky and have great flavor." Likewise, 2006 in Burgundy was considered difficult because of a July heat wave and a wet August that brought rot. After the massive, structured wines of 2005, it was a letdown. Nevertheless, says Raj, "2006 is a drinker's vintage. The wines are fairly soft and integrated, and have nice aromas. Many are delicious now and some of them could end up becoming better than the 2005s."

By purchasing wines from the same producer every year, you ensure that your cellar is diverse when it comes to the styles and vintages you have on hand. This, you'll find, affords much more drinking pleasure than a cellar crammed full of monolithic wines that always seem hard, closed, jammy, or tannic.

Buying by producer is also valuable in the interest of quality. The reason is simple: a handful of producers in every region are more talented, work harder, and care more than everyone else. They make the best wines—often in spite of the pedigree of their *terroir*—so they are the producers whose wines you want. "Great winemakers make great wine, period," adds Bohr. "Great vintages don't make bad winemakers great."

Of course, the established, universally acclaimed producers will already have followings, and their wines will be both expensive and hard to find. But every region has its young up-and-comers, so it is important to identify them as early as possible. Many of the most highly allocated, expensive, and scarce cult wines of today—Screaming Eagle from Napa, Quilceda Creek from Washington, Henri Jayer of Burgundy—didn't debut as cult wines. They started off small and high scores from critics or insatiable demand from buyers blew them up. How do you get in early on the great wines of tomorrow? You do it by getting out, chatting with sommeliers at restaurants, importers at tastings, collectors. Ask the producers whose wines

BARRIQUES, BURGUNDY

you already purchase who their most talented neighbors are. Even if you do not rely on the ratings they print, books and magazines can be excellent sources of information about the styles and methods of producers that interest you. Ask big wine buyers like Rajat if they have tasted anything new or exciting from the Sonoma coast or Burgundy or Sicily. Most good sommeliers or wine-shop clerks will have an answer for you. And, remember, once you taste the wines and find that you like them, buy them every year.

KNOW THY IMPORTER

What you'll likely learn after asking sommeliers for tips is that many of the great, unheralded wines come to their attention thanks to enterprising, peripatetic importers, the real heroes of wine discovery. The relationship is symbiotic: the importers are the source of much of the sommeliers' best wine, and the sommeliers not only sell the importers' wares, but also promote them and educate customers.

In wine buying at any level, it is essential to know who the best importers are and what makes them tick. "The vision of each importer is critical," states Rajat. "The best ones have a theme, a personality, a guiding principle about the wines they import." Maybe it's a specialization within a certain region, or maybe it's a selection of wines from all over the world, curated with a certain ethos. But one way or another, the wines always represent in some way the personality of the importer. "If they don't or if there's no personality, the wines are probably not worth buying," says Rajat.

What defines a guiding principle? Not surprisingly, many of Rajat's favorite importers have a vision similar to his, favoring producers who make so-called noninterventionist wines— that is, wines that are not heavily manipulated, made with excessive oak or commercialized yeasts, or subject to other practices that result in a contrived or confected taste. Rather, certain importers work exclusively with artisanal producers who farm mostly organically or biodynamically, and who insist on harvesting their grapes by hand, vinifying them with wild yeasts, using minimal sulfur, and employing little new oak.

When the wine buyer and importer find they can trust each other, the relationship can be a highly fruitful one. And the influence of an importer with vision cannot be overstated. He or she can set in motion trends that can come to dominate entire segments of the market. The best example of this phenomenon is Rajat's favorite importer, Kermit Lynch, who in his 1988 book, *Adventures on the Wine Route*, described his travels in and out of the cellars of old France, searching for wine authenticity. Lynch, whose Berkeley, California, shop, Kermit Lynch Wine Merchant, has been stocked with wines he has been selecting since the early 1970s, sets the standard for small, specialty importers by insisting on the highest quality in the wines he sells and in the way they are transported and stored.

The name Kermit Lynch became synonymous with producers like Domaine Roulot and Coche-Dury in Burgundy, Vieux Télégraphe in Châteauneuf-du-Pape, and Domaine Tempier, the most famous wine from Bandol, in Provence. And Lynch's promotion of traditional, estate-bottled French wine has contributed to the evolution of California cuisine. In the 1970s, he became friends with Alice Waters, whose culinary philosophy—simple, seasonal, local— corresponded with his notion of "natural" wine, in other words, wine produced with minimal shaping by the hand of the winemaker. Lynch's philosophy also guided a generation of serious sommeliers like Rajat, who says, "When I see that the wine is from Kermit Lynch, even if I've never heard of it before, I take it seriously." Rajat feels this way about several other importers, as well.

How an importer treats his or her wines also influences the level of trust a buyer should accord an importer. After all, one of the main functions of the importer is to get the wines from their country of origin to the country of destination. Yet, until Lynch in the 1970s, it was common for importers to pay little attention to how wines were transported. Lynch was the first to insist on refrigerated shipping. Before then, wines were typically packed in shipping containers without air-conditioning, which made them subject to damaging extremes of heat and humidity. Today, refrigerated shipping is customary among serious wine importers, but it is still worth noting the care with which importers look after the condition of their wines. Jorge Ordóñez, the great importer of Spanish wines, for instance, is famously meticulous about the transport of many of his wines. When sending important bottles on a plane, he goes as far as sealing the capsules with wax so the wine won't be affected by the unpressurized hold.

Discovering which importers your tastes jibe with and which ones they don't can be a valuable tool when buying wine. When you taste a wine you like, check to see who imported it, then try a different wine from the same importer. If you find two or three great producers in a single importer's portfolio, it's a safe bet that you'll find many more.

Here are Rajat's favorite importers and a few notes on their portfolios.

KERMIT LYNCH WINE MERCHANT: The original and the best, offering minimally manipulated, *terroir*-focused, and, when possible, organic wines of France and Italy. The wines always have a distinct personality, whether it is a twenty-dollar bottle or a five-hundred-dollar bottle. Lynch's *Adventures on the Wine Route* is a poetic, entertaining, and informative evocation of his philosophy of wine and life—one of the great wine books of all time—and his monthly newsletter is among the best in the business. Selection of top producers: Roulot, Coche-Dury, Raveneau (Burgundy); Clape, Allemand, Vieux Télégraphe (Rhône); Lapierre, Foillard (Beaujolais); Tempier (Provence); Joguet (Loire).

ROBERT KACHER SELECTIONS: Kacher is known for his French wines, particularly from the southwest and south of France, but he has great producers from all over the country. If his wines share a certain style, it is big, rich, and opulent, with ample fruit and a fair bit of oak—French wines that appeal to the American palate. Selection of top producers: Dugat, Monnot (Burgundy); Jamet, Ogier (Rhône).

ROSENTHAL WINE MERCHANT: Neal Rosenthal is a passionate and outspoken devoté of old school winemakers, and his portfolio, mostly focused on France and Italy, reflects that. The wines are full of character, honesty, and devotion to the principles of *terroir*. Selection of top producers: Fourrier, Barthod (Burgundy); Cuilleron (Rhône); Pradeaux (Provence); Brovia (Piedmont); Montevertine (Tuscany); Bea (Umbria).

ROBERT CHADDERDON SELECTIONS: Similar in ethic and direction to Rosenthal, Chadderdon is interested in distinctive, *terroir*-driven wines that are traditionally made. His book, though not big, is impeccably chosen and contains many of the finest producers of their respective regions. Selection of top producers: Billecart-Salmon (Champagne); Marc Colin (Burgundy); Trénel (Beaujolais); Rocche dei Manzoni, Bartolo Mascarello (Piedmont); Quintarelli (Veneto).

VINEYARD BRANDS: A big company with over sixty producers in countries from South Africa to Chile, Spain to Germany. But its great strength is in France, and it boasts one of the best Burgundy portfolios around. Selection of top producers: Vincent Dauvissat, Michel (Chablis); Mongeard-Mugneret, Sauzet, Ponsot, Girardin (Burgundy); Beaucastel (Rhône); Cotat (Loire); Weinbach (Alsace).

BECKY WASSERMAN SELECTION: Wasserman is a famous player in Burgundy and Champagne, with clients in other parts of France. She is known for representing a legion of boutique, very high-end producers. The wines are reliably stylish, balanced, and wonderfully satisfying. Selection of top producers: Bachelet, Mugnier, Liger-Belair, Lafarge, Lafon, Jobard (Burgundy).

MARTINE'S WINES: Martine Saunier is one of the pioneering women in wine in America. Born in France, she moved to California in the 1960s, and started her own import house in 1979, signing up some of the greatest names in French wine. Saunier's top wines are known for their sophistication and the almost regal nature of their quality. She also harbors a handful of characterful small wineries. Selection of top producers: Leroy, d'Auvenay, Denis Mortet, Rouget (Burgundy); Coquillette (Champagne); Pegau, Rayas (Rhône); Uroulat (southwestern France); Niepoort (Douro, Portugal).

80

TERRY THEISE: A true visionary, Theise was as groundbreaking in introducing Austrian wines and grower-producer Champagnes to Americans in the 1990s as Kermit Lynch was for French wines in the 1970s. Theise, whose selections are imported by Michael Skurnik, has also been central to the promotion of German wines. He is an intellectual and a philosopher, and his wines often have their own brainy complexity. But they also all show tremendous purity, grace, and character. Selection of top producers: Peters, Geoffroy, Chiquet (Champagne); Dönnhoff (Nahe, Germany); Leitz (Rheingau, Germany); Müller-Catoir (Pfalz, Germany); Nikolaihof (Wachau, Austria); Nigl (Kremstal, Austria); Schröck (Burgenland, Austria).

LOUIS/DRESSNER SELECTIONS: Another great importer with wines primarily from France and Italy. Again, the viticultural approach is for natural wines and the favored wine making is rigorously traditional and noninterventionist. Many of the wines come from lesser-known appellations in France, but they are always clean and precise and tend to favor acid and structure over fruit and unctuousness. Selection of top producers: Larmandier-Bernier (Champagne); Chidaine, Breton, Clos Rougeard (Loire); Occhipinti (Sicily); Radikon (Friuli).

JORGE ORDOÑEZ: No one has played a bigger role in the introduction of the vast panoply of Spanish wines to Americans than Malaga native Jorge Ordoñez. He set up his import house, Fine Estates from Spain, in 1987, with the desire to make his country's wine industry competitive on the world stage. At the time, Spain had more old vines than any other country, but wine making was woefully archaic and unclean. Ordoñez helped create the new taste of Spanish wine, by finding and promoting producers who typically make native Spanish varieties in a modern, New World style emphasizing oak and extraction. His wines are very different in style and intent than those of the French wine importers listed here, but Ordoñez is just as influential and carries some remarkable offerings, including some he produces himself. Selection of top producers: Muga, Remelluri, Sierra Cantabria (Rioja); Alto Moncayo (Campo de Borja); El Nido (Jumilla); Botani (Málaga).

ERIC SOLOMON SELECTIONS: Another player in the Spanish revolution, Eric Solomon has created a portfolio that covers many of the same regions as Ordoñez's. Solomon is smaller, however, and focuses less on high-volume, inexpensive wines than Ordoñez, emphasizing instead a greater percentage of boutique, high-end wineries. Selection of top producers: Aalto, Hacienda Monasterio (Ribera del Duero); Clos Erasmus, Scala Dei (Priorat); Rafael Palacios (Valdeorras); Pazo de Señoráns (Rías Baixas).

RARE WINE COMPANY: Founded in 1989 by Mannie Berk, the Rare Wine Company does as its name suggests: sources and imports some of the world's rarest and finest wines. The portfolio is not based around one country, but a general idea of great wine. An advocate of traditional wine making, Berk also imports a few of the flashier modern wines. The unifying element is that they are all made by hand with great attention to quality and detail—and they are all hard to get. Also, no one has delved as deeply into or stood up more stoutly for the wonderful and unusual wines of Madeira, which have become a spiritual cornerstone for Berk's business. His newsletter is perennially educational and tempting. Selection of top producers: Alvaro Palacios (Priorat); Descendientes de José Palacios (Bierzo); Pingus (Ribera del Duero); Jacques Selosse (Champagne); René Rostaing (Rhône); Giacomo Conterno (Piedmont); D'Oliveira (Madeira).

KNOW THY SALESPEOPLE

In 2009, Wilf Jaeger, the successful doctor, venture capitalist, and celebrated wine collector, decided to make the thirty thousand bottles of his personal cellar available to customers of one of his new investments, restaurant RN74, where his partners are Rajat and Michael Mina. While continuing to fashion his collection, he has also taken on some of the responsibilities for purchasing wine for the restaurant. About that task he says, "The important thing to know when it comes to buying wine is that it's all about relationships."

Sommeliers fully know the importance of good sales reps. "They're huge," says Robert Bohr. "I do business with very few reps, and the ones who I do see are the ones who understand and respect my time and know what I specifically care about versus twenty of their other clients." Sommeliers rely on their reps not just for rare and allocated wines but also for the quotidian ones. As always, trust is key to the relationship. "Sometimes I don't have the opportunity to taste a certain wine, but there are times when I need, say, a Sancerre," Bohr continues. "I don't really care what it is, but I need a twenty-dollar bottle of Sauvignon Blanc from the Loire Valley. My best rep is the first guy I call. If he says he has something I'll like, I trust him to deliver. All these reps are given one chance to screw you over, and over all the years I've worked with this guy, he's never screwed me."

For anyone who typically purchases wine directly from the shelves of retail stores, it is easy to believe that there is no relationship in the buying of wine besides the one between your credit card and the cash register. But for buyers who take the time to interact with their wine sellers, greater pleasures and bargains may be in store. For one thing, not every wine that goes into a shop or into a restaurant makes it onto the shelves or onto the list. In fact, many of the most prized bottles are held back and will be waiting for the people who specifically ask for them or for those who the sellers deem worthy to buy them. The job of the successful wine buyer is to become one of those people.

"It's about getting to know the seller, because the wines that we often want are allocated," says Jaeger. "And typically the people who are really selling wine, the owners of the wine shops, don't interact with the clients." The people you deal with are the salespeople. "And what motivates wine salespeople?" Jaeger asks. "They want customers who are genuinely interested in wine, who can appreciate it, who they can have conversations with, and who they like. Whether I'm buying wines from merchants in France or distributors or retailers I've gotten to know, it's almost always a relationship. I like to talk wine with them."

The point is valid: people who work in good wine shops are not the same as clerks who work in department stores or supermarkets. They usually accept their ten-dollar-an-hour paycheck just for the opportunity to be around wine full-time. This enthusiasm, this motivation on the part of the clerks works to the advantage of the savvy shopper.

"I take interest in the people selling the wine," Jaeger says, "because, frankly, often they're not individuals who get a chance to taste a whole lot of great wine. If I buy a lot of DRC [Domaine de la Romanée-Conti], for instance, I'll say, hey, let's try a bottle, so we'll pop a bottle of Grands-Echézeaux or Echézeaux, and we'll just taste it. It gives me a chance to see how the wines are and it gives them a chance to experience wines they'll quite often never taste. This turns out to be very important when it comes to old wine. As a buyer you want to be sure the wine is in mint condition and represents what it ought to be for its age and appellation. So, almost inevitably, if I'm buying eight bottles of something, I'll open one and taste it with the staff and leave it for them to enjoy."

Jaeger's practice is both considerate and smart. But the wine does not need to be DRC caliber to warrant sharing one bottle of a case with your retailers. It can be any wine of significance, value, or rarity that the staff doesn't get to taste on a regular basis. "There's a tendency among buyers, particularly high-end collectors, to treat the people who are selling to them as inconsequential," Jaeger says. "They don't see that there's someone at the other end of the discussion who's really interested and who may well be like they were twenty to thirty years ago. It's the forty-, fifty-, or sixty-year-old guy who is able to afford serious wine. It's the twenty-two-year-old guy who is working at a wine shop to put himself through college or to get to the next level in life who is selling the wine."

GETTING THE MOST OUT OF AUCTIONS

Retail shops mostly provide access to younger vintages of wine; for older bottles, sommeliers and collectors turn to the auction market. Most people find wine auctions intimidating. They worry that the unwitting scratch of an earlobe may seal the deal on a $10,000 case of old Bordeaux. In fact, wine auctions are more benign than that and can actually be enjoyable.

For one, if you attend in person and have registered to bid, you often get the opportunity to taste a selection of older wine, which can be educational for anyone who doesn't typically get the chance. If you live in San Francisco, Chicago, Los Angeles, or New

York, wine auctions are common. Famous houses include the Chicago-based Hart Davis Hart and Chicago Wine Company; the San Francisco–based Bonhams; Christie's in New York and Los Angeles; and Sotheby's in New York and London. All of the companies post their catalogs online or will mail them for free. Attendance and registration are likewise free, though shipping charges and a "buyer's premium"—usually 10 percent of the sale—that goes to the auction house will add to the cost of any wine you buy.

While it is possible to bid remotely by phone or Internet, being present at an auction is more than just entertainment. "Attending auctions," says Robert Bohr, an auction-buying whiz, "is great for the open-minded value seeker. If you're looking to maximize the deals, especially as a restaurant buyer, you need to show up. There is always some lot that you figured would generate a great deal of interest, but then you're there and notice that no one's bidding on it. Sometimes, you can snap it up at the reserve. If you're an absentee bidder, you don't see that." (The reserve price Bohr speaks of is the minimum price a seller is willing to accept for an item. If a bid does not meet or exceed the reserve, the item will remain unsold. The reserve price is only revealed if it is not met after the initial round of bidding.)

The notion of direct contact is also why Bohr, buying as a sommelier, has little interest in online auction sites like winebid.com or winecommune.com. "I have relationships with the auction houses I use, whereas I really can't with an Internet program," he explains. "If I have a problem with the wine down the line, I have a person who I can call." Just as with wine sales reps, Bohr recommends locating trustworthy liaisons at auction houses. "Find that person who's going to handle everything, from sending you catalogs to helping you collect your wine," he says. "If you have some questions about the wine collection being sold, your contact might give you good information like, 'Hey, I was in the warehouse, this guy's collection is legit, every bottle we looked at was amazing, all the capsules spun, bottles were great.' It's nice when you get that inside testimony."

Looks can be deceiving. Bohr, for one, could care less about torn or missing labels, nicked capsules, or the like. Larry Stone agrees. During his auction-buying days, Stone liked to taste at least one bottle from the cellar being sold. From his Charlie Trotter days, he recalls the sale of one lot of 1945 La Tâche. "The fills were described as low," he recalls, a sign that the aging conditions might not have been stellar and that wine had leaked or evaporated. "Well, when I saw them I saw that the fills were scarily low. But one bottle was open at the preauction tasting, so I tasted it and it was incredible." Stone asked how the fill was on the bottle he had just tasted. The answer was that it was the lowest of the whole lot, so low that the auctioneers didn't want to include it. Because of the ullage, no one bid on the wines, and Stone got them for the reserve at $125 a bottle. When Charlie Trotter saw the wines later that night, he couldn't believe that Stone had spent money on such ragged-looking bottles. Stone countered that the wines were good, so Trotter insisted that they open another one on the spot. "It blew him away," Stone remembers.

84

Auctions can be like a game, with the pros seeing how big they can score. "The general rule is, you buy three cases, sell two of them for more than you bought them for, and thus drink the third for free," says one Bordeaux collector from New York. He even challenges himself: "I try to buy three cases, sell only one, and drink two for free." As an auction junkie, this collector is fluent in the current prices and qualities of hundreds of wines and vintages—knowledge the amateur wine buyer most likely will not have at his or her fingertips. But the amateur need not compete with the likes of that guy, who trades in expensive high-end wine. Most auctions have great range when it comes to the price and exclusivity of the wines.

"It doesn't take a genius to spend a lot for a top-tier wine," says Wilf Jaeger, who buys regularly at auction. "What takes knowledge and passion is to spend a moderate amount for an outstanding wine. The great thing about auctions is that you can do that if you are an astute buyer. Particularly with Burgundy and lesser-known Bordeaux, the market is not efficient."

Auctions are obviously geared toward reaching the highest possible price for any given wine. Apexes are usually reached for the most desirable wines. That's what Jaeger means by efficiency. But most auctions are also vast, loaded with hundreds if not thousands of individual lots, many of them of little interest to the big collectors. For every $20,000 case of DRC, there might be five or six lots of wines that are far more obscure.

"You can find that Premier Cru Chablis, or the lesser-known Vosne-Romanée Premier Cru," continues Jaeger. "And remarkably those wines are often ignored. At some of the very big auctions where you have a single, well-known cellar, the lesser wines are usually passed over, because the people who are focused on those auctions are interested in the heavy hitters. So, if a Domaine de la Perrière Gevrey-Chambertin Petite Chapelle 1978 were to come up at auction, it would probably sell for no more than $50 or $60 a bottle. That wine is gorgeous. And often what happens with a single cellar sale, where the wines have been accrued over a lifetime by one knowledgeable and passionate collector, is that you'll find those gems."

Rajat doesn't buy much wine at auction, preferring instead to source older wines from private cellars or directly from wineries. But for smart buyers, he sees both good opportunities and convenience on the auction market. "You don't have to actually go to the auctions to make good deals," he says. "I once put a casual, lowball bid on a couple of cases of Vouvray from the 1970s, and I didn't even know I'd won until the wine arrived at my doorstep. It was cheap and simple, and the wine, which was amazing with cheese, remained on the list for almost a year."

Rajat agrees with Jaeger that the best auction deals are outside the mainstream. "Amazing bargains can still be found on Napa Cabernet from the 1970s. Sometimes you see it going for $30 a bottle. Not every bottle in a lot might be in good shape, but if you get eight transcendent bottles of thirty-five-year-old wines and only paid $360 for the case, I'd say it was a good deal." Likewise, Rajat counsels to look out for older wines from the Loire, Rhône, and Beaujolais; well-stored Chianti; and classic Rioja and Madeira. "All of those wines age, and sometimes even the humblest bottle can be stunning if it was well cared for."

85

OVERLEAF: CELLAR AT DOMAINE CLAPE, CORNAS >

Old red wine is always a much safer buy than old white wine. That said, the complexity and nuance of well-stored mature white wine is one of the greatest pleasures on earth. The quality of the older whites sold at RN74 since its opening in April 2009 has been exceptional. Everything from older white Burgundies to forty-year-old Riesling to Champagne from the 1980s has been praised as drinking ten or more years younger than it actually is. This is not a coincidence. Wilf Jaeger, from whose cellar most of the older whites come, and Rajat both exercise great discretion when buying older whites.

"I'm extremely cautious about white wine," says Jaeger. "I can probably count on two hands the number of times I've purchased white wine at an auction." Red wine, explains Rajat, has much more to protect it. "The tannin, the anthocyanins that provide the color. It's more resistant to light, to heat, to movement. When you think of all the things that white wine doesn't have to protect it, it seems naked."

Jaeger recommends setting two conditions before making a decision to buy an older white wine: only buy if you have the ability to look at every single bottle, and train yourself to recognize the shades an older white wine can take when seen in the bottle.

"I'll admit to being anal about this. I need to see the wine's color," says Jaeger. He's not talking about the color of the wine when it has been poured, but rather the color through the glass of the sealed bottle. "If I go in to buy an older white wine from a cellar that I know, in France or here, I line all the bottles up and I check every single color. Within a case there can often be two or three variations in color."

Jaeger cites the 1979 Domaine Ampeau Meursault Perrières. "That wine is gorgeous, right? Well, it is not always gorgeous. I've seen probably ten cases of the wine in my life and purchased only three. The color varies anywhere from a beautiful light green-yellow to quite dark. The latter wines are not likely to be terribly exciting. We recently put on the list the 1989

Jobard Meursault Genevrières. I bought thirteen bottles for the restaurant. That was out of four total cases. I looked at every single one before deciding which to buy."

Color is important in all older whites, but it has been especially relevant in the case of Burgundy. White Burgundy experienced an iffy period beginning around 1989. A variety of factors, from vineyard regimes to sulfur additions to cork treatments, contributed to the premature oxidation (often shortened to the term *premox*) of many of the wines. "Wines that should last over fifteen years have only been good for five," says Rajat. "The issues seem to be rectified right now, so it's not as big a worry for recent vintages. But every wine from 1989 to 2004 needs to be examined closely."

According to Jaeger, you can train oneself to judge the color of white wine in the bottle. "It takes a little bit of work because white Burgundy bottles come in many shades, from very light yellow to fairly dark green, so it's important that you learn how a wine should appear through various shades of glass." As practice, he suggests procuring a few white Burgundy bottles in different-colored glass to get a sense of how wine looks in each.

The technique for surveying the color of the wine is simple, says Jaeger. "The neck of the bottle provides the clearest view because light shines through it better than it does at the thick base. Turn the bottle upside down to fill the neck with wine and then examine the wine. Look for bottles with the lightest-colored wines; these will be the most pristine." And always use incandescent light, he adds, as fluorescent light alters the perceived color of the wine.

Finally, Larry Stone has this basic, reluctant advice for buying older whites. "If you have to do it," he says, "make sure the storage was perfect. And also try to buy from powerful, high-acid vintages. If the wines are going to make it, they're not going to be the high-alcohol, low-acid whites."

Another option for finding high-quality but less expensive versions of the great wines is to look for "second labels." For the sommeliers, Rajat says, "these wines are very important. They bring pedigree, name recognition, and wine-making expertise at a fraction of the cost of the *grands vins*. More than anything, these wines are excellent options for restaurants."

A second label is composed of parcels of wine that a producer decides are of good quality, but perhaps not good enough or just not compatible to blend with the producer's premium wine. These lots often come from younger vines that yield a wine that is perfectly acceptable, but doesn't have the depth and complexity the winemaker is trying to achieve with his or her *grand vin*. The practice of the second label is most common in Bordeaux, where it has been around for centuries, and producers around the world have followed the model. While these wines do not have the pedigree of their stablemates, they are an excellent way of enjoying the style, expertise, and superior farming of the world's great estates. And in fantastic vintages when vast amounts of the fruit is of uniform excellence, a second wine can occasionally rival its premium counterpart in quality.

Second-label wines have some advantages over their superior siblings. First, they usually cost a fourth or less of the price of the top wine. Second, they are ready to drink much sooner. And they are becoming better with each passing vintage, as the quality of the juice that goes into them has risen because of the competition among the houses. Pursuit of precious points from the dominant critics has spurred producers to be more exacting about the composition of their *grands vins*. As the selection of the lots for these top wines becomes more rigorous, the quality of what is relegated to the second label is likewise elevated.

Better, more popular second wines have brought higher prices, of course, but the price differentials are still astounding. At the beginning of 2010, Les Pagodes de Cos from vintage 2005, the second label of the famed Château Cos d'Estournel, could be found for a mere $40 a bottle compared to the $270 that the *grand vin* was fetching. The 2005 Château Bahans Haut-Brion, the second wine of First Growth Château Haut-Brion, can be found for one-tenth the cost of its first-class kin ($70 rather than $700). Most critics would not describe the wine as having only one-tenth the quality. Can't afford Château Palmer at $400? Try Alter Ego for $60.

The second wine is not the exclusive intellectual property of Bordeaux. The famed Château Rayas of Châteauneuf-du-Pape makes a second label called Château Pignan. Pignan comes from vines on a strip adjoining the Rayas vineyard, and, like the top wine, it is 100 percent Grenache. It is generally slightly coarser than Rayas, but alluring in its own right, with aromas of dried flowers, wild blackberries, fresh pepper, and grilled meat—and it is about half the price. Château Rayas also offers two other alternatives to its grand vin: Fonsalette, from a different estate (a blend of Grenache, Cinsault, and Syrah), and Pialade. They are two of the best wines of Côtes du Rhône. Coudoulet de Beaucastel is a worthy second to the great Châteauneuf-du-Pape of Château de Beaucastel. Clape's Cornas "Renaissance" is the domaine's young-vines cuvée, but it is no slouch even when compared to the regular bottling. Of course, Delamotte is its own brand of Champagne, but it is widely known that it is the sibling of the ultra-high-end brand Salon, and that the fruit of years in which the vintage-only Salon is not made goes toward improving Delamotte. Tuscany has also gotten into the act: Le Serre Nuove is the second of Ornellaia, Guidalberto is the second of Sassicaia, and Montevertine is the second of Le Pergole Torte.

Increasingly, American vintners are finding the benefits of an alternative label. A few years ago, Peay Vineyards, one of the top producers on the Sonoma coast, started a second label called Cep, under which it bottled various lots of Pinot Noir and Syrah that didn't fit into its estate blends. No mention of the connection to Peay Vineyard appears on the Cep label, so you have to be in the know. Although not as powerful or complex as Peay's eponymous wines, Cep is nonetheless delicious, and in many years is preferable to a number of the more expensive California Pinots. Dominus, the Napa home of Bordeaux icon Christian Moueix, makes a second wine called Napanook. Sonoma's Laurel Glen Vineyards, home to one of the greatest (but least heralded) Cabernets in California, has a wonderful second label, Counterpoint, that is one of the better deals in American wine. At just over half of the $50 that owner Patrick Campbell charges for Laurel Glen, Counterpoint is among the rare second wines that can age almost as long as its sibling. On the other hand, Napa's king of cults, Harlan Estate, has a second wine, The Maiden, whose release price is still usually north of $200.

OFF THE BEATEN PATH

Sommeliers pride themselves on their wine finds, on being the first to offer and promote some new great producer, some new wine bargain. "If you're reading about a wine in the *Wine Spectator* or hearing about it in a shop and it's a wine that I have bought," says Rajat, "I hope that I've already been pouring it for months, if not years, before it entered the mainstream. That's why people come to my restaurant. I must always be looking for the next thing."

Often the "next thing" that Rajat or other sommeliers find ends up becoming trendy, and it is usually a great bargain early on. So it behooves even the casual wine buyer to taste and explore lesser-known wines from all over. Grüner Veltliner from Austria is a good example of a sommelier-ignited trend. Those earthy whites were showing up as a versatile by-the-glass pour at restaurants for quite a while before the press started hyping the grape. Some restaurants have made their name by finding an obscure niche and occupying it. San Francisco's A16 had the first southern Italian–dominated list in the country, and the city's Slanted Door made its wine name by stocking a majority of German and Austrian wine to go with its Vietnamese cuisine. In Chicago, Taxim supplements its modern Greek food with an all-Greek wine list.

THE ROAD NEAR VOSNE-ROMANÉE

Rajat sometimes gets kidded about his obsession with Burgundy and the northern Rhône, even though he has always been an open-minded buyer. (Years ago, he may have been the first major sommelier to put Domaine Sigalas Assyrtiko, from Santorini, on the tasting-menu pairing). While he gets more than his fair share of praise for the list at RN74, Rajat's competitive streak was awakened when critics started lavishing praise on a few lists in town that dove deeply into the esoteric. Wryly, Rajat notes that "sommeliers are sometimes criticized for filling their lists with obscure or otherwise unknown wines." Nevertheless, to remind himself that he could play at that game, too, Rajat diversified his winter 2009–2010 list at RN74 with an array of more obscure wines from France. Long overlooked by most drinkers, Beaujolais made a determined incursion onto the list (Rajat organized a special night that featured wine from all ten Crus), as did more obscure wines like Roussette and Mondeuse from the Savoie region, Pineau d'Aunis from the Loire, Sauvignon Blanc from Saint-Bris in Chablis, and the Grenache- and Mourvedre-based wines from Pic-Saint-Loup in Languedoc. In late 2009, Rajat began preaching about the Corbières, a rugged, craggy appellation of the Languedoc, from the tiny producer Domaine Sainte-Eugénie.

Rajat likes to point out, however, that even tried-and-true regions like his beloved Burgundy still have discoveries to offer. "People ignore the lesser wines of Burgundy, but they can give a lot of pleasure," he says. "In areas like Saint-Aubin, Auxey-Duresses, Santenay, Savigny-lès-Beaune, Beaune, Fixin, Pouilly-Fuissé, Saint-Véran, and Hautes-Côtes de Nuits, a generation of talented young winemakers are producing some spectacularly good wines."

THE BIG BUY

Championing an obscure wine involves a certain level of risk for a sommelier, but skilled buyers know that to build a world-class cellar, you can't be afraid to take such risks—and often much larger, more costly ones. What qualifies as a risk when it comes to buying wine? For one, a case of good wine will usually be more expensive than a pair of pants or a toaster oven. On top of that, it's a guessing game as to if and how well a wine will age. You do the best you can with the information you have: your own conclusions (if you've tasted the wines), the opinions of critics (if you follow them) and winemakers, and your knowledge of the vintage and the region. But even armed with the best of this information, things can still go awry, as exemplified by the premox issues that have plagued the last two decades of white Burgundy.

As with any good risk, you also have the prospect of great reward. An investment in an overlooked vintage, producer, or region can pay dividends if the wines end up rising in value. Top sommeliers are always ready to drop some cash on good wine at a low price, even if it requires a large upfront investment. For some sommeliers, these buys have occasionally been career defining.

Larry Stone had one of those buys in his early years at Charlie Trotter's in Chicago. The offer was from Martine Saunier of Martine's Wines, and the product was the 1990 red Burgundies from Domaine Leroy, which was a new estate founded with exceptional vineyard holdings by the famous and controversial Lalou Bize-Leroy (she is one of the owners of the Domaine de la Romanée-Conti, but was ousted from her management role in 1992). Today, the wines are some of the most expensive and hard to get in all of Burgundy.

"Sitting in the office at Trotter's, I was looking at the list, asking myself how much I could afford to buy," recalls Stone. "I was thinking, maybe ten thousand dollars' worth. I could get a number of different wines, break up the order, going heavy on the less-expensive village wines with a few Grands Crus sprinkled throughout. But even back then it was expensive; a village Nuits-Saint-Georges was twenty-five to thirty dollars wholesale.

"Charlie comes into the office, sees me, and asks me what I'm looking at. 'You've been here all day hunched over this list,' he said, 'so what's up?'

"'Well,' I explained, '1990 is perceived as a great vintage in Burgundy. I don't know if it really is. The wines are powerful, but they're a bit overripe and maybe lack a little acidity. You have to be really careful with this vintage. These wines from Leroy, though, are terrific. They're ripe and structured and powerful, but also balanced and extremely well made. It's only the second vintage of Domaine Leroy, and the wines are already pretty hard to get. But I'm thinking maybe we should buy some because I don't think we can lose. They'll probably just go up in value.'

"Charlie said, 'Buy as much as you want.'

"I said, 'I'm already looking at ten thousand dollars' worth. That's a lot of money, and I don't know how much room we have.'

"'Larry, I want you to buy as much as you want, and get as much as you can of the most expensive wines.'

"'But, Charlie, that could be forty to fifty thousand dollars' worth of wine if I get everything I ask for.'

"'I don't care. Will the wine improve in the cellar?'

"'Yes.'

"'Will it increase in value?'

"'Yes.'

"'Well, then, why are you thinking so hard on this?'

"'Because everywhere else I've worked I've had a budget!'

"'If I have this wine for ten years, and I drink it myself and enjoy it, that'll be worth it.'"

Stone bought a whole truckload—so much wine he didn't even know where to put it. Ironically, just before the shipment of Leroy arrived, Stone had the chance to buy the entire cellar of a restaurant outside of Chicago that was going out of business. He was enamored of some of the wines, but not all: "They had fifteen cases of Duckhorn Merlot and I already had plenty of Duckhorn. I was trying to figure out a way to get them to sell me only the older wines that I really wanted and keep the rest. And Charlie asked, 'How much would it cost if we just bought the whole thing?'

"I said, 'We don't need fifteen cases of Duckhorn Merlot.'

"'Is it a good wine?'

"'Yeah, it's very good—and popular.'

"'Just sell it by the glass. Even if you buy the wine at a loss, it might be worth it to get it off the guy's hands. Tell me what you think he might take. Come up with an offer.'

"'A couple hundred thousand dollars.'

"'Let's do it.'"

A few weeks later, Stone and Trotter had the whole kitchen staff get up one Saturday morning and load a moving truck with the entire restaurant cellar. There was no room in the restaurant's storage area, so the wine went into Trotter's parents' basement. When the Leroy arrived, it also went there. "The basement was so full, you could barely move around in it," Stone recalls. "His parents had to get air conditioners for it. But that restaurant cellar was a huge addition to Charlie Trotter's wine program. And the 1990 Leroys aged beautifully and were a foundation of the list for years to come." Stone's bet on the 1990 Leroys not only contributed to his own reputation, but also helped solidify Charlie Trotter's as one of the top restaurants for both food and wine in the United States.

"Obviously, Charlie deserves a lot of credit," says Stone. "He was willing to do whatever it took to make the restaurant better, no matter the cost. And with that kind of support, I was able to go out and make the kind of buys that people remember you for."

The lesson is clear: when you believe you see a good deal, go for it, as long as you are reasonably confident that the wines will increase in value and quality. Even if the cost is a little more than what you wanted to spend, it may be wise to pay it and get the wines. Sometimes such risk taking can pay off bountifully.

In 1997, when he was wine director of The Little Nell in Aspen, Bobby Stuckey had such a buy. A huge cellar came up for sale; the owners needed cash and called for a decision within forty-eight hours. Stuckey saw the inventory list and thought it was a bargain. "I had to go to The Nell and ask for a cashier's check for a variance of forty-eight thousand dollars that had not been budgeted." Stuckey wrote a prospectus of why it was a good buy (he thought the cellar was worth at least a hundred thousand dollars) and made the winning bid.

Strangely, thought Stuckey, the most aggressive bidder against him was the guy who had bought all the wines for the owner. He soon found out why. "When I get in there, the inventory sheet said twenty-four bottles of 1982 Mouton," he remembers. "Well, there were forty-eight bottles. There was Soldera Brunello that wasn't listed, and unlisted 1989 Gaja. All the wine that was listed was there, but tons of extra wine was also there."

Stuckey reinventoried the whole cellar, which contained hundreds of thousands of dollars of extra wine. "It looked like the guy who had been managing the cellar had been stealing from the owner, yet was keeping all of his loot in the owner's own cellar." Stuckey reported the inaccuracies to both the wine's original owner and The Little Nell, which ultimately received all the wine at no extra cost. Lauded by both parties for his honesty, Stuckey was offered any bottle from the collection he wished to drink and enjoyed a year of not having to worry about going over budget.

THE KEYS TO GOOD WINE STORAGE

To spend a lot of money on fine wine and skimp on the details of its storage is a recipe for disaster. Consider a tale from Belinda Chang, wine director at New York's The Modern, though this incident dates to when she was a sommelier in Chicago. "It's my worst story," she confesses, and it begins in 1998, with the famous salvage of the Swedish freighter *Jönköping*, which was sunk in the Baltic by a German torpedo in 1916. About two thousand bottles of intact Heidsieck Champagne, vintage 1907, were found on board, and they were sold individually at auction for high prices around the world some years later. "The proprietor of the restaurant I was working for purchased ten of the bottles," Chang recalls. "They were stored in individual straw-lined wooden boxes, and we had the boxes beautifully displayed in our cellar. Whenever we needed to turn a table, we would offer the guests a cellar tour to get them up."

Most of the bottles were lying down, but a few were standing upright in their boxes, each wrapped in a garland of straw. "Maybe eight months after we'd purchased these bottles, I was doing inventory and decided to investigate them a little more closely," Chang says. "They were just waxed on top; they didn't have the capsule. And I realized to my horror that three of them had completely leaked. We hadn't noticed because they had leaked into the straw." Chang worked feverishly to try to once again salvage the bottles, even attempting to reseal them with candle wax. She called Larry Stone for a suggestion (as one does in these situations), but he had none. "We did lose three of those legendary bottles," Chang says, adding, "so please store all bottles horizontally instead of vertically. That's wine storage 101. And I failed it with some really expensive bottles."

Of course, not all big buys are so dramatic. Sometimes, a great buy is just swooping up something that you see gathering dust at an old store. "We've all left wines on the shelf that we knew we should have bought," says Rajat. "The thing about wine that's different from most other products is that when you see a great wine at a great price, you may never see it again. I once saw bottles of a superior Rhône on a store shelf at an expensive yet still reasonable price. I bought two, because that's what I thought I could afford. Now, the wine costs five times as much if you can find it, and I wish I had bought all the bottles. Today, that's what I would do."

The fundamentals of proper wine storage are simple but crucial. A good wine cellar should be dark (little or no natural light) and free of vibration. Temperatures may vary within a small spectrum. For long-term aging, Rajat prefers a cellar at the classic temperature of 55 degrees. "It's tough to have that at a restaurant, though," he says, "because the wines are too cold to serve. So we keep our restaurant cellar closer to 60 degrees." A good cellar also requires humidity, but it should not be too damp, as moisture foments mold. Mold will not harm the bottle, but it will cause the label to rot and ultimately disintegrate. The cellar temperature must be consistent, too. Big swings in temperature will wreak havoc with certain bottles, especially delicate whites and Champagne.

Bottles should be stored on their sides, labels facing upward. That's because corks are porous (especially ones from 1907 . . .) and will dry out if not kept in contact with the wine. When the cork loses moisture, it shrinks and stiffens, letting air in, wine out, or both. Wines meant for long aging should be stored in a peaceful location, where they will not be continually jostled or moved.

Finally, whether you are using a notepad, a spreadsheet, or online management software like CellarTracker, keep an inventory of what you have. For professionals, it is an imperative, and sommeliers typically do a full inventory on the first day of every month, including New Year's Day. But even if you have only a small wine collection, you can easily fall prey to forgetting about bottles and letting them get past their prime. "It is a great feeling to run across something wonderful in the cellar that you forgot you had," Rajat says, "but it is a terrible feeling when you can't find an important bottle that you *know* should be there."

CAFÉ DES MUSÉES, PARIS

CHAPTER FOUR

PAIRING WINE
WITH FOOD

Eleven Madison Park was hot. The restaurant had just received its coveted fourth star from then *New York Times* critic Frank Bruni in August 2009, and the staff was still reeling from the effort it took to get it. "We were on lockdown for almost four months," says sommelier John Ragan of the period leading up to the review. "Thank goodness we're closed on Sundays, because none of us took a night off for months. We had no idea Bruni was going to come, but the first time he visited, we got lucky. Someone spotted him at the door. And from that day forward we knew it was game on."

After the excitement of becoming one of only six restaurants in New York to own four stars, Ragan turned his attention to the wine pairings for chef Daniel Humm's autumn menu. One of the dishes presented a particular challenge: suckling pig confit with crabapple chutney, cippolini onion soubise, and cider jus. A signature preparation of Humm's, it had been named "Best Pig" in *New York* magazine's Best of 2007 issue, which described it as "part indulgence, part high-minded haute cuisine showpiece, part pure barnyard pleasure."

Ragan takes his wine pairings exceedingly seriously, which is one reason why New York restaurant impresario Danny Meyer snatched both Humm and Ragan from San Francisco's Campton Place restaurant in early 2006. He also isn't afraid of change. A strapping, all-American-looking fellow in his midthirties, Ragan first visited California on vacation at twenty-three, never having even seen the ocean, and impulsively decided to stay, giving up a job as a city planner that he was to begin in a matter of weeks in Kansas City. Thrilled to find himself literally minutes away from vineyards, he rented a room in the town of Napa and waited tables for eight years before transitioning into the wine department of the Martini House, a St. Helena restaurant. From there, it was only a few years before he was wine director of one of New York's finest restaurants.

For Ragan, the process of narrowing down a pairing involves both trial and error and good taste. "Sometimes just by seeing a dish on paper you have an idea that a specific wine is going to be the perfect fit. And then you try it, but it's like a guitar that's slightly out of tune. You know you're in the neighborhood, but something's off. Other times, you need to take another turn entirely." In the case of Humm's suckling pig, the pairing challenge came from the crabapple chutney garnish. "The chefs had to make the chutney pretty sweet because the crabapple is so tart," Ragan recalls, "so they went for an aggressive sweet-and-sour thing. The dish was going to be on the chef's menu for three months, which meant a lot of guests were going to order it, and because many of them would take the pairings, too, choosing the right wine had to be taken seriously." A white wine—a Riesling perhaps—would have been a natural choice, Ragan acknowledges. "But it's the main course, so you've already been through a couple of whites. And at that point in the meal, people want red wine." He tried Burgundy, another natural choice, but it didn't work. Beaujolais, with its up-front fruitiness, juicy acidity to cut the richness of the pig, and earthy side to counter the tartness, seemed promising. "I'm not a huge fan of Beaujolais," Ragan admits, "but we thought maybe a really good one, say, a Morgon Côte du Py, would work. But it didn't."

Ragan started over by taking both the dish and the wine back to their basic elements. "I asked myself, what else has a lot of up-front fruit but has a little more body, a little bit more backbone, and still really effusive fruit? Then I tasted a range of wines, and all of a sudden I found myself pretty far away from my original idea, and also pretty far away from a wine that I would normally gravitate to. But when you stumble on what works, you have to go that way."

The drawing board took Ragan in some new directions. In his search for copious fruit married with both a stiff spine and a fleshy body, he found himself looking at a truly obscure category: reds from northeastern Italy. "We tasted through Merlots from the foothills of the Alps, and then Lagreins and Teroldegos," he says. "Going through three different flights of four northern Italian reds, I started whittling it down." Some may question whether these wines are worthy of being the spotlight red. To a sommelier, however, it is the pairing that counts, not the grandeur of the wine. "I'm not the world's biggest advocate for wines from Trentino–Alto Adige, and they might seem a bit humble for a four-star restaurant's tasting menu," admits Ragan. "But at the same time, they were perfect. So when you figure something like that out, you have to take it."

The winner was Teroldego, a grape from Trentino. Ragan solved his "worthiness" issue by selecting the most exalted Teroldego of them all, the 2004 Granato from Elisabetta Foradori. Lush but firm, fruity but not unctuous, it solved the problem. "In a lineup of courses with traditional wines," Ragan recounts, the Teroldego "turned out to be a sleeper hit—people were excited to discover the wine."

Wine and food pairings don't have to be that rigorous, of course. In fact, Rajat says, "I take wine and food pairings very, very seriously, except when I don't." Indeed, Rajat once went through one hundred wines before finding the perfect pairing for Michael Mina's miso-marinated sea bass with bok choy and shiitake mushrooms. "Previous sommeliers had all poured Pinot with this dish, which was terrible," he recalls. "The only wine in the world that paired well with it was Heidi Schröck Muscat from Austria. We ended up buying close to the entire U.S. allocation just to go with this one dish." At the same time, Rajat has been known to drink what he wants with what he wants. Big northern Rhône Syrahs paired with the legendary roasted chicken at San Francisco's Zuni Café is one of his favorite meals, and not a classical pairing to be sure. "But I love both things, and what you love to drink is never better than when it's drunk with what you love to eat."

Rajat's sage advice notwithstanding, the matching of food with wine has become a mania in culinary circles. Dozens of books on the subject have come out in recent years, putting forth a stream of analysis and information more complicated than the Premier Cru vineyards of Burgundy. To get too technical about the combination of wine and food, to stress about it that much, can diminish the enjoyment of the wine before you ever take the first sip. In other words, don't let anxiety over a pairing ever ruin a meal.

That said, it is the sommelier's job to create wine pairings that sing. And for the home sommelier, sometimes employing a healthy dose of geekiness over a pairing can be fun—an intellectual challenge as well as a sensual pleasure. So, if perfect pairing is your inclination, have at it with abandon, and what follows is advice both specific and technical to help you along your way.

ESTABLISH A PHILOSOPHY

When considering how to match wine with food, the first order of business, Rajat states, is to determine your overarching philosophy for the pairing. "You must decide on the focus," he says. "Is it the food, or is it the wine? If it's the food, the chef has to do the menu and we select the wines. If it's the wine, food has to be a backdrop."

Most people think of the food first, but it's not uncommon in the world of sommeliers for the wine to take precedence. At restaurants, wine collectors often bring in wines and ask for meals to be served around them. And when sommeliers get a hold of special bottles to drink at home (which is all the time), they will usually script a meal around the wine.

"Wine and food pairing is generally straightforward," says Rajat. That is, the elementary rules work nearly all the time. Most important—more crucial than flavors or colors—is weight. A heavy dish will clobber a light wine, and likewise a light dish will be destroyed by a heavy wine. "But the old color codes—white wine with fish and red wine with red meat—don't always mean something today, because we have access to so many different kinds of wine," explains Rajat. "We have light reds that are great with fish, and richer whites can pair with certain meats. The only color code that seems consistently valid is green. White wines with a touch of green in them—Albariños, Sancerres, some Greek whites—are usually good paired with green foods like salads and vegetables."

How do you cook for a wine if the wine is very old? Daniel Boulud, the great four-star chef of Daniel in New York, answered that question when he was asked to prepare a special dinner. "A few years ago, I cooked for an incredible Latour tasting that was organized by Christie's auction house," he recalls. "All the biggest collectors from across the country were there, about twenty people. The wines were the best vintages of Château Latour from 1861 to 2000."

A chef needs to understand the wines for which he or she is cooking. Are they shrill or soft? Are they savory or do they have some fruit? But Boulud was flying blind here. "At first, I had no idea what the wines would be like. I know what the 1961 is like, maybe. Perhaps I'd tasted a teaspoon of a 1945 that someone had shared with me." But he had never tried to cook for wines that were close to 150 years old. The first thing he did was gather information. In addition to digging through ancient recipes and techniques and any records he and his staff could find on menus served with other old wines, he asked the wine collectors and the auction house for tasting notes, for "as many reference flavors for the wines as possible, be it toasted shallots or burnt papers or leather." His foremost concern was to avoid cooking anything that would step on the toes of the old wines, which he knew would be delicate.

Boulud made some unusual decisions, such as serving lobster with old reds. "At one point, they had four different wines for one course, and I did four different tastes of lobster to go with them," he says, noting that lobster has both richness and delicacy, which is how the texture of the old Bordeaux was described to him. He also knew that lobster's richness could flourish in a variety of settings, from light, bright, and tropical to a darker, earthier environment with mushrooms and even red wine. Thus, Boulud chose not to emphasize the seafood flavor in the lobster, but rather a richer, roasted flavor that he achieved by roasting the shells and then making a savory sauce with them. "It went very well with the wines, I heard." The point is less what Boulud cooked with the wines, but how he went about it: learn as much as you can about the wines. "And always remember," Boulud adds, "your job as chef is to make the wines taste better, not to crush them in an attempt to show how good a chef you are."

Rajat says that *Michael Broadbent's Vintage Wine* is the best reference available for finding out how an old wine should taste. "He has tasted everything and taken copious notes," Rajat explains. If the exact wine you are cooking for is not in the book, he says, cross-check it with other vintages of the wine and with similar wines from the same vintage. "It is not difficult to get a mental image of a wine," he says, "and it is important. You might think that a 1928 Petrus would be dried up and old. But the last time I tried it, it was quite the opposite: fruity, fleshy, and youthful. That's what you need to know if you are cooking for that old wine."

In general, Rajat doesn't like to clutter old wines with too many flavors. "The more complex the wine," he states, echoing Boulud, "the less complex the food needs to be. Never try to match the wine in complexity. Simple is always safe and usually best."

WINE WITH FISH

"Fish is the category with the most misconceptions about pairing wine with food," says Rajat. "It's much more complicated than most people think. White wine with fish is simple and safe, but the right red wine is often the more exciting pairing," he says, giving credit to *Red Wine with Fish*, the seminal book by Joshua Wesson and David Rosengarten, for liberating modern pairings from the fusty old ways. But beyond the question of red versus white, Rajat believes the mistake most people make with fish is failing to consider the cooking details. How is it cooked: grilled, steamed, sautéed, or salt baked? Skin on or skin off? Is it a pungent fish or a mild fish? Is it an oily fish from cold water or a nonoily fish from warm water? So many permutations exist that it is difficult to come up with hard-and-fast rules.

That said, Rajat—who has spent years working with seafood and has opened two restaurants in Las Vegas, Seablue and American Fish, that specialize in fish—has developed some strong opinions. The first is simple: Cabernet Sauvignon almost never goes with fish. "If you must pour it," he says, "only one fish, and that's monkfish, can stand up to it, and the monkfish must be prepared with mushrooms and a red wine sauce." Beyond Cabernet, Rajat is decidedly more flexible. Here is a collection of Rajat's tips and observations on matching fish and wine.

- -

SALT BAKED: At home, Rajat likes to bake fish inside a thick crust of salt, which imparts a textural moistness and a delicate infusion of salt flavor. "White wines are no problem with this preparation, but a red can often be the more interesting partner. Choosing one, however, is tricky, because salt makes red-wine tannins tighten up and come forward," explains Rajat. Tasting the tannins in a wine will obliterate the silky texture of most fish and clash with the flavor, so you need to pick a red that doesn't have much tannin, such as Pinot Noir, Gamay, Valpolicella, Schiava, or a light Dolcetto.

- -

POACHED: "When fish is poached," says Rajat, "it almost always requires white wine. That's because poaching typically involves no added flavor, unlike if the fish was sautéed in butter or roasted with olive oil or cooked on a grill." Poached fish is invariably very light, very pure. In this case, you need a wine that matches the fish in weight. Chablis, white Bordeaux, Pinot Grigio, and Riesling are excellent for ocean fishes of light to medium body like sardines, snapper, and sole. White Burgundy and other rich whites go well with oilier and meatier poached fish like halibut, salmon, monkfish, cod, or grouper (or even something more delicate like sole if it is slathered in butter). With freshwater fish like trout, pike, or even catfish, Rajat likes a white with an earthy edge, such as Chenin Blanc or Grüner Veltliner, or something with a hint of sweetness, such as a German Riesling.

- -

SAUTÉED AND GRILLED: One night at RN74, Rajat was tasting wines with a new menu item, grilled *loup de mer* (sea bass), its char standing out as blackened stripes across the skin. He tried three different ones to find the right pairing: a Pinot Noir, a Côtes du Rhône, and a Bourgueil. The surprise winner was the last wine, a Cabernet Franc from the Loire Valley. "Grilled fish is the perfect opportunity to serve red wine because of the smoke," Rajat advises, noting that he takes a similar approach to fish sautéed in a superhot pan. "Even a wine with a little oak is apt." Again, it is fish, he cautions, so don't go for a heavy wine. Pinot, Chianti, and Gamay all work, and you can even try some bigger wines like an old school Rioja, a Bierzo from Spain, or a Barbera. "With the *loup de mer*," Rajat reflects, "the Cabernet Franc was medium bodied and bright with acid, but still had that cherry fruit that just loves the smoke and char on the fish skin."

- - - - - - - -

SKIN ON: If the skin is left on, the fish will probably be grilled or sautéed, which means, as has just been said, this is red-wine territory. "I like the skin," Rajat says, "if it has been thoroughly cooked. It has to be dry, salted, and maybe a bit wrinkled." If it has been grilled with the skin, especially on a smoky barbecue, he adds, you can bump the wine up into a bigger category, because the skin adds more oil and more fat. Try a Syrah, Grenache, Sangiovese, or even a bigger Cabernet Franc (like a Joguet Chinon)—wines with more intense flavor, a bigger body, and even a little oak, which will echo the smoke and char of the skin.

- - - - - - - -

RAW: "There is one hard-and-fast rule with raw fish," says Rajat. "Never use an oaked wine." That obviously encompasses red wines, but also whites such as most New World Chardonnays (unless the label explicitly announces that the wine is "unwooded" or "unoaked"), white Burgundy, some high-end Champagnes, and most white Bordeaux. The toast in the wood, he says, offends the delicacy and purity of the raw fish. "The wine needs to be transparent to the fish, something that will not offend its flavors yet cut through its fat to refresh the mouth. Riesling and Champagne—high-acid, clean, pure wines—are the best options."

- - - - - - - -

SALMON: Salmon is a common fish but not so easy to pair, says Rajat. "Most people default to Pinot Noir, maybe because of the pink–light red color connection, but it rarely works." That opinion definitely cuts against the grain, at least at Oregon's International Pinot Noir Celebration, where the Salmon Bake with Pinot Noir is the highlight event. Nevertheless, Rajat asserts that salmon—rich, often fishy, and even a bit oily—offends the red fruit and oak notes of most Pinot Noir. Rajat's solution is to pair pink with pink. "With salmon, I love a great rosé," he says. "It can even be a heavier one like a Bandol or a rosé Champagne."

WINE WITH CHICKEN AND PORK

"I wrote the wine notes for *Charlie Trotter's Meat and Game*," says Belinda Chang, wine director for The Modern in Manhattan, "and we got the monster packet of recipes for the book the week before the kitchen was scheduled to test the dishes. We were supposed to take each recipe and choose our two best-guess pairings to match with the food. We were wrong almost every time. What we learned from the experience was that the protein often doesn't matter. Instead, it's all about the sauce and the accompaniments. And that is especially true for chicken and pork."

While it is true that deciding on what to drink with chicken and pork depends on what surrounds them, a few generalizations apply. With heavily roasted, browned chicken served with a highly caramelized demi-glace, Chang (whose grandfather owned a chicken farm in Taiwan) is inclined to go with red wines, from Pinot Noir and Nebbiolo to light Rhônes. Extremely rich, aged white Burgundies can also work in that situation, she says. Lighter chicken preparations—"think grilled with fiddlehead ferns, snap peas, and other spring vegetables—call for an herbal, garigue-laden rosé." Chicken dishes "with a good dose of acidity, such as lemon juice in the sauce, might take you to Sauvignon Blanc territory. So, you see, it's all relative," Chang says.

Chang follows rules similar to those for chicken when pairing pork. "In some cases, the cut of pork will influence the choice of wine. Is it a really meaty chop, a juicy tenderloin, or a fatty belly?" For the meaty chop, she counsels red wines with good acidity, such as Pinot Noir, Nebbiolo, Sangiovese, or Rhône Syrah. With the tenderloin, which typically does not have as definitive a pork taste, she suggests a light red or a medium-bodied white. And with the pork belly, "you can use the tannins in a tannic red to cut through the fat," she says, "though a high-acid white like Riesling is always a great pairing." For smoked pork, Chang likes to find wines that have a hint of smoke "from the *terroir*, not from oak." Among the wines that fit that profile she counts some from the southern Rhône like Châteauneuf-du-Pape, some Spanish reds like Priorat, and some reds from southern Italy.

WINE WITH GAME

"People wonder," notes Rajat, "why wine and food seem to go together so much better in Europe than they do in the United States. Well, a number of reasons can be cited, led by the fact that the cuisine and the wine have grown up together. We don't have that in the United States." The United States does indeed lack the sheer number and diversity of provincial

MA CUISINE (APRÈS), BURGUNDY

cuisines that have evolved in Europe over centuries. And even the culinary traditions that do exist have not developed alongside mature local wine industries, as they have in Europe. So it's no wonder, as Rajat points out, that people vacationing in Europe invariably find that wine and food taste great together (not to mention that leisurely escape tends to bring out the best in everything).

"And," he adds, "they also eat a lot of game, much more than we do in the United States. And game is a brilliant match for wine."

- -

GAME BIRDS: According to Rajat, this is the greatest category for matching one grape, Pinot Noir. "Pinot is often named the most versatile grape, and it is," he says. "But it was made to go with squab, quail, partridge, duck, game hen, and goose. Any of these birds, cooked in almost any way, will be more delicious with Pinot Noir than with any other grape." He cites the combination of Pinot's pure red fruits, lighter tannins, and earthy edge as being the perfect mix with the finer flesh and lighter flavors of game birds. Heavier, meatier birds like goose and duck can take heavier Pinots, such as New World wines (as long as they have good acidity); bigger Burgundies, such as Gevrey-Chambertin; younger wines; or wines from powerful vintages like 2003 and 2005. Lighter birds, like squab and quail, benefit from more delicate Burgundies, such as Chambolle-Musigny, or wines with significant age.

- -

GAME MEATS: Red wine is great with beef, agrees Rajat, but adds that "powerful, Old World reds never taste better than when paired with meat that is as feral and wild as the wines are." Wines that frequently have a gamy or meaty component, like Brunello di Montalcino, Côte-Rôtie, Rioja, Barolo, and aged Bordeaux, are beautiful with strongly flavored meats like venison, rabbit, boar, or lamb (not exactly game, but gamy). Often these Old World wines work better than New World ones (California Cabernet Sauvignon, Australian Shiraz) not only because their flavors are a little more woodsy and earthy, but also because the acidity is better. Acid is a counter to fat. Although game meats are never as fatty as the meat of long-domesticated animals, high acidity is likewise the knife that will help cut through sinuous, lean, or otherwise more densely muscled meat, as game often is.

BEEF AND BIG RED WINE

The classic reasoning behind the pairing of red meat and red wine is based on the fact that most big red wines are tannic—especially America's most popular red, Cabernet Sauvignon—and to have an enjoyable food and wine experience, those tannins need to be balanced by

110

something. Full of tannin-cutting protein and fat, a nice cut of beef negates any harshness or grip in the wine, leaving your mouth with a lovely combination of sweet fruit and savory meat.

But on closer inspection, this is more complex than meets the eye. For instance, cooking styles matter. As Evan Goldstein, master sommelier and food-wine pairing guru (his books, *Perfect Pairings* and *Daring Pairings*, are two of the best on the subject), says, "People don't think about this, but good red wine and meat pairings have everything to do with fat content, which involve both the cooking style and the nature of the beef itself." When you cook a steak until it is well done or nearly well done, he points out, you not only dry out the meat, but you also burn off a lot of the fat. Without that fat, the wine has less to cling to, so the tannins don't get absorbed the way they would with more fully marbled meat.

RARE AND UNAGED: Goldstein's rule of thumb is that since younger, juicier beef is redolent of blood and fat, it pairs well with slightly older Cabernets or Syrahs. "Obviously, you still need the tannins," he says, noting the gentler tannic profile of aged reds. "But when time has softened the wine, desiccating the fruit and emphasizing bottle bouquet and maturity, the juiciness of the meat will compensate for what has been lost in the wine."

WELL-DONE AND AGED: Conversely, with well-done, dry-aged, or stewed meat, Goldstein says, it is best to serve a young wine that can replace the juiciness that has been removed by stewing or aging. The meat will be dense and lack moisture, which means it will need the younger, fresher wine. And because you have cooked off a lot of the fat, he says, "the wine's tannins must be kept in check so the meat will not be overwhelmed—go with a juicy Merlot or Cabernet Franc, instead of a Cabernet Sauvignon." Other softer-tannin wines, like Grenache and Syrah, are also a nice option.

GRILLED: "Grilling acts on meat in two ways," Goldstein says. "It imparts a smoky character, yet it also adds an acrid char to the exterior. Smoke works with oak in the wine, no problem. But that bitter character in the char is not going to offend the tannin—it doesn't counterbalance tannin, but it also neither echoes nor accentuates it." His advice is to pair grilled steaks with younger reds that contain a generous amount of both tannin and new oak, such as young Bordeaux, California, and Washington State Cabernets and Merlots; New World Syrahs; and Malbec from Argentina.

CORN-FED VERSUS GRASS-FED: In the past, you did not have much of a choice when it came to buying beef—it was corn-fed or nothing. But these days, grass-fed beef is both popular and easy to find. It has a different flavor and texture than the classic corn-fed beef of the Midwest, which means different wine considerations, too.

Goldstein points out that grass-fed beef tends to be a lot leaner than corn-fed, so a wine that features less tannin is preferable. The challenge of grass-fed on the grill, he warns, is that if you cook it too quickly, it can tighten and dry out. Argentinean cooks typically deal with this by grilling over lower temperatures for a longer time, so the meat does not get too tough. But it always threatens to toughen, Goldstein notes, which is why when you are in Argentina, juicy, fruit-forward Malbec, which has none of the austere and drying tannins of Cabernet Sauvignon, pairs so well with the local grass-fed beef.

Grass-fed beef often boasts an earthier, gamier flavor and a coarser texture, however, so it needs wines that have a more earthy and savory component. A Cabernet Franc–Merlot blend from the right bank of Bordeaux or a northern Rhône–style Syrah will do the trick.

Corn-fed beef, by virtue of the cow's diet, is a bit sweeter and more marbled. The steaks are richer, fattier, and more unctuous. Try a full-flavored, even tannic young Bordeaux or Napa Valley Cabernet, because the fat calls out to be cut by youthful tannins and the sweet flavor will pick up on the fruit of the wine. Grilling—adding that layer of toasty, bitter char—is also a nice way to balance the sweetness of the beef and play to the strengths of young, oaky reds.

CHEESE

In the last few years, centuries of food and wine pairing tradition have been invalidated all because of a single discovery: red wine is generally not a good match with cheese. In the 1999 *New York Times* article "Why Red Wine and Cheese Have Stopped Going Steady," Roger Dagorn, wine director of New York's Porter House (though famous for his thirty years at the late Chanterelle), says it all: "Red wine with cheese is an old myth. White wine is livelier and has more acidity, which balances the fattiness of the cheese." There you have it. Stop breaking your tongue in half by trying to force Bordeaux into your mouth after its just held Camembert.

Of course, as the article notes, the custom exists for practical reasons. Most diners will still have a half glass or so of red left after the main course and will simply continue drinking it when the cheese is served. This is not the sommelier way. Here is a better plan: With the first course, have a nice bottle of white wine, such as a white Burgundy, Chenin Blanc, or Sancerre. But rather than finishing the bottle, drink only half of it and set it aside. After the main course, have a light *salade verte* or other palate cleanser. And then, when the cheese course comes out, your wine will be waiting for you on the sideboard.

Even though the white wine and cheese assertion is largely true, it cannot be assumed in all cases. The world of both cheese and wine is so nuanced and diverse that pairing them must be approached on a case-by-case basis. Here are a few that come up frequently.

GOUR NOIR

GOAT'S MILK AND SHEEP'S MILK CHEESES: Goat's milk cheese, or chèvre, has a pungent, herbaceous grassy flavor, as does Sauvignon Blanc, and thus the classic pairing is Sancerre or another dry Sauvignon Blanc. Coincidentally, or perhaps not, chèvres are closely associated with the Loire Valley, which is also the cradle of Sauvignon Blanc. Another Loire grape, Chenin Blanc (Vouvray, Savennières) is also a good bet.

Sheep's milk cheeses are fairly versatile, though their tanginess generally offends big, oaky whites and reds. It's better to stick to crisp, fruity whites, like Chablis or Soave, with younger sheep's milk cheeses, like a salty pecorino. For their aged kin, such as Manchego or Roncal, both light reds—Pinot Noir and Beaujolais—and medium-bodied reds—Rioja and Rhône—work nicely.

- -

STRONG WASHED-RIND CHEESES (AFFIDELICE, ÉPOISSES): These potent cheeses go well with dry Riesling. But the best choice is aged white Chardonnay, which can often develop complementary aromas. Go big: try older Meursault, which has rich, earthy, mushroomy aromas that perfectly complement the organic "stink" of the ripe cheeses. And, despite its age, Meursault keeps its acidity, a helpful knife through the richness of the cheeses.

- -

SOFT-RIPENED, CREAMY CHEESES (CAMEMBERT, BRIE): You need something with acidity to pierce the unctuousness of these rich, smooth cheeses. Chablis, a crisp white Burgundy, or even a Chenin Blanc will work well.

- -

BLUE CHEESES (STILTON OR GORGONZOLA): Port or Sauternes is the popular choice for these strong, tart cheeses, but the sweetness in those wines often covers up the nuances of the cheeses. Instead, try a medium-aged Madeira. It is less sweet, more transparent, and wonderfully nutty.

- -

SEMIHARD COW'S MILK CHEESES (GRUYÈRE, COMTÉ): You can actually drink red wine with these cheeses, as long as it is a soft and fruity type, like Beaujolais, Pinot Noir, or a light Nebbiolo. Also, crisp, fruity whites like Riesling, Albariño, and even Muscat pair successfully.

"IMPOSSIBLE" VEGETABLE PAIRINGS

Vegetables and fruits are sometimes the most challenging ingredients to pair with wine. Why fruits are difficult is obvious: wine is made from fruit, and the simple accrual of acid on the

114

tongue from too much fruit can be painful. Vegetables offer their own difficulty. Unlike meat or cheese, they lack the fat to welcome wine's acidity and tannin. Also, the flavors in some vegetables contain compounds that are actually repellant to most wines. These are known as the impossible pairings. But while these vegetables neutralize most wines, a few choices work.

ARTICHOKE: It is common knowledge that cynarin, a compound found in artichokes, has a particular effect on the taste buds: it causes anything you taste afterward to seem sweet and ruins the true taste of your chosen wine. One recommended solution is to cook your artichokes in water with lemon and salt, which mitigate the effect of the cynarin. Another suggests sautéing the artichokes and using their hearts as an accent with other dishes, which makes pairing with a white or a light red sometimes possible. If you must eat them straight, try a fino or a Manzanilla sherry. The natural, slow oxidation of these wines seems to make them defiant of the cynarin, yet they still have plenty of acidity and herbal flavor to match the artichoke's unique taste.

ASPARAGUS: Despite its impossible-pairing reputation, asparagus is actually quite easy to match. Just avoid wines that taste like fruit. When they come up against the wickedly herbaceous flavor of asparagus, such wines taste bitter. Instead, take the bitter, green flavor right to the asparagus with a New Zealand Sauvignon Blanc (which often tastes like asparagus) or, better yet, with a Grüner Veltliner from Austria, which has a beany, green, peppery character that nicely offsets the asparagus. The latter, a sommelier success story, was little known beyond its homeland until the late 1990s. That is when sommeliers recognized its "miracle" pairing potential with difficult foods and placed it prominently on their by-the-glass lists, catapulting the grape into minor celebrity (if not household fame).

FRIED FOODS AND SOUPS

The question of what to pair with these two unrelated foods has the same answer: Champagne. In both cases, the partnership works not because of flavor, but because of texture.

The sensation of foods with a crispy, fried crust—fried chicken or french fries, for example—is perfect with Champagne or, really, any sparkling wine. Both the food and the drink delight the mouth in different but compatible ways. And any crispy crust is also full of oil, making Champagne's high acidity a welcome relief. Texture also defines the classic pairing of Champagne and soup. The prickliness of the wine provides the perfect counterpoint to silky broths and creamy purées.

ERIC RAILSBACK AT RN74, SAN FRANCISCO

CHAPTER FIVE

SERVING AND ORDERING WINE

Consider the following scenario: A guy's on a date. He got the reservation he wanted, and his date looks luminous from across the candlelit table. Everything is under control, until he is handed the wine list, which is about as accessible to him as the Dead Sea Scrolls and probably has more pages. Not to mention it features mostly wines that are more expensive than a tourist-class seat on a Soyuz spacecraft. He feels a droplet of sweat form on his forehead. All of a sudden the fate of the evening hangs on something he had not expected: the wine selection.

Fortunately, the smiling sommelier, his savior, is standing by. The night is salvaged for the guy. But for the sommelier, it is another game of high-stakes poker. What if the customer doesn't like the wine? What if the wrong choice ruins his night? But that is what the sommelier is there for. That's why he has studied the vintages of Château d'Yquem back to 1881. That's why he knows the particulars of the 1961 vintage of Bordeaux. That's why if you say you like Merlot and Chardonnay, but are interested in expanding your range, he will know the perfect New Zealand Pinot Noir to pour for you. The greatest feat a sommelier performs is not matching wine to food, but wine to diner.

"Service," says Bobby Stuckey, "is the most important thing a sommelier needs to understand. Before he's a wine geek, before he puts on a fat tie and smart-looking glasses, he needs to learn to take care of people." Stuckey, a veteran wine director who opened his own now-acclaimed restaurant, Frasca, in Boulder in 2004, seems to have service in his DNA. In his teens, he told his grandfather that he loved being a busboy, and his granddad replied, "Well, you better be the best busboy you can be." He still cleans tables, takes orders, and runs food every night that he is on the floor of his own restaurant, evidence that he has never lost that inner busboy. But he worries that others in his profession have, noting that "sommeliers have gotten away from the mission of service in the last ten years."

Larry Stone confirms this: "Too many people come into the business today and don't see that it's easy to lose the trust of the customer, which is the thing that makes them valuable. Customers need to trust you enough to accept your recommendations and to recognize that you are trying to help them. How to gain trust? Try recommending cheaper wines. If you only recommend high-priced wines, it won't work. But the most important way to ensure trust is to listen, to make them understand that you are listening to what they want even if they themselves don't know. If you do that, you'll be successful, because the customer will come back for your advice and will feel comfortable spending money in that environment."

"Sommeliers must, must consider things from the guest's perspective," Stuckey asserts. "We must be compassionate. We must take into account what they did to get a reservation, how far they have come to get here, how much they feel comfortable spending, and what kind of experience they are having at their table. Reading the guest is key."

These are the reflections of veteran sommeliers. But, as you will see, it was not always as easy as it sounds. The road toward understanding guests is filled with potholes.

118

Following three simple sommelier rules, however, can make the difference between a successful and an unsuccessful night for both the customer and the wine steward.

Rule number one: expect the unexpected. A guy walked into Rubicon wearing a Hawaiian shirt and flip-flops. "Flip-flops!" recalls Sarah Floyd, an assistant sommelier at the time, who now is a master sommelier and successful wine broker. The man was with his family, who were all—to put it kindly—improperly dressed for a fine-dining restaurant in San Francisco. "We all thought, 'Oh my god,'" says Floyd. Luckily, however, the sloppily clad family wasn't seated in a back corner and offered a low-end Merlot. Rather, they were treated (at least outwardly) with the same respect given businessmen wearing Armani. And "the guy proceeded to order all these amazing wines," recalls Floyd. "By the end of it, he had spent something like five thousand dollars. The guy knew everything about Burgundy and Champagne, had an incredibly sophisticated palate, and had dined all over the world. It just goes to show."

It just goes to show that being a top sommelier requires being a good judge of character, and a lot of tact. Clearly, visual cues are out. Better to use the ears. "Sometimes you have to listen to what the customer means and not what he says," advises Eugenio Jardim, the sommelier at San Francisco's Jardinière. "Because often my vocabulary for wine might be very different from theirs." Ask a customer who wants Chardonnay if he or she would like something very dry or something fruitier and richer. "The customer might say, 'Oh, I like my wine very, very dry. You know, creamy and oaky,'" says Jardim. "But to me, a creamy and oaky Chardonnay is not what I'd consider especially dry."

Rule number two: it's the guest's dinner. A sommelier has to keep his or her own enthusiasms and ego in check, nodding in agreement at some of the most egregious pairings: oysters and Cabernet? Absolutely. A just-released Château Latour in front of a delicate Vouvray? Why not? "If the customer is happy, that's what matters," says Jardim. Rajat agrees: "You want to do what's best for the customer, but often what you think is best might not be what they want."

Larry Stone learned this early in his career. He recalls a night when he did a poor job of reading both the table and the wine. An unassuming older couple came in and insisted on ordering the best white Burgundy on the list, an eight-hundred-dollar Montrachet. Stone had a hard time believing they meant their request. Nevertheless, he poured it for them, and they seemed content.

But, tasting it himself, he decided that it was not performing up to standard. "I had sold this poor couple a bottle of one of the most expensive wines on the list, and I just didn't want them to be shortchanged," he explains. So he went back out and told them that he didn't think it was performing well. "'But Mary and I like this wine,' the man said," recalls Stone. "Still, I convinced them to give me back the second half of the bottle, and I gave them something else that was very good, which they reluctantly accepted. When they left, they said the second one was good, but that they liked the first one better."

Even half-drunk bottles of wine can cause nightmares. "Later, when I got home, I tasted the wine again, and it was beautiful. I felt so bad that I woke up in the middle of the night and told my wife what had happened. I kept thinking of that man saying, 'But Mary and I like this wine,'" Stone says, obviously still haunted by the memory.

Of course, things can go in another direction, too. Rebecca Chapa, a former sommelier at Jardinière and now a wine educator and consultant, recalls a time that she gave some customers a bottle of wine that she quickly discovered was horribly corked. "But they were loving it," she recalls. "I went back up to them and asked if they were sure they were happy with it. They said they were, so I let it be. What am I supposed to say? 'Moron! This is the worst corked bottle I've ever tasted in my life'?"

Rule number three: know when to hold and when to fold, especially with expensive bottles. One evening, a couple dining at Michael Mina selected a fifteen-thousand-dollar bottle because it was half the price they had seen it for in Las Vegas. It was a 1945 Mouton Rothschild, one of the most legendary wines of the twentieth century. For one, it was the first of the now-iconic Mouton artist labels, in which a different artist paints the label each year. On this inaugural label, designed by Philippe Julian, a golden V sits at the top, along with the words *Année de la Victoire* (Year of the Victory), to acknowledge that this was the first wine produced after the end of World War II. But the wine is not significant only for what is outside the bottle. The liquid inside caused Michael Broadbent to gush in his book *Vintage Wine* that it's "larger than life, immediately recognizable, complex, endlessly fascinating, unforgettable." Its nose, he wrote, is "one of the most astonishing smells ever to emerge from grapes grown out of doors." Michel Bettane, the great French wine critic, has waxed equally superlative, writing in *La Revue du Vin de France* that "sometimes the myth may be more impressive than the real quality of the wine, but I have to admit that I kneel every time before the great 1945 wines, especially the most legendary of them all, Mouton."

But apparently, the customers didn't agree. "They just said it wasn't what they expected," says Rajat. "It was too heavy, too portlike. But I had to stand behind this wine because it was tremendous." And here's the kicker: they didn't finish it. They just paid for it and left. "I knew they were upset," recalls Rajat. "I was upset." So, of course, Rajat called Stone, his mentor, and asked if he had tasted the 1945 Mouton. And Stone said, "Oh my goodness. Yes, I've tasted that wine. It's tremendous. It's majestic. That's one of the best wines I've ever had."

Rajat was pleased to have the corroboration of a more experienced palate, but he still felt queasy about the situation. "The money makes it horrible," he says, "but what makes it worse is that they didn't have a satisfying time. Even if it wasn't my fault, when it's on my watch, making sure that people are happy is what I live for."

Conversely, there are many stories about when a sommelier offers a guest a great wine, but one that fails for one reason or another to satisfy their expectations or desires. Rajat tells the story of a woman who came into the Fifth Floor, his first job as a head sommelier, and asked for the best Chablis in the house. Rajat's mind reflexively arrived at one wine: 1986 Raveneau Les Clos, a rare wine from a top producer. This was one of Rajat's epiphany wines. Indeed, a taste of it years earlier had spiritually confirmed for him that he was on the right path. When the woman tasted the wine, however, she all but spat it out. "This is not Chablis," he remembers her saying. He realized that he had given her a bottle of something that was not typical of Chablis. It was rich, powerful, dense, and complex, whereas she was hoping for something crisp, bright, and zippy. He apologized, ate the two-hundred-dollar cost of the bottle, and served her a more conventional Chablis.

So what happens to these rare bottles that get sent back? "We drink them," says Jardim, "usually with the staff or with colleagues." Stone reaped the rewards of the Mouton. When Rajat told him there was some of the wine left, he headed right over. Rajat isn't sure he heard the phone hang up. "He must have left it dangling," he says.

THE PRACTICAL ART OF WINE SERVICE

In a fine-dining restaurant, good wine service is clearly essential. In a more informal restaurant, such as Frasca, seamless wine service elevates the entire experience of a meal, taking it that step above "casual dining" that Bobby Stuckey insists on. And at home for a dinner party, confident wine service adds a level of grace and sophistication to the evening in a way that nothing else can.

No matter the setting, the key to elegant wine service is an appreciation of the mechanics that go into it. As Christie Dufault, who teaches the wine-service class at the Culinary Institute of America (CIA) in the Napa Valley, explains, "The physical act of wine service is an overlooked art. You can take a wine class anywhere in this country, from your neighborhood recreation center to your local university. But few of those classes tell you how to handle the wine before and during service. You can memorize a wine encyclopedia, but if you don't understand the practical application, you're not getting it."

Every act of wine service, no matter how small, exists for a practical reason, and the choices the server makes can have profound consequences on the wines being poured. In the pages that follow, you will learn exactly how the top sommeliers in America feel about and perform the core part of their job.

A guest's first experience of wine service and first experience in a restaurant are often one and the same: the presentation of the wine list. This is also the guest's first, albeit indirect, communication with the sommelier. The wine list is a sommelier's principal method of self-expression. "A professional, or someone in the business," says Belinda Chang of Manhattan's The Modern, "can go into a restaurant, ask to see the wine list, and then tell you who put it together." Good lists are more than just inventories of wines for sale; they are indicators of a sommelier's taste and knowledge. They can also be literary documents unto themselves, capable of both entertaining and educating.

First and foremost, it is the duty of a wine list to be honest. "The first time I met with Danny Meyer," says Chang of her hiring at The Modern, "he sat down with me for three hours. He took my predecessor's wine list and marked it all up. It must have taken him hours, it was solid red ink, and it told me everything he wanted to change."

On the list, Meyer had seen some biases toward particular distributors or importers, or perhaps specific wineries, where he felt the sommelier might have listed wines for reasons other than their quality or applicability (currying favor, repaying debts). "He was basically saying," Chang recalls, "'I know that you wouldn't have had a vertical of this wine on your list because you think it's great. You probably just have a vertical there because you're trying to make someone else happy. But it's not making the owner happy, and it's not making the guests happy. It's there for another reason.' He just didn't see the kind of integrity that he wanted." For the record, Chang found Meyer's directive refreshing and now, years later, she hopes that the list reflects her point of view and the kind of integrity Meyer was seeking.

Good lists also have diversity. The best wine directors have a democratic sense, wanting everyone to love wine as much as they do, so they will make sure to stock their list with lots of styles at lots of different prices. "I don't want anyone to feel excluded by one of my lists," says Nicole Burke, wine director of San Francisco's Town Hall, Salt House, and Anchor & Hope. "So, there need to be choices at both ends of the price spectrum." Even small lists, she says, should include both a couple of inexpensive bottles and a couple of pricier choices for people looking for a more extravagant time.

And, finally, many lists today seek to educate, inform, and entertain. Some contain quite a bit of writing. How much, and the balance of text to inventory, are up to the sommelier. "Sometimes when customers open a list and find a lot of verbiage on the page, they don't want to deal with it," says Burke. "But then when a list is just that—a list—and there is nothing to guide them, they similarly don't want to look at it."

Rajat's lists for the Mina Group restaurants around the country are balanced between verbosity and inventory, in the style of the lists of his mentor, Larry Stone. Besides simply listing wines, they offer text describing the various regions, villages, grapes, and/or producers

PIERRE CLAPE, CORNAS

that are important to each restaurant's unique wine program. By carefully reading these lists, a diner gains a window into Rajat's entire view of wine: which regions and grape varieties are important to him, how he considers them in the context of one another, and the producers he values most as agents of expression of these grapes and places. Under the heading of red Burgundies from the village of Gevrey-Chambertin, you will find the following text:

The historic town of Gevrey-Chambertin is known for producing the most powerful wines in Burgundy. Power, muscle, and rich, jammy fruit—tending to start compact and needing time to unfold broadly—characterize these wines. In recent years, this commune has seen a number of excellent "new" domaines. Some of these producers include Denis Mortet and Claude Dugat. While these young producers have taken a modern step in wine making, the old-timers have also learned to keep pace. Producers like Domaine Armand Rousseau and Joseph Roty (making wine since 1710) recently have been producing some of the most interesting and long-lived wines from their prime vineyards.

It's a mini primer on an important village in Burgundy. Even if a diner knows nothing about Burgundy before coming in, he or she will now have concrete knowledge on one of the most important villages in the region.

An educational list can also offer "insider" tips about various wines. Consider Peter Kasperski's massive list for Cowboy Ciao, his Scottsdale, Arizona, restaurant. Under the listing for the Champagne Pierre Peters NV Brut Blanc de Blancs, he writes, "Fans of Krug and Salon drink these when they're slumming—same vineyard region, pennies on the dollar (or is it fractions on the franc? Iotas on the euro? Whatever, they represent a terrific value)." That's a good annotation on an excellent Champagne. It is candid information that could help anyone navigate his otherwise huge, intimidating, and unruly list.

Paul Grieco's wine lists at New York's Hearth and Terroir, his restaurant and wine bar, respectively, are well known for their eccentricity and entertainment value. His incredibly verbose lists are often full of rants and raves ("Let's all be honest, we New Yorkers are all in one big Goddamn hurry. . . . So, for those of us who can't get away, the above list is a means to lift us above the monotony of the day, and taste our way into one of the world's most beautiful and unknown wine houses: Styria's Weingut Neumeister"), personal jokes ("10 Reasons to Drink Rosé Wine. . . . 9. It's all the Yankee payroll can afford"), and well-written disquisitions on various grapes and bottles. The list is mostly full of largely obscure European wines, many of which most people have never heard. Yet, on reading his whimsical, highly personal list, they are probably willing to put themselves in Grieco's hands, because anyone who would take this much time to scrawl all over his wine list, to amuse and educate us, would seem to care too much to lead us astray.

124

What is most important is that customers engage, whether by easily finding something they want to drink or by savoring a wine list as they might a good book. When Burke has taken the time to write educational passages on her list, she says, "It's unbelievable how well people respond. What's most gratifying is when I ask if I can take the wine list away and they say no, because they have not finished reading it yet."

THE SOMMELIER'S TOOLBOX

When it comes to equipment, you can be as minimalist or maximalist as you like. Most sommeliers prefer the former. As Dufault says to her classes at the CIA, "Besides a bottle of wine, the only three things you need for good wine service are a corkscrew, a wineglass, and a side cloth." A cloth, you say? Only three things are needed for wine service and one of them is the cloth? "Yes," she says, "because you will drip wine in this world, and you must *never* drip it on a guest."

Of course, full wine service is performed with more than the minimal provisioning. Here's a rundown of what you will want to have around.

CORKSCREWS: You'll need at least two. Forget the Rabbit, the butterfly (aka wing), and all the other gimmicky versions. Sommeliers don't use them, as they are either too cumbersome or too slow, or do a messy job. The two preferred types for sommeliers are sleek, simple, and functional. The first is best known as the waiter's corkscrew, which folds up and fits in the pocket. It's the fastest and most reliable way to get a cork out of a bottle. It should have a sharp blade for cutting the foil, a strong, tight bore (some say "worm") for penetrating the cork, and a good lever on the end opposite the blade for extracting the cork. Ninety percent of the sommeliers interviewed for this book prefer the classic Laguiole corkscrew from France (though that pick seemed almost sentimental, since they all complained that it breaks rather easily).

The other kind of corkscrew you'll need is an ah-so, otherwise known as the butler's friend. This is the strange-looking device with a handle and two thin prongs extending from its base. If there's any doubt about the integrity of the cork, this is the tool to use, since it doesn't puncture the cork and thus risk pieces of it crumbling into the wine. Its two prongs are slowly wiggled into the neck of the bottle, one on either side of the cork, until the handle of the corkscrew is nearly flush with the rim of the bottle. You then pull upward on the handle, usually while gently rocking it from side to side. This squeezes the cork between the prongs, allowing it to be extracted in a single piece.

DECANTERS: Decanting is addressed below, but just be aware that you will want a few different shapes and styles for different kinds of wine. In casual situations, anything can be used for a decanter (at home, Rajat favors the déclassé style of glass milk bottles from Marin County's Straus Family Creamery). But for more formal or stylish dinners, nothing adds a touch of grace or sparkle like wine in a handsome decanter.

- -

CRADLE: A wine bottle cradle is useful for carrying a bottle from the cellar without jostling it and thus disturbing any sediment. Use of a cradle presumes that the bottle is a wine with sediment that has been lying on its side.

- -

LIGHT SOURCE: Decanting an old bottle of wine that is likely to throw sediment must be done over a light source. Most sommeliers use a traditional candle, for both presentation and purity of light.

- -

COASTERS: Larry Stone insists on a coaster at the table, as does Rajat, who learned it from Stone. When the bottle is on the table, keep it on an attractive coaster. It looks good and keeps the table spotless.

HOW TO REMOVE A CORK

Use a blade to remove the top of the foil, cutting below the second lip to keep any shards of foil away from the wine. Removing the entire foil is inelegant. As you cut the foil, don't move the bottle too much (this is where a sharp blade helps), and try to keep the label facing forward. Twist the bore in; attach the lever to the side of the bottle's lip, fastening it with your off hand; and pull the corkscrew straight up. With the cork mostly extracted, grab the bulk of it with your hand and ease it out of the bottle. Take the cork off the bore and place it on the table.

When opening an older bottle of wine, wipe around the lip of the bottle with your cloth after removing the cork. Often, especially in the case of Sauternes, there can be some mold around the rim, which can severely damage a wine if it is not removed.

If the bottle has a wax seal, some people heat the wax with a steamed cloth or in hot water. Others chip away at it with the blunt end of a corkscrew, like an archaeologist chipping the dirt off an artifact. All of this is unnecessary. To get at the cork through a hard wax seal, you must be bold. Go hard with the bore directly into the wax, as if you are going straight into the cork. And then open the bottle as if there was no wax. When you get the cork out, make sure to wipe inside the lip and neck of the bottle to clean away any wax shards.

Good glassware is essential to enjoying good wine. That said, you do not need to own a different Riedel (or Schott Zwiesel or Spiegelau) glass for every variety or region that you might drink. In fact, there is a rising sentiment among sommeliers against the somewhat overbearing specialty glass movement. Sommeliers polled for this book resoundingly said that they prefer to use only a couple of different styles of glass. And, if they were restricted to only one glass from which to taste all wine for the rest of their lives—red and white—a majority named the Riedel Riesling glass as their vessel of choice. Some added that they already use this glass exclusively for both red and white. It is compact, has a thin lip, has enough dimension for easy swirling, and delivers the wine neatly and gracefully into the mouth. This choice indicates a movement toward an all-around, least-common-denominator glass that shows off many wines well, but none greatly. Of course, all red Burgundy partisans would be remiss not to own Burgundy bowls, whose wide mouths and ample volume seem to catch and project the complex aromas of Pinot Noir better than any other glass.

STORING: Be as careful about how you store your glasses as you are about how you store your wines. Glasses kept inside freshly painted, lacquered, or plain wooden cabinets will absorb the smell of those materials. The odor will ruin the aroma of any wine and can be difficult to wash out of glasses once it has infected them.

POLISHING: Use a lint-free polishing cloth; linen is a good choice. The trick to polishing is to have clean glasses in the first place. This is achieved with a hot-water rinse. You can use detergent, but very little is needed. The interior of a wineglass doesn't get particularly dirty. It is mostly the lip of the glass and the outside, where fingers make their mark, that need a soap cleansing. Every table should be set with glasses so clean that they sparkle. It makes an impression.

CHAMPAGNE GLASSES: "Flutes," Rajat says, "should be abolished." Why? Because the reasons they are used are superficial: to lengthen the duration of the bubbles and to show them off as they rise from the base. If you care about Champagne as wine and not as a visual prop, then you will want to use smaller white wineglasses or broad tulip-shaped glasses for your bubbles. Whereas a flute fatally constricts the aromatics of a Champagne, a white-wine glass actually allows you to smell them in all their vinous glory. Tulip-shaped glasses are expensive, hard to find, and not suitable for restaurants. But if you drink a lot of Champagne at home, you should invest in some. What about the argument that glasses other than flutes lose Champagne's bubbles too quickly? If your Champagne out of a white-wine glass is going flat, you are drinking too slowly.

HOW TO POUR FROM A BOTTLE INTO A GLASS

A graceful pour sounds easier than it looks. Here is a case in which practice makes perfect.

Hold the wine bottle from the bottom. Have your neatly folded cloth in your nonpouring hand. Aim the top of the bottle for the center of the glass. Start pouring at a good, rapid tilt. Don't be tentative, be confident. When you have filled the glass to the desired level, raise the neck of the bottle smoothly to an upright position, twisting your wrist inward toward your body at the same time. This simultaneous raising of the neck and slight twisting motion spreads the wine at the lip of the bottle and pulls it back in, rather than having it gather mass into a drop and fall out of the bottle. After pouring the glass, retract the bottle and lightly wipe the lip with the cloth.

TEMPERATURE

Another extremely important aspect of wine service is temperature. Most white wines are served too cold and most reds are served too warm. Rajat has an easy formula: "The lighter the wine, the colder it should be," he says. "The heavier the wine, the warmer it should be. This is true for both whites and reds." So, a light Albariño should be pretty cold (50 degrees), but a heavier, aged white Burgundy should be just under room temperature. Likewise, Gamay is served chilled (unless it is a tannic Morgon), and Napa Cabernet is served just under room temperature. "The one constant," Rajat adds, "is that red wine should not be served over 65 degrees. If a white is too cold, you can warm it up in the glass, but warm red wine is a travesty."

At The Modern, wine director Belinda Chang has wine cabinets set at five different temperatures: Champagne and other sparkling wines at 44 to 48 degrees; lighter, high-acid whites at 48 to 50 degrees; heavier whites like Burgundy and Chardonnay at 50 to 52 degrees; lighter, thin-skinned reds such as Pinot Noir at 52 to 55 degrees; and bigger reds like Syrah, Cabernet Sauvignon, and Bordeaux at 55 to 58 degrees (the last group is "definitely on the cooler side," she admits, "but allows for tempering after decanting").

TIMING

The timing of wine delivery is an extremely underrated aspect of the job of sommelier. "The wine must go down before the food," says Christie Dufault. "If it doesn't, it's a huge disservice to both the food and the chef." The first bottle of the night is easy, she insists. "But after the

first course and before the second, it's challenging to get the timing right." Often, she says, the second course is poised to arrive and the guests have no idea that they are almost out of wine, usually because they are deep in conversation. Then the food comes and suddenly wine is needed. The wine list is promptly requested, but by then it is too late.

How to spur the guests to notice that their first bottle is almost gone and they need to order another before the next course arrives is a subject of internal debate among sommeliers. "Two schools of thought exist," says Dufault. "I always pour out the last ounce of the first bottle into the host's glass so that he or she observes that the bottle's empty and realizes that it's time to order more wine. Other sommeliers think differently. Their idea is that you pour out the last bit into the glass of the person sitting directly next to the host. The host watches this happen and realizes that he or she is not going to get any more wine. So that next bottle? The host is all over it."

DECANTING

Decantation disaster stories can take on a dramatic, even tragic, bent. "I was once having dinner with [wine collector] Wilf Jaeger, who had generously brought a bottle of 1971 La Tâche to the restaurant," Rajat recalls. To ensure a quick, easy decantation, the famed bottle of Domaine de la Romanée-Conti, worth many thousands of dollars, had been standing upright in Jaeger's cellar for at least twenty-four hours to settle the sediment in the bottom. "The sommelier calmly walks up to our table with a decanter," says Rajat, gracefully opens the bottle, and proceeds to dump the entire bottle into the decanter. Wilf and I were so shocked that all we could do was look at each other." The bottle of wine was pretty much ruined, Rajat says. "Our glasses were filled with sediment that was completely mixed into the wine. Why pour it into a decanter if you're not going to decant it?"

Indeed, even though that bottle of La Tâche was dumped into a decanter, it was not in the most fundamental sense of wine service "decanted." In that situation, however, the need for proper decantation was obvious, but that is not always so. When it comes to serving wine, the most basic question is whether to decant or not to decant. It is a decision that causes a lot of confusion, not only among amateur wine drinkers, but also among professionals. And it is a serious question, as a lot can be at stake.

"There are four reasons to decant a wine," says Christie Dufault. "Sediment, aeration, temperature, and presentation."

SEDIMENT: As described above, taking a wine off its sediment is the primary reason to decant. It is common for old wines to have sediment, but sometimes relatively young, tannic wines will, too. An elegant decantation, says Dufault, is worth appreciating. "When you go down to the wine cellar to retrieve an older red wine that has been still for a long time, especially if it has not moved for four or five years, and you gently put it in a cradle and bring it upstairs, it is an act of grace." (When using a cradle to transport the wine, leave the bottle unmoved in the cradle when you open it, and carefully pour the wine with the bottle still resting in the cradle.) Decanting it over a candle is easy, Dufault notes, when the bottle has been still for so long. "The sediment will be settled and possibly hardened, the wine crystal clear. This is the Holy Grail of wine service," she says emphatically. "How often do you see perfectly clear old red wines? It's a beautiful thing, and it happens very rarely."

For the record, when you decant a wine off the sediment you put the candle under the shoulder of the bottle, not the neck. If you are watching only the neck and see the dark grain of sediment start to flow through it, it is already too late. "You stop when the sediment hits the shoulder," says Dufault.

Pour wines with sediment that don't need oxygenation (older wines) into a narrow-necked decanter to keep them from oxidizing too quickly. For young wines with sediment, use a wide-bodied decanter, to encourage aeration.

- -

AERATION: Separating a wine from its sediment is the traditional reason for decanting, but today, when so many wines are being drunk young, more people decant for the sake of aeration. Which wines need to be decanted and which don't? There is no single formula. Certainly, wines with off aromas caused by sulfur, reduction, age, or a host of other factors (not corkiness, which will never go away) would be candidates for decantation. The need for aeration can differ not only from wine to wine, but also from year to year with a specific wine, depending on what stage of development it is in. That said, in general, wines to be decanted are old wines, big red wines, and tight, young reds and whites. Wines not to decant include young or old Pinot Noir, older white wines, and fragile wines on the edge of being too old.

If you are unsure whether to decant a wine for aeration or not, taste it. Look for the presence of off aromas and ask yourself if you think they might blow off. If the wine seems tight and constricted or its aromatics are muted, aeration in a decanter might be a solution. Remember, however, wines take in the most air once they have been poured into a glass. It is just as common for sommeliers to pour a slightly tight wine and let it open in the glass.

These days, you might observe a sommelier decanting a bottle of Champagne. "This might seem trendy," Rajat says, "but decanting the right Champagne into the right decanter can improve the experience of the wine." The decanter, he adds, should be a narrow-necked, tall one, "as close in shape to a bottle as possible." Sparkling candidates for decantation include young, austere Champagnes that have high acidity. "Decanting aerates and opens up a Champagne," he says, as it would any other wine. "But it is especially good for Champagnes with no dosage, as they are more austere." The final reason to decant is to release some of the pressure in a young, tight, intense Champagne, which will make its aromatics more available.

132

- -

TEMPERATURE: The importance of wine temperatures is addressed above, but decantation can slow or speed the change in temperature of wine. If a wine comes from an extra-cold cellar, decanting it will help it warm faster. Likewise, when put on ice, a wine in a decanter will cool faster than a wine in a thick glass bottle.

PRESENTATION: Wine, red and white, looks beautiful in a decanter. "Few people appreciate a wine's color anymore," bemoans Dufault, who says that a moment to appreciate the nuanced, layered color of older wine should always be taken, first in a decanter and then in a glass. Decanters are frequently highly crafted, beautiful objects and can enhance the dining experience by being on the table or near it. Most are also, she adds, "designed to be poured from, and thus make for clean, graceful wine service when you are pouring at the table."

PREPARATION COUNTS

The key to great wine service is being so prepared that the moment of service is all action, no thought. It is much easier and more graceful to prepare things ahead of time and have them on hand, than to have to fumble around when presenting or pouring a wine.

Good sommeliers take a few moments to envision the imminent wine service, to decide what tools will be needed, and to calculate the time required to complete each step. If you will be serving a lineup of wines at a single dinner, it is important to take a moment to consider the order in which you want to serve them. "Some people always want to drink the youngest wines first, moving progressively to the older wines," says Rajat. "And some like the opposite: start with the oldest, most complex wines, enjoying them when your palate is fresh, and then move toward the younger, simpler wines." The order of the wines, he says, is the diner's choice, but the decision merits some predinner consideration.

Likewise, being prepared with stemware is paramount. "If you open a bottle, have a glass ready to pour it into," says Rajat. "It's never good when people have to chug or dump a wine they are enjoying to get a taste of the new one. Have extra glasses if people want them."

Perhaps most important to good preparation is having a staging area. Anyone who has dined at a restaurant with great wine service has probably noticed a sommelier prep table or even a wheeled cart in the dining room, where the sommeliers can decant, warm, cool, and generally prepare the wines. The one at RN74 is a long wooden table in the middle of the dining room. Glasses are stored underneath, and sommeliers open and taste wines at the table, often keeping guests' bottles and decanters there instead of on the crowded dinner tables. It is a good idea to have a staging area at home, too. If your guests bring a wine or you have one for later in the meal, placing the bottles on a sideboard to be admired and anticipated is a nice touch. Plus, a staging area is the ideal place to keep your corkscrew, cloth, and extra glasses.

MARCO PELLETIER OF HÔTEL LE BRISTOL, PARIS

CHAPTER SIX

THINKING LIKE A SOMMELIER

Paul Grieco, owner and wine director of the esteemed New York establishments Hearth and Terroir, grew up in a restaurant family in Toronto, Canada. In 1961, his grandfather opened La Scala, Toronto's first formal Italian restaurant. It was a true family business: Grieco's father started working with his grandfather on the very first day the restaurant opened. Paul was born in 1965, and his earliest memories include going to La Scala on Saturdays and polishing silverware, cleaning glassware, setting tables, and vacuuming floors. At the restaurant, "all the men were dressed in tuxedos," recalls Grieco. "It was very formal. I had to wear a jacket and tie to go in, and we only dined there on our birthdays. It was a rarefied world for me."

Ironically, the Griecos' existence centered around food-filled tables—just not their own. "There was no elaborate culture of the table in my family," says Grieco. "I saw very little of my father. He worked during the day and then came home around dinnertime, had a bite to eat with my mom, and then went back to work."

Although he did not grow up wanting to be in the restaurant business, Grieco was attracted to certain aspects of it, one of which was wine. "From a young age, I loved the idea of wine," he says. "I loved looking at wine labels. I was aware that wine could take you to another place in a very different way than a lot of things could."

Thanks to a penchant for partying (what he calls "a little too much hospitality"), Grieco was kicked out of university. Without a job, he was drawn back into the family business. "My father took me by the scruff of my neck and said, 'Okay, you're going to work here.' Kicking and screaming, I started behind the bar."

Shortly after he began working at La Scala, his father came to him again with a stiff and domineering order. "Okay, Paul, in September you are going to go to Italy for twenty-eight days," Grieco recalls him saying. "You are going by yourself. You are spending two weeks in Tuscany, one week in Piedmont, and one week in the Veneto. You are going to visit these restaurants and these wineries. . . ."

Grieco objected, to no avail. So in 1986, the twenty-one-year-old Grieco flew to Italy on his own, landing in an Italian wine world undergoing a renaissance. "This incredible world of wine was in the process of joining the modern world. There were a lot of dynamic personalities," Grieco recalls, "but they were not yet *known* in the broader sense of the word." Grieco was presented with opportunities that even for the scion of an Italian restaurant family would probably be impossible today, given the growth in popularity of Italian wines and in the celebrity of the people who make them. He spent three days with the Antinori family at their palazzo in Florence and their castle in Umbria. He stayed in Angelo Gaja's condominium in Barbaresco and began each day over espresso with the great winemaker.

"I went over a relative ignoramus and came back four weeks later a relative genius compared to the other people in my family's restaurant," Grieco says. "Most important, I fell in love with wine. My mind was stimulated to discover that wine really does touch on a number of different disciplines." He also saw firsthand that beyond the gustatory pleasure in wine exists a complex and captivating blend of history, religion, philosophy, sociology, and culture. And it thrilled him.

"When you are with the Antinoris, you realize, my god, this family has been here for six hundred years. It was palpable," Grieco says. "You pick up that bottle of Chianti and you understand you are drinking history. That is what put things over the top for me. Not just the grape juice or how the juice tasted, but the history. And it was the sense that when you are at the table, everyone is equal. It doesn't matter if you are a *marchese* whose family has been doing this for centuries or a farmer who finally took his small crop of grapes and made some delicious little wine. In Italy, everyone sat at the table, everyone was equal, and everyone could talk." Through travel, Grieco had found his home—a home in wine, and a home in restaurants.

THE IMPORTANCE OF TRAVEL

For any sommelier—indeed, for any wine enthusiast—travel can be both a reward and an obligation. "It's simple," says Rajat, "if you love a wine, you must see where it comes from. And, if possible, meet the winemaker and walk the vineyard. You can learn a lot by drinking a wine, but to really know it, you have to go to the source."

Chefs and restaurateurs, at least the enlightened ones, recognize this and support the continuing education of their wine staff. "The connection to the winemakers is important for a sommelier," says Daniel Boulud, who, unlike many chefs, holds winemakers in unusually high regard, seeing in their hard work, dedication, and craftsmanship a reflection of what goes on in a three-star kitchen. "Out of respect to the customer, the chef, the winemaker, and the wine itself," he says, "the sommelier must be able to represent that wine as intimately as possible on the floor." To that end, Boulud extends a fairly free hand when it comes to allowing his prized wine employees to explore wine beyond the restaurant. "I've always supported the touring of my sommeliers," he says.

Michael Mina shares Boulud's viewpoint, which means that Rajat travels a lot, more than most sommeliers. At least twice a year, he visits Burgundy and the northern Rhône, and while there, he often manages to tack on a trip to another favorite region, such as Champagne, Beaujolais, the Loire Valley, or Provence. He also always goes to Paris for a rendezvous with Marco Pelletier and Manuel Peyrondet, the sommeliers of the Hôtel Le Bristol, for hours of late-night blind tasting at the Café du Passage. "The French somms are driven," Rajat marveled after a recent visit. "It's inspiring to drink with them. These guys taste old Jurançon, old Chinon, off-vintage white Burgundies, old Sancerre. That's how I learn. My list often changes because of what I taste with them."

Rajat also typically takes one trip a year outside of France. Greece, Argentina, Italy, Spain, Germany, New Zealand, and Austria have all been destinations in the past. And, finally, Rajat travels to the major wine regions of the United States. He makes wine in Oregon, so he is up there a few times a year. And even before he began making wine in Santa Barbara County five years ago, he was visiting the area at least half a dozen times a year, spending time with Jim Clendenen of Au Bon Climat, Bob Lindquist of Qupé, and Sashi Moorman of Stolpman, Evening Land, and Piedrasassi.

Of course, for the budding sommelier, there is more to visiting a wine region than just the wine. Wine, as Grieco notes, is at the intersection of many factors—history, religion, philosophy, sociology, culture—and it is to the sommelier's benefit to observe how these forces have shaped wine, to see it in context. In such knowledge lies not only the key to understanding wine when you taste it, but also to making it come alive for others, whether on the floor of a restaurant or for guests in your own home. Not everything about wine travel needs be so intellectual, however. Tasting is also a huge part of it, as are dining and the pure enjoyment of the landscape and its people. Following are some tips on how to get the most out of a visit to a wine region.

- -

TRAVEL WITH AN EXPERT: Whether you are putting together your own trip or you are traveling with a preorganized itinerary, you never want to be the most knowledgeable person in the room. "The first thing I do when choosing a trip," says Laura Maniec, master sommelier and beverage director for the New York–based B.R. Guest Restaurants group, "is to make sure there will be people who know more than I do. In any wine region you spend a lot of time in a car. Don't waste that time. Travel with someone who knows the region and can talk about it as you are driving through it."

It was this logic that drove Maniec to make the unusual decision of taking an organized wine trip to Greece before she ever even set foot in Burgundy. "All my friends said, 'You are crazy to go to Greece before you have been to the motherland.' I replied that, of course, I want to go to Burgundy, but I'm also surrounded by people who know a lot about Burgundy. I have a chance to go to Greece with one of the foremost experts on Greek wines. And that's exactly what I did."

- -

TRY TO SET UP A TASTING APPOINTMENT: In some regions, such as Bordeaux, Tuscany, Rioja, Andalusia, Willamette Valley, and Napa Valley, it is not too hard to get a tasting appointment. In regions of smaller, high-end production, like Burgundy, Piedmont, and the Rhône, however, it can be difficult if not impossible to see favorite cellars. Years of relationship building are often required to get in at the more elite domaines. How to build these relationships? As discussed earlier, become a loyal customer and friend to your local wine specialist. Develop a rapport with a good and well-connected sommelier. Even with that groundwork done, securing a tasting appointment may not be achievable. But never let the fact that you cannot get into a favorite winery stop you from visiting a region. During your time there, you will usually discover ample and affordable ways to drink your sought-after wines, plus an opportunity to visit the winery may turn up unexpectedly.

OBSERVE THE PROTOCOLS AT A WINE-TASTING APPOINTMENT: If you are lucky enough to get a tasting appointment at a great winery, four commonsense protocols must be followed. (1) Always be on time. The winemaker might be late, but you never should be. (2) Do some research. If you are not familiar with the wines, read up on them so you at least appear worthy of the winemaker's time. (3) Ask intelligent questions. Winemakers like to discuss the specific nature of each wine they make, but some familiarity and wine knowledge on the part of the visitor is usually required to draw them out. (4) Before you spit, find out where to do it. Winemakers will often provide a bucket or a spittoon, but not always. Sometimes you are directed to spit into a drain on the floor or directly onto a dirt or gravel floor. Some small producers like you to put your unfinished wine back into the barrel, so ask before you dump.

WALK THE VINEYARDS: "It's quite possible," Rajat says, "to go to a wine region and not see any vineyards." You get shuttled from cellar to cellar, he explains, and don't get to look at the vines. This can easily happen in Bordeaux, and even in Burgundy, where the cellars are surrounded by vineyards. "One time," Rajat recalls, "I was in Burgundy and it was cold and rainy the entire time. No one wanted to walk a vineyard row. But I still went out with a hat and a coat, because it is sacrilege to taste the wines without seeing the vines."

Indeed, any good winemaker will insist that it is the quality of the grapes that makes the wines. And there is no better way to comprehend the grapes and the wines than by seeing the vineyards, walking the rows, feeling the soil in your own hands. Sometimes this requires a little extra effort, but it is imperative that you do it.

TAKE NOTES ASSIDUOUSLY: It may seem obvious to recommend careful note taking, but when tasting or drinking wine on a wine trip, it is easy to forget to do it. "When you are new to the experience, it is tempting to go and party and eat and drink," says Maniec. "And that's good. But be studious. I just did a trip to Austria. Every single time we sat down to taste with a winemaker, I wrote down almost everything that was said. When you get back home, it's hard to remember the soil types and the vineyard sites, and good notes allow you to share what you learned with other sommeliers or with guests."

On that same trip, Maniec recalls a specific tasting with the winemaker from Leth, a winery in the Wagram. "He was doing wood trials with his Zweigelt, and he spent two hours with us pulling out wines from barrels of various forests and toast levels," she says. "If I don't

140

take notes, how am I going to remember this stuff? I was just talking with a winemaker the other day about the cooperage Vicard. So I pulled out my notes from Austria, and there they were—all my impressions of those Leth barrels."

FIND OUT WHERE THE WINEMAKERS EAT: And go there. Every wine region or village has a restaurant or a bar where the local winemakers go to socialize, drink wine, taste the latest vintages of their colleagues, or just hang out. This place is in many ways the heart and soul of the region. In Burgundy, for instance, the place is Ma Cuisine in Beaune (see page 189). In Piedmont, it is La Salita in Monforte d'Alba. In the Willamette Valley, the place is Nick's, in McMinnville.

Rajat's first tasting trip to Burgundy (his second overall) was in 1998, just two years into his Rubicon stint. The trip's most significant moment happened at Ma Cuisine, then a new restaurant, where he was having his last dinner, alone. "I'm drinking a 1991 Lafon Perrières and a half bottle of 1988 Dujac Charmes-Chambertin," Rajat recalls, "and in walk Dominique Lafon, Christophe Roumier, Jacques Seysses, and Alain Graillot. It was their Burgundy tasting group, and they were tasting wines blind." They noticed Rajat sitting by himself in the corner and decided to send the wines over to him, blind. Rajat, of course, nailed them. "Then one wine is opened by the restaurant owner, Pierre," says Rajat, "and no one knows what it is." Rajat tastes it and thinks it is 1993 Dujac. Jacques Seysses vehemently disagrees. "He agrees that it was a wine made by him," remembers Rajat, "but says 'no way it is 1993.'" The wine was 1993 Dujac Echézeaux.

A friendship may have formed that day, but it was the mood in the restaurant that inspired Rajat. "As I saw how excited they were, I said to myself: these are real lovers of wine. So much energy among them, drinking and eating together. That was it. The spirit—that one dinner, those people, that place. Maybe they have all forgotten, but I'll never forget it."

CHECK OUT THE HOME COOKING AND THE LOCAL FARMERS' MARKET: Restaurant food isn't always indicative of the way the wine producers of a region eat day to day. Knowing what they serve at home to their families and their guests when they want to show off their wine can give important clues for pairing it in your own home. So, first, never refuse an invitation to be entertained at a producer's home. Invariably, these will be the best meals you will have in a region. Second, visit the markets. A farmers' market (usually on Saturday morning) presents in one place the bounty of the region, and it is an important context in which to see wine. Third, if you are visiting a region for more than just a few days, consider renting a house or an apartment with a kitchen. Some of the best times can be had by shopping at the markets and preparing a local delicacy, whether it be Bresse chicken, Argentinean beef, or Portuguese shrimp. That way you will see firsthand how the wine interacts with the food at your own table.

141

OVERLEAF: RAJAT WITH ÉTIENNE DE MONTILLE >

THE SOMMELIER'S BOOKSHELF

Taste, taste, taste is often the first commandment when it comes to learning about wine. But as Joseph Spellman, former head of the Court of Master Sommeliers, says, "neither tasting without studying nor studying without tasting will ever get you very far."

Indeed, anyone who has amassed any sort of respectable wine knowledge has spent considerable time with his or her head buried in books. Sometimes it is paging through encyclopedias like the Oxford or the Sotheby in search of definitions for such terms as *volatile acidity* and *Marzemino*. Other times it involves perusing atlases like those by Oz Clarke or Jancis Robinson and Hugh Johnson, or regional books like John Winthrop Haeger's *North American Pinot Noir* or Clive Coates's *An Encyclopedia of the Wines and Domaines of France*.

Sommeliers often like to sit down with more general-interest wine books, too. "I recommend books like *Wine and War* [by Donald and Petie Kladstrup] and *The Billionaire's Vinegar* [by Benjamin Wallace]," says Laura Maniec. "Just as important as the history they contain are the stories. They give you something to talk about with guests, anecdotes to share on the floor that will make the wine and the meal come alive for people when they learn that the bottle they are drinking is connected to decades and decades of history."

So, read for study, but also read for color and enjoyment. Here are seven books that have been important in animating Rajat's quest for wine knowledge.

CÔTE D'OR by Clive Coates: Many books offer in-depth explorations of Burgundy, but none has the character detail about both the vineyards and the people who own them that Coates delivers. This book is for readers who want a brief, witty glance into the personality of Burgundy, along with all the raw data they will ever need.

MICHAEL BROADBENT'S VINTAGE WINE by Michael Broadbent: With its thousands of wine impressions, this book is the ultimate tasting note compendium. No one has tasted a catalog of so many great wines from the 1800s to the present and kept such scrupulous notes. The book is a first-rate reference guide, of course, but it is also illuminating to sit down and read entire sections. Great information about vintages and producers is couched in the notes, by one of the most open and curious wine minds in the world.

THE OXFORD COMPANION TO WINE edited by Jancis Robinson: The most thorough coverage of wine, including its grapes, regions, personalities, chemistry, history, tools, and more. Basically, here is everything you need to know in one place. Indispensable.

144

THE WORLD ATLAS OF WINE by Hugh Johnson and Jancis Robinson: A crucial part of understanding wine is understanding geography. That makes a good wine atlas essential, and this is one of the best (Oz Clarke's is also good). Outstanding maps of all the world's important wine regions clearly show how land, sea, and wine are related. A wealth of information about wine styles, viticulture, and history is impressively smuggled into the long, thorough text accompanying the maps.

WINDOWS ON THE WORLD COMPLETE WINE COURSE by Kevin Zraly: One of the first books written by a sommelier for budding wine drinkers. It is generally considered a book for beginners, but Zraly's focus on the classics, and on accessibility and enjoyment as well as erudition, makes it worthwhile for even the most experienced sommelier to revisit now and again.

VINO ITALIANO by Joseph Bastianich and David Lynch: In the last decade, the sprawling, diverse, and exotic world of Italian wines has become more well known in the United States. This book sheds light not just on the wines and grapes, but also on the provincial cultures (gastronomic and otherwise) that produce them. Although not exhaustive, its recipes and travelogue are wittier and more fun to read than most any other wine book.

THE NEW FRANCE by Andrew Jefford: The greatest and most exciting wines in the world still come from France, but not all of them are made by the producers and methods hailed in the old wine books that might be sitting around your house. Jefford, a thoughtful and searching writer, travels France to uncover the most cutting-edge regions, winemakers, and philosophies. This is an engrossing and enlightening book for anyone with even a modicum of interest in French wines.

SOMMELIERS WHO MAKE WINE

One bright winter day a couple of years ago, a half dozen or so sommeliers headed up to Hanzell Vineyards in the hills above Sonoma Valley to taste. Obviously, nothing is unusual about sommeliers sampling wine, but this occasion was highly unusual as it was perhaps the first formal tasting for sommeliers of wines solely made by sommeliers. In the room was then–Spago wine director Kevin O'Connor (Lioco), John Lancaster of Boulevard in San Francisco (Skylark), and Rajat (Parr Wines), as well as former restaurant sommeliers

Greg Harrington (Gramercy Cellars) and Larry Stone (Sirita). The tasting was organized by Hanzell's winemaker at the time, Michael Terrien, who, after observing the growing trend of those who buy wine becoming those who make it, said that he was "curious to see how a sommelier thinks about making wine."

It is an understatement to characterize the trend of sommeliers who make wine as growing. In fact, exploding is a better word, as there are now more than thirty sommeliers or former sommeliers across the country making wine under their own labels, including, in addition to the names mentioned above, such prominent figures as Bernie Sun of Jean Georges, Bobby Stuckey of Frasca, and Kevin Vogt of Delmonico Steakhouse in Las Vegas.

The list of sommelier wines shows a wide spectrum of engagement. Some wines are nothing more than a sommelier helping to create a blend of available wines and slapping his or her own label onto the bottle. Yet the most interesting of the wines show a willingness on behalf of their makers to try techniques and practice styles that mainstream producers would deem commercially unviable. Indeed, many of these stylistic choices involve going to lengths to subvert the very hallmarks of mainstream wine: richness, fruit-forwardness, overt oak, high ripeness. Inspired most often by the great wines of France and Italy, these sommeliers are taking both commercial and stylistic risks that other winemakers (who, it must be said, don't have prominent sommelier positions at influential restaurants to fall back on) cannot or will not take.

Commercial gain was not the primary inspiration for many of the sommeliers. For Rajat, the wine-making impulse is about a challenge and finding truth. "I wanted to see if I could do it," he says, referring to the idea of making wines using the techniques of the French producers he most admires on California fruit to achieve restrained, low-alcohol wines that are still ripe and flavorful. "So many California winemakers have been selling me high-alcohol wines for a long time, saying that it's impossible to have low-alcohol, ripe-tasting wines, that I wanted to see if it could be done."

In a mere half-dozen vintages, Rajat, who concentrates on Chardonnay, Pinot Noir, and Syrah with his brand Parr Wines, has answered his question. Consider his Cuvée Anika Syrah, which he has managed to harvest at a staggeringly low 22 Brix, yielding wine of a mere 12½ percent alcohol (most California Syrah is between 14 and 16 percent). He routinely makes most of his Syrahs 100 percent whole cluster (using the stems as well as the grapes in the fermentation) in the style of Domaine Jamet of Côte-Rôtie. Yet even using such rare and, by modern California standards, "reckless" techniques, Rajat's Syrahs are dark, dense, and meaty, with overtones of violets and wild blackberries. "This wine will work at the table," says Rajat. "That's what I care about most." Parr's Purisima Mountain Syrah is usually picked at a low 23.5 Brix and fermented 100 percent whole cluster for an alcohol level of around 13½ percent. Its flavors emphasize savory dried herbs and black olives, and the moderate alcohol makes it exceedingly easy to taste.

146

HARVEST 2009, SANTA BARBARA COUNTY

Rajat began making his wines under the auspices of Jim Clendenen and Sashi Moorman, but in just a few years he has learned so much that he has taken over most wine-making decisions himself. Today, his wines are made at Moorman's facility in the Santa Rita Hills of Santa Barbara County. Rajat drives down regularly during harvest to oversee selection and fermentation. Moorman, a brilliant winemaker, handles the labor and the technical expertise while acting as a consultant and guide.

Before he went into wine making full time, Kevin O'Connor was the longtime wine director of Spago in Beverly Hills. A few years ago, he teamed with former North Berkeley Imports specialist Matt Licklider to form Lioco, a brand that focuses on steel tank–fermented, unadorned Chardonnay, as well as Pinot Noir and a Carignan-based blend called Indica. The early success of Lioco allowed O'Connor to leave Spago and dive headfirst into his brand.

At the heart of Lioco, as with Rajat's wines, is a question. As O'Connor puts it: "Can winemakers in this country make wines that have typicity?" While he denies that Lioco is an attempt to influence or rebuke anything in the California wine industry, a criticism is implicit in his question. "Many American wines are compelling, but do they speak of a specific place or about their varietals?" he asks. To that end, the two partners and their winemaker, Kevin Kelley, source grapes from a variety of top vineyards in the Chalone AVA in Monterey County up through Mendocino, and vinify the wines with minimal intervention. The Chardonnays, for instance, are all steel tank and native yeast–fermented, aged in tank without *bâtonnage*, and bottled unfiltered and unfined. "We are much more interested in the vineyard coming through in that particular vintage than in having someone say, 'I love that Lioco style.' Each wine should speak of this place, this vintage," says O'Connor.

The incursion of sommeliers into wine making begs a question: can a sommelier-made wine of restraint and/or typicity convince mainstream winemakers to do the same? To be sure, the sommeliers are not the first or only winemakers to attempt to make low-alcohol, whole-cluster wines. Winemakers like Bob Lindquist of Qupé and Jim Clendenen of Au Bon Climat have been making such wines for years. Nevertheless, Rajat's wines are pushing the boundaries. As Moorman says, "Ideas that Rajat has brought to the table have changed things that I do in programs I run outside of Rajat's project. And I think his ideas are also going to move the conversation forward about how to make balanced wines in California." He cited Rajat's frequent trips to France to learn from master winemakers as an invaluable source of knowledge and wisdom that most California winemakers are unable to duplicate. "What gives Rajat the most confidence, though," says Moorman, "is when he gives his wine to winemakers or sommeliers in Europe and they say, 'I didn't think a wine like this was possible in California.'"

The sommelier-as-winemaker trend may complicate the sommelier-winemaker relationship, however. After all, sommeliers are supposed to be selling a winemaker's wines, not competing with them. Moorman says that at first he was "lukewarm to the idea of

TRAILBLAZING WINE FROM SOMMELIERS
(OR FORMER SOMMELIERS)

BASTIANICH: Joe Bastianich, the wine side of the Batali-Bastianich empire (Babbo, Del Posto, Lupa, Mozza) was a pioneer of sommelier-made wines. He was also perhaps the first to go abroad to make his wines, in this case in the Italian region of Friuli. His portfolio includes a Tocai Friulano, Sauvignon Blanc, Vespa Bianca (Chardonnay, Sauvignon Blanc, and Picolit), and Vespa Rosso (Merlot, Refosco, Cabernet Sauvignon, and Cabernet Franc).

GRAMERCY CELLARS: In 2005, master sommelier Greg Harrington left the profession to start a winery from scratch in Walla Walla, Washington. He makes Syrah, Cabernet Sauvignon, and Tempranillo in a balanced, nuanced way that belies the blockbuster style popular in Washington.

LIOCO: Former sommelier Kevin O'Connor and wine salesman Matt Licklider are already making some of the best Chardonnay in California, as well as a good Pinot Noir and a Carignan-based blend. The wines—moderate in alcohol, restrained, food friendly, and evocative of *terroir*—are part of the vanguard for new California wine.

PARR WINES: These ambitious California wines—Syrah, Chardonnay, and Pinot Noir— follow the model and the advice of some of the most famous winemakers of Burgundy and the Rhône. And they succeed. True to Rajat's tastes, they are low alcohol, high acid, restrained, food friendly, and intriguing.

SKYLARK: John Lancaster and Robert Perkins of San Francisco's Boulevard restaurant make excellent Syrah, Pinot Blanc, rosé, Grenache, a Rhône blend, and a crowd-pleasing Chardonnay called Alondra. Lancaster and Perkins do almost all the work themselves, yet somehow hold down one of San Francisco's busiest wine programs.

helping a sommelier make wine," but he eventually embraced it because of the fruitfulness of the collaboration. Great sommeliers spend so much time studying wine and learning in minute detail how each producer grows and makes his or her wine, it seems inevitable that, presented with the opportunity, they would want to try their hand. And the benefits of such undertakings may outweigh any potential conflicts if these restrained, low-alcohol wines of *terroir* are able to crack the tyranny of the high-alcohol fruit bombs that have reigned nearly without challenge for almost twenty years. Moreover, sommeliers of integrity will always sell the most appropriate wine to each customer. For instance, though Skylark wines are on the list at Boulevard, Rob Perkins, who makes the wines with co-sommelier Lancaster, insists that he goes out of his way not to sell them. He and Lancaster also avoid mentioning their restaurant connection when dealing with potential grape sources or even when making sales calls to the retailers and restaurants that buy Skylark. "It is important to us that the wine is sold on its own merits," adds Lancaster.

Several avenues are open for sommeliers—or anyone—interested in making small amounts of their own wine. For example, it is possible to go the route that Rajat took. Ask a winemaker with whom you have a close relationship if you might try your hand with his or her guidance. In making such a request, just be sure to explain to the winemaker that your passion is driving the pursuit and that you are not setting out to undermine him or her. (This is thin ice, so be careful.) Another option is to find a custom-crush wine-making facility, buy grapes, hire a consultant, and do it yourself. Or, you might befriend someone who owns a winery and ask if you can pay a fee to make use of space, equipment, and expertise. Alternatively, many consumer-oriented wineries-for-hire are operating in America's wine-growing regions, from California's Central Coast Wine Services in Santa Maria to Crushpad in the Napa Valley to City Winery in New York.

═══════════════════════════════════════

WINE EVENTS

Imagine ten long tables filled with great bottles of Burgundy that have to be shifted around to accommodate the serving of a multicourse meal prepared by celebrated chefs like Daniel Boulud and Michael Mina. Imagine a singing troupe periodically roving the room, harmonizing on classic folk tunes of Burgundy. Sitting next to you is one of the greatest living Burgundy producers, perhaps Jean-Marie Fourrier or Anne-Claude Leflaive. And then imagine your meal being interrupted every few minutes by one of the best sommeliers in America (who has volunteered to work the event) offering a taste of an incredible wine, such as a 1990 Raveneau Les Clos or a 1978 Domaine de la Romanée-Conti Grands Echézeaux—or something even better. To make room for the wine in one of your glasses you are faced with the uncomfortable choice of either dumping or slamming the wine that is already in it, which probably almost matches the quality of the one you are being offered. The choice ends up not being so tough after all: you drain the wine and accept the gift.

This is a common occurrence at the Saturday dinner of La Paulée, the one-day gathering that is, at least for Burgundy lovers, the best wine event in the country. Staged annually by Daniel Johnnes in New York and San Francisco on alternate years, it draws twenty or so top-flight Burgundian producers for a grand afternoon tasting of their current vintages, followed by dinner. It is overkill to be sure, but all this indulgence is countered by one presiding ethic: sharing is the order of the day. Every guest is asked to bring a great bottle of great Burgundy to share with the other diners at his or her table or beyond. The craziness starts with the big collectors and wine producers, who all bring cases of the finest, rarest wines in the world. Inevitably, some of that bounty gets shared around, and you are bound to taste a revelatory wine (or ten) before you stumble home.

The catch? Tickets to the afternoon tasting and evening dinner cost a whopping fourteen hundred dollars. This might seem a steep sum for a day of Burgundy swilling, but when you consider that two cases of a midlevel, current-release Burgundy will cost about the same, what you will undoubtedly taste at La Paulée seems like a bargain, not to mention the meal and the camaraderie. Furthermore, proceeds from the charity auctions at La Paulée have benefited Meals on Wheels and the Hospices de Beaune in Burgundy.

If you are a fan of Napa Cabernet, you might consider attending the Auction Napa Valley in June. A full, three-day package will set you back twenty-five hundred dollars, but it includes a wine-soaked dinner at a top Napa winery, an invitation to an exclusive barrel tasting, dinner and lunches at other Napa wineries, and dinner under the tent at the glamorous Napa auction. (The auction is also one of the top philanthropic events in the country. In 2009, it raised $5.2 million for a variety of Napa County programs, including ones aimed at children's health insurance, mentoring, and affordable housing.) July's Central Coast Wine Classic, held at the exquisite Dolphin Bay resort in Pismo Beach, California, is a more laid-back version of the same, featuring wines from all over the world, cooking demonstrations, lectures, and, of course, lots of eating and drinking. Individual events range in price from forty dollars for a barrel tasting of fifty California wineries to two thousand dollars for a special 1982 Bordeaux dinner. Pinot Noir lovers will benefit greatly from a weekend spent attending lectures, tastings, and dinners at one of the two great Pinot events in the country, World of Pinot Noir (WOPN) in Pismo Beach, or the International Pinot Noir Celebration (IPNC) in McMinnville, Oregon.

Of course, sommeliers who are invited to volunteer their time and expertise at La Paulée do not pay an entry fee, but the event is so special, so grand, that they willingly pay their own transportation costs in order to taste rare wines and rub elbows with the greatest winemakers of Burgundy and with their fellow American sommeliers. Many of the other organizations (WOPN, for instance) offer sommeliers invited to work a stipend that is typically just enough to cover budget travel and lodging costs.

The benefits of working these events go far beyond simply tasting a few excellent wines. Some, like La Paulée, offer tastings and seminars exclusively for the sommeliers—knowledge that they would be hard-pressed to get elsewhere. Most events include plenty of unstructured casual time with great winemakers and chefs, and the bigger gatherings offer unparalleled opportunities for networking, ideal for sommeliers looking to make a move and in need of connections in a new city or with a new restaurant group. "You learn a lot in the seminars, but really it's more just in the sitting around talking, the camaraderie of it," says Dana Farner of Los Angeles's CUT. "I also find that it's therapeutic. To be around a group of people that you're just getting to know gives you remarkable perspective on everything you are doing."

Another benefit is the free-flowing exchange of notes among comrades. "It's amazing to connect with other sommeliers about the guests you have in common," says Farner. "We see some of the same guests at these events that we see regularly in our restaurants, whether it is my restaurant in Los Angeles or a restaurant in San Francisco or New York. For instance, I have one big wine collector who likes his wineglasses primed with a few drops of the wine he is about to drink. I've shared that detail with other sommeliers whose restaurants he visits."

Parties, which are nightly and sometimes raucous, are another attraction. Sommeliers working these events for the first time are advised to practice some restraint at the evening affairs for two reasons. One, morning call times are often early and a day's work can be long, with only minor breaks. Two, wine (and often more) always flows freely at the parties. "Remember, you are representing your city, your restaurant, and your chef at these events," cautions Rajat. "I've seen more than one sommelier injure his or her career by getting drunk and out of control."

That said, the benefits of attending or working one or several of these events generally far outweigh the possible downside. What follows is a list of five of the top sommelier-oriented wine events in the country. Not included, though important as well, are the major auctions and one-day tastings that are also good opportunities for tasting and sommelier interaction.

LA PAULÉE (alternating between San Francisco and New York; February/March): The premier Burgundy event in the world. Well worth every cent, as once-in-a-lifetime wines and the most exclusive producers are on hand, as are great chefs (www.lapaulee.com).

WORLD OF PINOT NOIR (Shell Beach, California; March): California's best Pinot Noir event. The top producers from all over the world convene in beautiful Pismo Beach to drink and talk Pinot Noir for two days, while lounging on California's coastline and eating great food. Includes intellectually stimulating seminars, informative tastings, and a great La Paulée–style party at the close (www.worldofpinotnoir.com).

HOSPICE DU RHÔNE (Paso Robles, California; May): The top Rhône event in the United States, featuring great Rhône-variety producers from the United States, Australia, Spain, France, and anywhere else the grapes are grown. Held in laid-back Paso Robles, the event spans the spectrum, from simple, delicious rosés to some of the world's most expensive Syrahs and Rhône blends (www.hospicedurhone.org).

- -

CENTRAL COAST WINE CLASSIC (Pismo Beach, California; July): This annual auction and wine event on California's Central Coast features top wines from all around the world, with a special focus on producers from the state. Includes a remarkable dinner at Hearst Castle, other lunches and dinners, seminars, and tastings (www.centralcoastwineclassic.com).

- -

INTERNATIONAL PINOT NOIR CELEBRATION (McMinnville, Oregon; July): A relaxing, highly pleasurable weekend in the Oregon wine country devoted to Pinot Noir. Pinots of the world are featured, with a special emphasis on wines of the Willamette Valley. Tastings, lectures, and winery visits fill the program, and a grilled salmon and Pinot feast closes the event (www.ipnc.org).

JEREMY SEYSSES OF DOMAINE DUJAC

THE WINE LIST

Everything a diner needs to know about a sommelier's wine philosophy is revealed in his or her wine list. Rajat's lists are no different. A thorough reading of them offers a window into how he views wine: which regions and grape varieties he considers significant, how he thinks about them in the context of one another, and which producers he most values in each region.

What follows is a wine list of sorts by Rajat. Unlike his restaurant menus, however, it does not itemize labels for sale, but instead includes commentaries on his favorite regions. Often kidded that his view of the world of wine (in the spirit of Saul Steinberg's *New Yorker* cover "View of the World from 9th Avenue") begins in Burgundy and ends in Champagne, Rajat is in fact quite open-minded (he also enjoys the wines of the northern Rhône). But it is true that his focus as a sommelier is the great regions of France's east-central corridor, and this appendix reflects that, offering suggestions on how best to understand and navigate them. This "wine list" makes no attempt to be exhaustive—that is for other books—but instead is simply a decantation of Rajat's thoughts, in his own words, from a career spent in the passionate pursuit of great wine.

CHAMPAGNE

I give Champagne more attention than most sommeliers do for two reasons. One, I love it with deep feeling. Two, it is one of the most underappreciated wines in the world. Underappreciated, you ask? Absolutely. Although millions of people view a glass of Champagne as the ideal vehicle for celebration or as a simple aperitif, few of them ever consider it as a wine. No one ever thinks about Champagne in the same way they do the newest cult Cabernet from Napa: "I wonder what the vineyard looks like that made this. Who is the winemaker that produced this amazing liquid?" Rather, Champagne exists in our culture as a commodity, a brand, a thing. This is no accident. The mass-marketing of Champagne over generations masks the fact that as a wine region it is as diverse and compelling as any great source in the world. Simply stated, Champagne is unequivocally a wine.

The word *Champagne* literally translates as "open landscape," and to visit the region is to see why. A vast, unprotected series of low-lying slopes, it is visually an unremarkable place. It feels exposed to the elements, almost oppressed by the low, flat sky, which is often gray and overcast. Champagne is one of the world's northernmost wine regions and is therefore a marginal place for viticulture. Traditionally, only three out of every ten vintages have been considered great. Unsurprisingly, the Champenoise have a serious, somewhat dour cast. It is ironic, then, that this somewhat gloomy place is the origin of the most delightful, lively, and spirit-lifting wine in the world.

Those unremarkable-looking hills of Champagne happen to be made up of some remarkable soils that winemakers in, say, California can only dream of in their vineyards. The secret to the soils is chalk, a category of geology that the French call *calcaire*. Soils containing various concentrations of chalk are magic for Chardonnay, Pinot Noir, and Pinot Meunier, the three grape varieties of Champagne. The iconic process by which these grapes are made into wine involves two fermentations. The first is a standard fermentation, to create from fresh grape juice a basic wine; the second fermentation occurs inside a sealed bottle, where the famous bubbles are created and captured. Although much attention is devoted to this process, it is actually the region's white, chalky earth that is responsible for Champagne's potential to make as nuanced, expressive, and complex wines as Burgundy or any other great wine region.

To a large extent, however, that potential is not being realized. For generations, the region has been dominated by major brands owned by sprawling, international corporations—what together can be called Big Champagne. Their goal has not been to create diverse, surprising, and expressive wines. Indeed, it has been to do just the opposite: produce a homogeneous product. Homogeneity, by nature, is anathema to wine, which changes from season to season from the year of its inception to the very moment it is consumed. Big Champagne erases such diversity through the art of blending, which blurs distinctions in the interest of turning out products that are as identical from one year to the next as canned soda. Among other mass-production practices that compromise fine-wine standards are extreme chemical and mechanical manipulation of wines in the cellars, irresponsible agricultural practices, and yields aimed at quantity over quality. The wines of the top fifteen big brands account for over 85 percent of the market.

Opposed to the big brands in style, process, and philosophy are the small grower-producers. These are farmers who used to sell their grapes to the big brands—as most of the estimated fifteen thousand growers in Champagne do—but in the last twenty years or so made the revolutionary decision to start making their own wine. Although now hundreds of grower-producers exist, just a handful of them export their wines to the United States, where they make up only about 4 percent of the American market.

Grower Champagnes are real wines. They are not sweeping blends made from across the region, but instead come from smaller, specific places, which is reflected in the wines. Most of them are primarily made from a single vintage. Thus, their great beauty is that they enable us to look at Champagne through the lens of *terroir*. The importer Terry Theise deserves much of the credit for introducing these wines to the American market and challenging us to learn more about the soils, the exposures, and the styles from the different Champagne villages. Based on quality, the best grower Champagnes are as good as any wines produced in France, which is why the bulk of my wine lists' sparkling real estate is devoted to them.

That said, it is not always easy to find a grower Champagne or even to recognize which wines are from a grower and which are from a large factory. I list a number of my favorite grower-producers on pages 160–161, but it is helpful to know how to discern whether a bottle you pick up is from a grower or from a corporation. Look for the identification code, a lengthy number preceded by two important letters typed in small print on the label of every bottle of Champagne. Most often the two letters will be NM, which stand for *Négociant-Manipulant* and indicate a large house that buys most of its grapes. If given a choice, these are the wines I generally avoid. The code I prefer to see is RM, for *Récoltant-Manipulant*, which means that the wine is made by a grower-producer. Not often, but sometimes, you see CM, or *Coopérative-Manipulant*, which identifies a wine made by a large cooperative. These wines are typically inferior. And don't be fooled by the designation RC, or *Récoltant-Coopérateur*. These bottles might look like a grower-producer's, but in fact contain repackaged wine from a large cooperative and have been labeled with an individual grower's name. RM is the code of choice.

The producer code is not the only bit of information relevant to the savvy consumer of Champagne. A host of other information is often available to buyers, some of it useful. But a lot of insignificant or questionable facts are lobbed at the Champagne consumer, too. Below are my thoughts on some important practical issues that will make buying and drinking decisions easier for the discerning Champagne drinker.

INSUFFICIENT VINEYARD RATINGS

When pimping their wines, many Champagne houses brag that their grapes come from villages with high ratings on a 100-point scale. The ratings refer to a system enacted in 1927 that codified quality based on the centuries-old reputations of each village. In 1985, the system was updated, but it is still highly technical and confusing. It rates the wine-growing areas of Champagne on a scale of 80 to 100 percent. Villages with a rating between 80 and 89 percent are designated Cru, which means a specific vineyard area. The forty villages rated between 90 and 99 are labeled Premier Cru. And seventeen villages have the precious 100 percent ranking, earning Grand Cru status.

The system was instituted for reasons of commerce. (A single price for grapes was set each year; growers in villages ranked 100 percent would receive the full price for their grapes, growers with vineyards ranked 93 percent would receive 93 percent of the price, and so on.) Yet today, Champagne sellers often use village ratings for marketing. Houses will boast about their wine's rating of, say, 95; some even brag about a wine being comprised only of fruit from 100-point villages. These scores are not of finished wines, however, as the scores from a critic like Robert Parker are. I am sure the producers of the Champagne do not mind if they are misread as such, but the scores refer only to the ratings of the villages in general and do not take into consideration the viticulture, wine making, and so on of each house.

Other inconsistencies also riddle the system. For example, the village of Mareuil-sur-Ay has a rating of 99, but it is only a Premier Cru. That seems ridiculous. Vilmart is a grower-producer in Rilly-la-Montagne, a village rated at only 94. But Vilmart's wines are some of the best in all of Champagne. How do you rationalize that? Also, how can you rate a whole village? Would not some vineyard sites within an individual village be better than others? Now, it is true that the villages with 100-point ratings are among the best in the region. But the rating is only a small part of the story of any wine and should always be regarded with skepticism.

DISGORGEMENT DATES

Not particularly relevant in younger Champagnes, disgorgement dates are more important with older bottles. Disgorgement is one of the final processes Champagne goes through before it is finished. During the step, the wine's sediment, or lees (dead yeast cells), is collected in the neck of the upside-down bottle and expelled. The lees have been there for the entire life of the wine, protecting it from oxidation. Champagne kept on the lees can remain youthful for decades. Once the lees are gone, the clock starts ticking: the Champagne begins to age in bottle like any other wine.

The difference between a bottle of recently disgorged Champagne on a store shelf and a bottle that has sat on a store shelf for years is huge. The latter bottle has been aging—the wine becoming nutty, yeasty, and golden—whereas the former bottle will still be fresh and vibrant. One style is not necessarily better than the other, but it is important to have an idea of what you are getting. The solution? More houses must print the disgorgement dates on the back label. Terry Theise, the importer who brings in most of the grower Champagnes mentioned here, insists that his producers do it.

Late-disgorged Champagnes do not age well. A regular Champagne from a great vintage like 1996 or 2002 will age for ten to twenty years. But Champagne that has spent a long time on its lees will be at its best between three months and three years after the lees are expunged. Champagne houses keep great stocks of undisgorged wine in their caves and can disgorge it to order. When we opened Restaurant Michael Mina, Veuve Clicquot disgorged magnums of 1947, 1953, 1955, and 1961 for our list. Many houses also have programs that release late-disgorged Champagnes onto the market—Bollinger calls its wine RD (Recently Disgorged). Dom Pérignon calls its program Oenothèque.

I enjoy the mystique of old Champagne—some of it can be truly remarkable—but for me it has to have bubbles, and as the wine ages, the effervescence declines. A forty- to fifty-year-old Champagne will not have much carbonation left. Thus, I prefer a fresher style.

That a Champagne was grown and vinified by the small grower who owns the vineyard does not make it great. As in any region, the truly great producers are rare. These are the people who work tirelessly in both the vineyard and the cellar, whose dedication to their craft (and often whose talent) goes far beyond that of most producers. Below are some of the specific grower-produced Champagnes I regard as exceptional. Consider this, by extension, a recommendation of the houses that produce the wines, as almost all of their bottlings prove remarkable.

CHARTOGNE-TAILLET CUVÉE SAINTE-ANNE: Alexander Chartogne is one of the most dynamic of the rising young stars in Champagne. Modeling his practices after those of his mentor, the great Anselme Selosse of Champagne Jacques Selosse, Chartogne has been gradually evolving the style of his wines from that of his parents, making them drier and more minerally. His goal is to show the typicity of vineyard in the bottle. Chartogne-Taillet is in the town of Merfy—only 84 on the rating scale!—which is not considered the most stellar *terroir* in Champagne. But the wines from this house display what is possible when true passion guides the production. Cuvée Sainte-Anne is not Alexander's flashiest Champagne, but for a nonvintage brut, it is perfect. Chalky and gently perfumed, it is not about fruit, but about texture, about the flow of heavenly juice through the mouth.

HENRI BILLIOT CUVÉE LAETITIA: Champagne Henri Billiot comes from Ambonnay, a Grand Cru village famous for its Pinot Noir. This wine, Billiot's flagship, however, is made mostly from Chardonnay. But it does not necessarily drink that way. It is a rich and vinous, dense, serious wine. The base wine comes from a *solera*, a multivintage blend to which some new wine is added each year. The *solera* was begun in 1983, so each bottle of this wine has a trace of every vintage since then. That concentration of time and focus makes an incredibly intense and powerful wine. But it is also precise and well defined. It is reminiscent of Krug—the celebrated Grand Cuvée of old, rather than the Krug Grand Cuvée of today.

PIERRE PETERS CUVÉE DE RÉSERVE: One of the best examples of nonvintage blanc de blancs, this Champagne comes from Mesnil-sur-Oger, the village that renders the greatest finesse and purity of any Chardonnay in Champagne. The wine's beautiful brightness perfectly captures that village quality. It is not terribly expensive, yet it glitters and glows with a crystalline precision that is irresistible. (Another Pierre Peters wine, a rare single-vineyard bottling, is described below.)

CHAMPAGNE GASTON CHIQUET NV BRUT "TRADITION" AND BLANC DE BLANCS D'AŸ: Nicolas Chiquet is among the greatest of all the grower-producers, and his basic NV Brut "Tradition" is one of the most stylish and graceful bruts. Weightless, it just seems to float, first on a cloud of fragrance, then like a cool wind on the tongue, and finally as a graceful whoosh through to the back palate and the throat. The house of Chiquet, which first planted vines in 1746, was also, in 1935, the first grower to begin to produce, instead of just sell grapes.

Chiquet makes another wine that is highly notable, a wine that every sommelier and serious wine drinker should know about, Blanc de Blancs d'Aÿ. What is significant about this Chardonnay is that it comes from a Grand Cru–rated village that is known for its Pinot Noir. This is a reversal that makes little sense: why make Chardonnay from a place that is universally praised for Pinot? The wine tells you why. It is from a very old vineyard, and the wine proves the point about *terroir* in Champagne: it is not at all an expression of Chardonnay, but an expression of this place. If you are a *terroir* doubter, game over. *Terroir* clearly exists, and this wine proves it. Heavier and richer than other blanc de blancs, it drinks like a Pinot Noir— robust and juicy, speaking of berries, quince, and honey—even though it is not.

JACQUES SELOSSE BLANC DE BLANCS "INITIALE": Anselme Selosse, who makes the wine here, is perhaps the most important producer in Champagne. He is the visionary. I cannot say it better than Andrew Jefford did in his book *The New France*: "If the future of Champagne truly is going to be one in which terroir plays more of a role then the region as a whole will have to pay more attention to Selosse and less to its accountants and brand managers."

Selosse's wines, almost overwhelmingly rich and explosive, can be hard to understand. They are vinous, more wine than sparkling wine. Selosse single-handedly changed viticulture in Champagne by insisting on rigorousness and low yields at a time (the 1970s and 1980s) when such efforts were dismissed. Likewise, he was perhaps the first modern man to make Champagne as forward-thinking producers were making Burgundy: with indigenous yeast fermentations, with minimal sulfur, and aging the wines in barrel (less than 20 percent new). Selosse's use of barrel gives the wines oxygen at an early point in their lives, setting the stage for the remarkable textural things that happen. His obsessive vineyard work yields the lowest-yielding, ripest fruit in the region, leading to the wine's explosive flavors. "Initiale," Selosse's blanc de blancs brut, is a low-dosage assemblage of three vintages. It bursts with minerals, lemon, salt, and apples. Its texture is creamy and full. This is a Burgundy lover's Champagne.

Although I typically avoid the big-brand Champagnes, I admit that a number of estimable producers are found among the large *négocians*. For the most part, these wines are characterized not by a sense of *terroir*, but by a sense of "house style" achieved through the vinification and blending process. Nevertheless, the wines are good, and achieving consistency of style every year (which is what the houses want) is no simple feat. Below is a list of my favorite NM producers.

LOUIS ROEDERER: The beautiful thing about Roederer is that it owns most of its own vineyards. In fact, no house as large as Roederer owns as high a percentage, and it farms its land intensely and benevolently with as great a dedication as many of the top grower-producers. Famous, of course, for its incomparable prestige cuvée, Cristal, Roederer's basic brut is one of the best.

JACQUESSON: A small *négociant*, Jacquesson, like Roederer, owns most of the vineyards from which it sources, all of them in Grand Cru–rated villages. Also, the direction of the house has changed from representing a consistent house style to one that expresses more fully the vintage of the base wine and the *terroir* of the vineyards. The nonvintage brut is excellent, as is the Dizy Terres Rouges rosé.

BOLLINGER: Rigorousness of vineyard management (Bollinger also owns a high percentage of its vineyards) and in the cellar characterize Bollinger's wines. But reliance on the Pinot Noir grape and fermentation in neutral barrels is what gives the brand its famous style, which is big, bold, and very rich. The Special Cuvée Brut NV, its basic brut, is finely wrought and earthy, and the prestige cuvée, La Grande Année, has lovely depth and admirable power.

RUINART: This is the oldest extant Champagne house and still one of the best. Its wines are very much toward the high end, and it specializes in Chardonnay, which makes up the majority of its blends, except for its entry level R de Ruinart. Its high-end series, called Dom Ruinart, features exquisite vintage Champagnes, including a rosé that is not to be missed.

SALON: Released only in exceptional years (about three times a decade), Salon is one of the greatest of all Champagnes. It uses only Chardonnay grapes from the Grand Cru village of Mesnil-sur-Oger, and only from reliable and long-established growers. Despite its reputation, this wine is not always a crowd-pleaser. Rather, its deliberate austerity, a product of high acidity and searing minerality, is for lovers of those qualities and ensures that the wine will last for decades.

162

DOM PÉRIGNON: Dom Pérignon is obviously a brand and not a house, but it has such a strong identity that I treat it as its own producer (ignoring owner Moët et Chandon). No one knows how much Dom Pérignon is produced, but speculation puts it at a very high number. Thus, it is amazing that Dom Pérignon's wines are so fine, crafted to excellence by the brilliant *chef de cave* Richard Geoffroy, year in and year out. The style is precise, floral, and dedicated to finesse, even though the wines typically need a decade to really show their stuff. Dom Pérignon's vintage rosé is a thing of beauty.

KRUG: This famous house has the reputation of being the ultimate Champagne. It broke the mold, upping the ante for the pricey Champagnes by turning its entry level wine, the Grand Cuvée, into a luxury brand. Through the 1990s, Krug's quality was among the highest in Champagne. But after it was purchased by LVMH (Moët Hennessey Louis Vuitton) in 1999, its quality began to decline. Krug is primarily a brand now. Its style has also changed: the Grand Cuvée used to have more reserve wine, giving it a lusher, nuttier style (the Krug signature) than it has today. Krug also has the ignominious distinction of producing what I consider to be the world's most overpriced Champagne: Clos d'Ambonnay. When it was first issued in 2007, it was one of the most expensive wines in the world at around three thousand dollars a bottle. How can this be acceptable, when the vineyard from which the wine comes was not even planted twenty to thirty years ago? The wine is good, but it is not worth the price tag. Indeed, it exemplifies what is wrong with Champagne: when marketing becomes the modus operandi, producers make luxury products rather than real wines.

BUYER'S TIPS

- In years that Salon is not made—roughly seven a decade—turn instead to Champagne Delamotte, its sibling Champagne house. Delamotte gets Salon's fruit most years, sells for less than half the price, and exceeds its own already highly respectable quality standards in Salon vintages with the addition of the finer fruit.

- Vintage Champagnes and prestige cuvées are two different high-end categories. Prestige cuvées are the houses' top wines, including bottlings like Perrier-Jouët Belle Époque (the iconic "flower bottle") and Pol Roger Cuvée Sir Winston Churchill. They are often vintage wines, though not always; Laurent-Perrier Grand Siècle, for example, is a blend of years. Vintage Champagnes are not branded like the prestige cuvées (no hand-painted bottles). Instead, they show the character of a certain year. In great vintages, these wines are often a much better value than the prestige cuvées and will sometimes rival them in quality. For example, the 1996 Louis Roederer costs about one-third of the price of Roederer's prestige wine, Cristal, but the quality difference is negligible compared to the price gap.

NON-DOSAGE CHAMPAGNES

Most Champagnes are slightly sweetened just before they are sealed with cork. This touch of sugar is meant to balance the wine, to keep it from being too austere. Non-dosage Champagnes are a special breed that are not sweetened at all. Sommeliers like these dry, crisp wines because of their raciness, acidity, and freshness. In a way, they are also more honest than typical Champagnes, as added sweetness is also a common way to mask flaws. Producing a balanced non-dosage Champagne is not easy. The wine must naturally have enough richness and ripeness to balance the acidity, and richness and ripeness are not easy to produce in Champagne's cool climate. Simply put, you must have exceptionally well-grown grapes to reach the level of ripeness required to make a balanced Champagne without adding a dosage, which is why these wines are so rare. But the good ones are among the most bracing and exciting Champagnes being made. Drappier Brut Nature is wonderful—and wonderfully priced. André Clouet, a top-notch but little-known grower-producer in Bouzy, makes the exquisitely dry Silver Brut. Very little of it comes into the United States, so buy it when you see it. And Larmandier-Bernier Terre de Vertus is an iconic wine, the model for *terroir*-driven, transparent Champagne.

MOST INTERESTING SINGLE-VINEYARD WINES

For a long time, Champagne was afraid of single-vineyard wines. The regional focus on blending was a shortcut, a way of getting around the work required to take a great vineyard and produce a complete and exceptional wine from it. That is changing. Krug started making Clos du Mesnil in 1979, and the success of that wine—both commercially and aesthetically— made waves. It is very good, but other single-vineyard wines are just as remarkable, and I hope that the trend of making these sparkling *vins de terroir* will continue. What follows are three of the most compelling single-vineyard Champagnes being produced today.

JEAN MILAN "TERRES DE NOËL" BRUT: This single-vineyard wine comes from the Grand Cru Chardonnay village of Oger, which some will tell you is the best *terroir* in the Côte des Blancs. Oger sits, collecting warmth, in a bowl between the hills of Cramant and Mesnil-sur-Oger. This is rich, intense Chardonnay that is lusciously velvety, yet held taut by an iron-clad minerality.

164

PIERRE PETERS CUVÉE SPÉCIALE "LES CHÉTILLONS": From a single vineyard in Mesnil-sur-Oger, this vintage bottling is, quite simply, one of the greatest Mesnil Champagnes. Vastly more affordable than Krug Clos de Mesnil and Salon, and yet every bit as good, if not better, it is, incredibly, unknown to most people. Complex as they come, it often recalls apples, mandarin oranges, bread, earth, and minerals.

PHILIPPONNAT CLOS DES GOISSES: Etched onto a steep hillside, something you do not often see in the region, the vineyard of Clos des Goisses is magnificent and yields one of the most underrated wines in Champagne. Philipponnat's 1996 Clos des Goisses was perhaps the best wine of a great, great vintage. Often serious and austere at first, the wine opens up to reveal racy citrus, pears, apples, and almonds, always on a creamy, yet intensely chalky palate.

===

BURGUNDY

My favorite wine, my obsession for many years, is Burgundy. And I am not alone. The fixation of the Burgundy lover is easily explained: at their best, the reds and whites of Burgundy are perhaps the greatest wines in the world. It is not just their sensual pleasure that makes Burgundy wines alluring, however. They also have an intellectual component that wines from many other regions lack. Like that elusive unifying theory of physics, great Burgundies at their best unite seemingly opposing forces: firm structure meets soothing gentleness, earthy minerality meshes with succulent fruit, immense power combines with ethereal delicacy. Is light a wave or a stream of particles? Great Burgundies—both white and red—inherently ask that same question.

The thirty-mile slope of the Côte d'Or is likely the most thoroughly examined strip of land on the planet. For centuries, the attendants of the vineyards were monks who focused on the land itself, discovering over generations how each section of hillside was different from the ones around it and which grape produced the best wines. Today's *vignerons* are the inheritors of the monks' work.

Famous for its geographic complexity, Burgundy's Côte d'Or is defined by its major villages and the mosaic of vineyards—hundreds of them, from very large to swimming pool sized—that surrounds them. To complicate things further, most vineyards are vinified by multiple producers, each with his or her own unique approach to the land. Therefore, to have even a tenuous grasp of Burgundy, you must know quite a bit about the distinctive character of each village, the specific vineyards, and the producers who make the wine.

Top Burgundian whites are the apotheosis of the Chardonnay grape, mingling an elemental mineral texture with pure fruit and an exquisite ability to age. The nucleus of Chardonnay in Burgundy is the Côte de Beaune, though it also grows well in satellite regions such as Chablis and the Macon. The Côte de Beaune stretches from Beaune south to the village of Chassagne. It is at the region's most southern reaches that the grape achieves its apogee.

CHABLIS

A fitting place for Chablis on a wine list is between Champagne and white Burgundy, for while Chablis is technically in the region of Burgundy, it is physically closer to the border of Champagne. The best limestone soils of Chablis are likewise almost identical to Champagne's. But the wines of Chablis contain no bubbles. They are made exclusively from Chardonnay, however, which makes them the bridge to white Burgundy.

Can Chablis ever be confused with white Burgundy? Yes. On a visit to Domaine Raveneau, I was told a story of when a famous restaurant in Burgundy bought a barrel of its 1978 Les Clos. When Monsieur Raveneau went to dine at the restaurant one day, he approached the owner, perplexed. "Where's my Les Clos? I can't find it on the list," Raveneau said. The owner replied, "Well, we sell it as Montrachet." The Raveneau 1986 Les Clos was my epiphany wine. In its complexity and fusion of power and elegance, it does remind me of some of the greater expressions of Montrachet, but it is even finer and more elegant. It actually has more vibrance and elegance than any Montrachet of a similar age—and to this day it is still more alive. That is the power of Chablis.

The greatest Chablis is Chardonnay grown in the soil that gives both Chablis and Champagne its distinctiveness: Kimmeridgian marl (first identified in Kimmeridge, England, where it also shows up), a blend of limestone and clay. With the unique property of holding enough water to sustain a vine, yet draining off enough to keep the vine from being overwatered, Kimmeridgian marl works wonderfully for white wines, imbuing them with a pronounced and unmistakable chalkiness on the nose and palate. Les Clos is the best (and biggest) of Chablis's seven Grand Cru vineyards, making a rich and luscious wine that maintains superb finesse and balance. Blanchot is the most delicate and aromatic Grand Cru. Valmur is similar to Les Clos in its power, but has perfume reminiscent of Blanchot. Montée de Tonnerre, the best Premier Cru, shares a geographic profile similar to the Grands Crus and is prized for its richness and complexity.

Chablis wines are typically austere. They do not have the flesh and roundness of fruit that you usually expect of Chardonnay. But that is not what you look for when judging the wines of Chablis. Acidity, aromatics, intensity, and, above all, minerality are the qualities by which great Chablis is evaluated. The combination of these factors over time is what makes the wines especially compelling. Young Chablis can be delicious, flaunting that signature chalkiness, married with lemon custard, spice, mushroom, and a certain greenish, herbal component. But it is as they get older that the wines begin to truly delight: the savory notes of mushrooms intensify, adding honey and butter, forest floor, and cheesy notes. Chablis can be drunk young, but the most powerful versions—the Premiers Crus and Grands Crus of the top producers—need five to fifteen years to soften and for their inner complexity to unfurl.

Chablis is famously flexible with food. The classic pairing is oysters, though older wines and ones that are fermented in wood—Grands Crus and some Premiers Crus, typically—work better with richer fare. For bivalves and other seafood, drink the lower designations, petit Chablis and village Chablis, instead. These wines are almost never oaked and are excellent house wines and great by-the-glass pours.

The three top Chablis producers are fairly well agreed on among sommeliers: François Raveneau, René et Vincent Dauvissat, and Louis Michel. People argue about which is better, Dauvissat or Raveneau. To me they are both excellent, but different. Raveneau is renowned for his barrel-aged Chablis. Only about 10 percent of the wood is new each year, but it gives the wines a rounded, variegated structure to contrast the linear, austere, and razor-sharp texture and acidity. Aromatically, I find Raveneau's to be the most complex wines in Chablis. Vincent Dauvissat, known for his use of biodynamics, is the most soil-focused Chablis grower, working tirelessly to handle his vineyards in a completely natural way for the good of the wines and the soils. This shows through in the wines, which have an unusual purity. They are more closed when young, but mature slowly into absolute gems. Louis Michel is the stalwart of stainless-steel, traditional, unoaked Chablis. I often think that Louis Michel, though not as highly regarded, may be the best of all of them. The wine is as pure, as transparent, and as direct as they come. The village wines of Louis Michel are amazing, and the Premiers Crus and Grands Crus have an almost blinding intensity that can take years to mellow enough for the wines to be drunk. Just behind this trio are two excellent producers, William Fèvre and Jean-Paul & Benoît Droin. Both make wonderfully fine wines from many vineyards at each level. Their wines display both precision and finesse, but they lack a touch of the defining personality of the leading trio.

BUYER'S TIP

- One of the best village Chablis for the money is not even a Chablis. It is La Châtelaine from Domaine de la Cadette, hailing from the town of Vézelay, about twenty-five miles south of Chablis. Citrusy, minerally, and fresh, the wine is good every year and is always inexpensive.

One afternoon a few years ago, some sommeliers were tasting the new 2005 vintage with Meursault winemaker Jean-Marc Roulot, one of the best *vignerons* in all of Burgundy. During the tasting, Roulot idly mentioned that he was in the process of procuring portions of a few new vineyards in Meursault.

One of the sommeliers, out of excitement and admiration for Roulot, asked, "Jean-Marc, why are you not buying up Grands Crus somewhere? A winemaker like you should have some Grand Cru vines."

Roulot replied, "Because that is not Meursault. That is not what we do."

The story is a way of pointing out that, famous as it is, Meursault surprisingly has no Grand Cru vineyards. Despite that lack of glamour, Meursault is one of the most popular wines of Burgundy and boasts arguably the most exceptionally talented and driven *vignerons* of any wine village in the world. Jean-Marc Roulot's point is well-taken. First and foremost, he makes Meursault; it is unique, and it is his. Second, why worry about whether or not something is technically Grand Cru or not, when you are already able to make Grand Cru–level wines in Meursault?

Meursault features calcareous soils— a blend of crumbly marl and chalk—perfectly suited to making rich still wines from Chardonnay. In addition, it benefits from an exceedingly low water table (compared to its neighbors), which forces its vines' roots to dig deeper in search of water. This causes much needed stress and creates a bigger root system for the absorption of minerals and other nutrients. The low water table also allows producers to dig cellars that are deep and cold, ideal for the slow, sure evolution of white wine. The result is Chardonnays that define the grape itself. Hazelnut, cream, butter mixed occasionally with mushrooms, citrus, pear, and gunflint begin to describe some of the flavors. And in the most compelling examples, the wines are underscored by a decided chalky minerality that provides an irresistibly gravelly texture and a firm structure.

Despite Meursault's nominal lack of Grands Crus, many sommeliers—including me— believe that the vineyard Les Perrières makes fine enough wine to be elevated from its Premier Cru status to Grand Cru. The soil in Les Perrières is the lightest and stoniest of Meursault's vineyards, yielding wines that are minerally, closed in their youths, and ultimately long-lived. Of course, it is somewhat irrelevant at this time, because the greatest versions of the wine— made by the likes of Coche-Dury, Roulot, Comtes Lafon—are as coveted as a Grand Cru and fetch commensurate prices. Meursault's other two great vineyards, Les Genevrières and Les Charmes, do not get the same play for elevation, but they are widely admired and in any given year can produce Grand Cru–level wines. The wines from Les Charmes are considered the fattest and richest wines of the village. Those from Les Genevrières exhibit some of the opulence found in Les Charmes and some of the stoniness in Les Perrières.

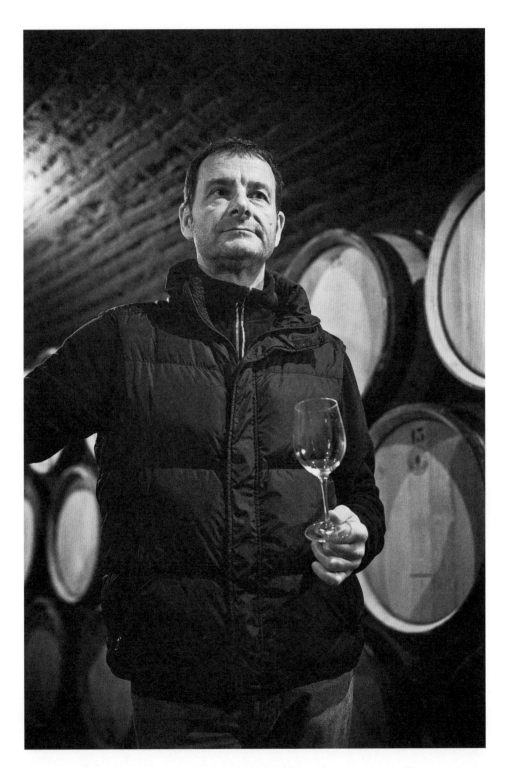

JEAN-MARC ROULOT

A number of the most well-known bottlings of Meursault are not Premiers Crus, but classified village wines called *lieux-dits,* or "named places." Although this is not aristocratic *terroir,* these wines are exceptional, especially in the hands of the great producers described above. The best *lieux-dits* are Clos de la Barre, En la Barre, Les Tessons, Les Narvaux, Les Chevalières, Les Rougeots, and Les Tillets.

BUYER'S TIPS

- Coche's wines are Meursault's most expensive, when they can be found. But in vintages where it is present, the Coche-Dury effect (see sidebar, below) turns up in all Coche wines. To experience the deliciousness at a lower price, seek out Coche's Aligote. It is not nearly as complex or substantial a wine as his Chardonnay, but it still bears his signature in a very attractive way.

- A limited area of Meursault is planted to Pinot Noir, and several producers in the area make a small amount of red wine. Look for wine labeled Meursault Rouge or even Bourgogne Rouge from respected Meursault producers like Domaine Roulot, Domaine Coche-Dury, or Domaine Comtes Lafon. These wines may not be as complex or meaningful as wines from dedicated Pinot villages in Burgundy, but they are charming, affordable, and delicious.

- Village-level Meursault is better than village-level Puligny. Buy village Pulignys for opulent, rich, but less complex wines. Buy village Meursault for minerally, taut, nuanced wines.

THE COCHE-DURY EFFECT

Many try to re-create it, but few can, or at least not with the same consistency that Jean-François Coche achieves. What is this effect? It is a controlled reduction of the wine, accomplished through wine-making techniques using grapes cultivated in Côte de Beaune soils. On some wines, the reduction is irresistibly attractive, smelling of gun smoke, matchsticks, and minerals. If the reduction is not done perfectly, however, it can leave a wine smelling dirty and decaying—something Coche's wines never do. When a wine is young, the Coche-Dury effect can stick out mightily, dominating the wine. Over time, however, it blends into the wine, adding complexity and a savory austerity to balance out the richness and intensity that always mark Coche's wines. The effect does not manifest in every vintage, but the ones in which it does are formidable indeed. (Domaine Leflaive, in Puligny, makes wines in a comparable style.)

172

For all of the love heaped on Meursault, there is no question that Puligny-Montrachet (despite being half the size of Meursault, as a village and in terms of acreage, and with fewer standout producers) is the greatest white wine–producing commune in the world. This is because the world's greatest white wine vineyard, Le Montrachet, lies at the southern end of town. But that is not all. As the sun is orbited by the planets, Le Montrachet is surrounded by lesser Grands Crus emanating from it and reflecting its light. So famous is Le Montrachet that three surrounding vineyards are named in its honor: Chevalier-Montrachet, Bâtard-Montrachet, and Bienvenues-Bâtard-Montrachet. Even the towns of Puligny-Montrachet and Chassagne-Montrachet saw the value of appending the celebrated Montrachet to their village names, linking them in the late-nineteenth century.

Montrachet is the apotheosis of white wine, where the minerality in the soil meets grapes on an optimal slope that gets sunlight all day until the last rays fade at sunset. The wines, which are grown on some of the most expensive real estate in the world, are further helped along by the care taken in every stage of their making. The hallmark of Montrachet is an extraordinary finesse and complexity, allied with great concentration, steeled by an awesome minerality and impeccable transparency. A well-matured Montrachet (perhaps ten to fifteen years) is one of the world's most profound and complex drinking experiences.

Chevalier-Montrachet, which sits directly above Montrachet, is considered one of the finest Grands Crus. Due to its elevation up the slope from Montrachet and its pure chalk topsoil, Chevalier is firm and masculine, and the wines are more austere than those of Montrachet. They are compact and tense in their youth, but in ten to fifteen years, the truly ethereal pure notes of limestone-grown Chardonnay emerge as power and perfume bound together with flavors of mineral and honeysuckle.

Bâtard-Montrachet, just below Montrachet, has heavier clay soil, which gives the wines more density and power and a heavier feel in the mouth, like the soil itself. The wines are robust and rich, with exotic notes of honey, butter, and popcorn. They age more quickly than Chevalier-Montrachet and Montrachet, and are best within five to fifteen years of the vintage.

Bienvenues-Bâtard-Montrachet, just below Bâtard, can, in the right hands, produce great wines that are rich, fat, and oily, with layers of tropical fruit. The wines can be clunky compared to their finer cousins, but they are also capable of seductive complexity and are accessible in their youth, with a capacity to age gracefully.

Alongside the Grand Cru vineyards are several often-forgotten, very good Premiers Crus. The best of them are Les Pucelles, Les Referts, and Les Folatières. The flavors you see in these wines and in Puligny in general are typical of the riper side of Chardonnay: ripe pear and tropical fruits like pineapple and coconut. Of course, the chalky substrate that props up what could otherwise be sometimes unctuously ripe is still there. The Premier Cru vineyard

Le Cailleret is surrounded on three sides by Grand Cru vineyards, but it is not Grand Cru itself. Why? No explanation exists, other than that the monks who mapped the vineyards did not think it was Grand Cru level. Nevertheless, it performs amazingly well and is a relative bargain. Its best producer is Domaine de Montille.

Some truly exceptional producers are found in Puligny, led by the celebrated Domaine Leflaive, whose owner, Anne-Claude Leflaive, is one of the most brilliant and outspoken characters of Burgundy. Other great producers include Domaine Étienne Sauzet, whose wines are delicate, nuanced, and serious (much like Benoît Riffault, the young man with whom I taste during every visit), and Domaine Louis Carillon. Carillon is a tiny estate and one of the quickest tastings I do each year, as there are just a few wines and not much talk. It is notable that the estate is dividing into two, each led by a different brother. Domaine Louis Carillon will remain, but Domaine François Carillon is new; François's first prominent vintage is 2010.

BUYER'S TIP

- Puligny Le Trézin is a *lieu-dit* village wine—indeed, the only village wine—on the hill of Montrachet. It is light but very stony and is one of the raciest, most mineral-driven wines of Puligny. It's always a great bargain; buy it when you see it. The best producers are Marc Colin, François Jobard, and Domaine d'Ardhuy.

CHASSAGNE-MONTRACHET

Chassagne is the last village of the Côte d'Or. While it technically enjoys half each of the vineyards of Montrachet and Bâtard-Montrachet, those vineyards are very much the *terroir* of Puligny. Chassagne is something entirely different. In the nineteenth century, the production of Chassagne was 80 percent red wine. This is not surprising, as the subsoils of the Chassagne are composed of oolitic Bathonian limestone, the same soil found in the red wine–producing Côte de Nuits. But the production changed over time because of the success of the white wines of the area. Today, Chassagne is still 50 percent red (the wine is not remarkable, and most of it stays in France), which explains why Chassagne is not considered as elevated a white wine locale as Puligny and Meursault.

Nevertheless, some wonderful white wines are being made in Chassagne. They tend to be softer, less dense, and less deep than the wines of Puligny or Meursault, though they still have a mineral edge, but also more floral and citrus notes. Chassagne has one Grand Cru entirely to itself—Burgundy's smallest white Grand Cru, Criots-Bâtard-Montrachet—and a handful of good Premier Cru spots. The Premiers Crus of Chassagne are all on a separate slope and have a different aspect than Puligny's. The best Premiers Crus—Les Chenevottes,

174

En Cailleret, Les Vergers, Les Morgeot, and Les Grandes Ruchottes—are on the upper slopes. Morgeot is considered masculine and assertive, whereas the others are known to be softer and more feminine. The greatest wine producers of Chassagne are Domaine Ramonet and the young, ambitious, and talented Pierre-Yves Colin, whose first vintage was 2001. Ramonet is quite famous, and famously eccentric. The domaine is run by two brothers who never leave Burgundy, despite the fact that they are regularly invited to represent their acclaimed wines around the world. Curiously, they also love to drink Bordeaux, especially Petrus. A friend told me that he once went to a soccer match in Lyon with the two brothers, and at a rustic café after the match, he was astonished to see them whip out a bottle of Petrus. My friend was expecting to drink beer.

Chassagne is also home to a slew of young producers making exceptional wines. The ones to watch are Domaine Bernard Moreau and Domaine Vincent Dancer.

BUYER'S TIP

- Saint-Aubin is a tiny village just behind Chassagne. It is generally not held up as one of Burgundy's great wine villages, even though it produces some of the best-value Chardonnays in the world. What makes Saint-Aubin special is its high elevation and steep, calcareous vineyards. It is on a hill next to Montrachet, and its soils are similar, though they contain more limestone. But Saint-Aubin does not have the exposition of Montrachet, and it makes more austere wines; in good years, however, they can be exceptional. Two great vineyards are Dents de Chien and En Remilly, and both are made wonderfully by Pierre-Yves Colin of Domaine Colin-Morey. Other good producers are Marc Colin and Hubert Lamy. Saint-Aubin is often an astounding bargain.

RED WINES OF BURGUNDY

The journey of Pinot Noir in Burgundy starts in the Côte de Nuits, the northern section of the Côte d'Or, just south of Dijon, and continues through the Côte de Beaune (skipping over white Burgundy) all the way to the bottom at Chassagne-Montrachet. Pinot's greatest expressions begin at the far northern towns of Marsannay and Fixin, however, and run like a red wave down to Volnay, south of Beaune.

Great red Burgundy marries wonderfully expressive, vibrant fruit with earthiness, spice, and minerality, while preserving acidity at a moderate alcohol level. Sommeliers like red Burgundy because it is one of the world's most versatile wines. From the delicious but relatively simple bottlings of Marsannay to the complex wines of Musigny, there is something for every palate and for every dish, at a vast range of prices. The challenge is that you must look long and deeply to find the finest examples. It is not enough to shop by the category of Burgundy or by the name of a village. Burgundy hides its riches well, but the dedicated detective will find great enjoyment in the hunt.

MARSANNAY

The village of Marsannay is the official beginning of the Côte d'Or, which seems surprising because when you drive through it, it feels like a suburb of the bustling city of Dijon. But not only does it have a sizable number of vines, it also boasts vineyard sites mentioned as far back as the seventh century. Marsannay has been known most widely for its rosé, which is made by vinifying Pinot Noir more as if it were a white grape. Otherwise, the wines are simple and fruity, cheap and pleasant.

Today, more value is found in Marsannay (and to a lesser extent, Fixin, the town right below Marsannay, whose wines are considered a bit more meaty and austere) than in any places producing red wines in Burgundy. Because of its proximity to the great village of Gevrey-Chambertin and the soil qualities they share, Marsannay makes a rustic but muscular Pinot Noir with plenty of tannin and lots of juicy fruit. Contemporary winemakers are able to make a darker, spicier wine from here than their predecessors made. The reason the area is not more highly regarded is because its wines are more angular, its tannins less harmonious than the crus of Gevrey. Its rusticity also makes it less expensive. At four to six years old, Marsannay can be delicious, having softened enough to be gulpable, yet still young enough to have resisted slackening. Most producers try to emphasize Marsannay's fruit. The best examples are from Domaine Joseph Roty, Domaine Denis Mortet, Domaine Bruno Clair, and Domaine Sylvain Pataille. Marsannay is famous for its rosé, which is the only rosé appellation in Burgundy. It is a great wine for a barbecue or with charcuterie at a picnic.

The historic town of Gevrey-Chambertin and its high concentration of clay soils is known for producing the most powerful, longest-lived wines in Burgundy. Muscle, richness, ripeness, dark fruit, spice, and a deep intensity characterize the wines, which are also tannic and need time in the bottle to unfold fully. Gevrey boasts the Côte d'Or's greatest number of old vines, which contribute to the wines' density and depth, and also has the largest number of Grands Crus, which are contiguous and closely set—like a line of dominos—across the midpart of its slope. Chambertin, a fantastic Grand Cru, shows the appropriate density and power—big, rich, bold—yet has an ethereally velvety texture. Clos de Bèze, a subparcel of Chambertin, makes the longest-lived, most substantial wines of Gevrey (followed by Richebourg, in Vosne-Romanée). Clos de Bèze needs a minimum of ten years before it becomes approachable. Sommeliers often have an affinity for the Grand Cru Griotte-Chambertin. It is the smallest, and although it may not have the depth and intensity of Chambertin, it is graceful, elegant, and sexy—more reminiscent of the wines of Chambolle-Musigny than Gevrey.

Disappointingly, Gevrey also has some of the most underperforming Grands Crus in all of Burgundy. Ruchottes, for example, does not have the same breed and class as the Clos de Bèze or the Chambertin. Mazoyères (typically today called by the name Charmes-Chambertin) is also disappointing. Latricières is a Grand Cru but rarely dazzles, with the exception of Domaine Leroy's bottling. The best expressions of Charmes-Chambertin are charming (as the name implies), but not what you would expect from wines with the lofty Grand Cru designation and price.

On the other hand, Gevrey has a Premier Cru, Clos Saint-Jacques, that outshines many Grands Crus. The only reason it is not a Grand Cru is because it is disconnected from all the others. (Domaine Armand Rousseau is the best producer, and if you go to his cellar, you will taste Clos Saint-Jacques right after a slew of Grands Crus, but still ahead of the Grand Cru vineyard Le Chambertin.) Gevrey has many other excellent Premiers Crus, too, like Lavaux Saint-Jacques, Champeaux, and Fonteny.

For people who like big wines or who are used to drinking New World Pinot Noir and cannot seem to develop an interest in Burgundy, Gevrey-Chambertin should be the first stop on an attempted crossover, as it is the commune with the greatest number of modern-style producers. The ripeness and power of the grapes achieved here tempt winemakers to extract more out of them, leading to bigger, richer wines in the so-called international style. Sometimes the wines get too big. Because of their size, they often also receive more oak, which should satisfy the palate of someone more used to drinking Pinot Noir from places like California, Oregon, or New Zealand. Producers for whom they should be on the lookout include Dugat, Dugay-Py, Mortet, Charlopin-Parizot, Perrot-Minot, and Geantet-Pansiot.

Wines with finesse and a lighter touch are generally made in Gevrey by the old-school producers, and sommeliers tend to prefer them. Domaine Rousseau is a particular favorite. On my first visit to Rousseau in 1998, I walked in and Charles Rousseau was hand labeling his Chambertin. Now that's old school. The style of the wines is pure and understated, not flamboyant. Rousseau's is the definitive Chambertin. Other great traditional producers that are popular with me and sommeliers in general are Domaine Leroy, Joseph Roty, Pierre Damoy, and Domaine Fourrier.

BUYER'S TIPS

- In the best hands, like Domaine Dujac's, Premier Cru Aux Combottes can outclass many Grands Crus. It is also a decisive example of how specific the delineation of Burgundy *terroir* is. Aux Combottes has Grands Crus on three sides, but is not itself a Grand Cru because it sits right on a little gap where the wind gets through. The cooling breezes result in lower degrees of ripeness, which make the wines slightly more austere and tannic.

- Domaine Fourrier is a small producer that languished for years, but thanks to the stewardship of Jean-Marie Fourrier, its stock is on the rise. Fourrier makes traditionally styled, finesse-oriented wines that are both wonderfully approachable in their youth and have great potential to age. He has worked in Oregon and Burgundy, and his wines, while rigorously old school, have a seductive, almost New World polish. Fourrier makes the best village Gevrey-Chambertin wines, as well as lovely versions of the higher crus.

MOREY-SAINT-DENIS

Traveling south on RN74 (now officially D974), you come to the village of Morey-Saint-Denis, whose wines are often described, depending on which side of the village the wine comes from, as reflecting the strength of Gevrey-Chambertin, to the north, or the finesse of Chambolle-Musigny, to the south. Because it is squeezed between these two ultrafamous villages, the much smaller Morey-Saint-Denis seems to have little character of its own.

Yet the wines can be very good. I think of them as earthy, mineral, and firm, but less so than Gevrey-Chambertin (indeed, the comparison cannot be avoided). And now, after decades of being touted as overrated, the wines of Morey-Saint-Denis fetch prices on a par with the other villages. Morey has five Grands Crus: Clos de la Roche, Clos Saint-Denis, Bonnes-Mares, Clos des Lambrays, and Clos de Tart. (The last one is a *monopole* under the sole ownership of Domaine Mommesin.) Clos Saint-Denis and Clos de la Roche are great vineyards, with the latter being more structured and mineral but less elegant than the former.

The pedigree of the vineyards is not the cause of Morey's lack of stature. Rather, it is because of the paucity of celebrated Premier Cru vineyards and relatively few great producers. The lack of notable Premiers Crus means that much of the wine from this commune is either Grand Cru or ordinary village, leaving a void of more accessible high-end wines. Plus, two of the Grands Crus are dominated by single producers, which limits the exposure of the wines, and the Domaine des Lambrays, which has a near *monopole* on the Clos des Lambrays, has been uneven, producing legendary wines in the 1940s, 1950s, and 1960s, but nothing equally spectacular since then. The best producers of Morey are Domaine Dujac, Domaine Ponsot, and Domaine Hubert Lignier. Laurent Ponsot is one of the latest to pick in all of Burgundy and uses no new oak. His wines are sui generis: dense and concentrated, presenting the most extreme, ripe version of Burgundy. They are delicious and visceral. Domaine Hubert Lignier (not to be confused with Domaine Georges Lignier) makes elegant wines in a balanced, nuanced, traditionalist style. And Domaine Dujac is inarguably one of the greatest producers in all of Burgundy—turning out wines in a traditional manner, but with a worldly polish and an intellectual sophistication. Dujac's style is unique, elevating purity and finesse over power and extraction. Purists might fault Dujac for having a recognizable house style that can sometimes trump vineyard expression, but to me the wines are magical.

BUYER'S TIP

- Clos de la Bussière is a Premier Cru of Morey-Saint-Denis and a *monopole* of Domaine Georges Roumier, one of the most sought-after producers in Burgundy. Of all of proprietor Christophe Roumier's wines, however, this is among the most affordable and available. It is worth the search to taste the hand of a true master.

CHAMBOLLE-MUSIGNY

I once served a bottle of Domaine Jacques-Frédéric Mugnier's Musigny to a customer at RN74 who was so moved by the wine that he wept. Tasting a wine of the stature of Mugnier Musigny can be a profound experience, of course, but I still could not believe that anyone would tear up over a glass of wine A few months later, I was visiting Mugnier, and I told him the story. He stood there blinking for a second, processing the tale, then said, "A bottle of wine could never make me cry. It's just wine!" He is not coldhearted. In fact, at the movies, it turns out, he tears up all the time.

The wines of Chambolle-Musigny can indeed be haunting, stirring in their transparency and fluidity. But that does not mean they are soft. They can also have a firmness, even a combativeness, surprising for such a fine-boned wine. Because of this multifaceted, modestly fickle nature and because of their elegance and sometimes pale, rosy color, many people think Chambolle is the ideal expression of Pinot Noir.

Chambolle may well be the favorite wine of sommeliers. It has a rich, velvety grace that rivals the finesse of Vosne-Romanée and the power of Gevrey-Chambertin. Sometimes the wines have a lighter color, but in red Burgundy, color means very little. Chambolle has only two Grands Crus, Bonnes-Mares and Musigny, but because of their high quality—and that of some exceptional Premiers Crus—this small village has an incredibly lofty reputation.

Ample chalk in the vineyards gives the wines higher acidity and sophistication, which expresses itself in the form of aromatic purity and finesse, like the finely drawn line of a fashion model's neck. The wine of Musigny is a mind-blowing combination of power and grace, garnished with effusive aromas that bring to mind strawberries and licorice. When fully mature (fifteen to twenty years), it becomes almost miraculous in its ability to maintain such intensity with such poise. Bonnes-Mares, which is shared between the villages of Morey-Saint-Denis and Chambolle, is the stepbrother of Musigny, masculine to its feminine. Sturdier, more tannic, and more forceful, it takes years to soften and merge into a pliant, often spicy wine.

The concentration of Premiers Crus in this town, given its size, is amazing, though many are very small and are not bottled under their own names, but blended together as generic Chambolle-Musigny Premier Cru. The wines express the grape and the typicity of the village at every turn. Those from the southern end, near Musigny, are more perfumed and gentler than wines from the northern end. The one standout Premier Cru here is Les Amoureuses, which usually commands higher prices than many Grands Crus. The northern end of the village, the steepest part of Chambolle, has some excellent Premiers Crus, which tend to have a little more grip and wildness. The top vineyards are Aux Beaux Bruns (Domaine Denis Mortet), Les Gruenchers (Domaine Dujac), Les Fuées (Domaine Jacques-Frédéric Mugnier), Les Charmes (Domaine Ghislaine Barthod), and Les Feusselottes (Domaine Mugneret-Gibourg).

BUYER'S TIP

- You are better off buying a village Chambolle than any other village wine in the Côte d'Or, as the quality is the highest among all the communes. Look for bottles from Dujac, Mugnier, and Roumier. Part of the vineyard of La Combe d'Orveau is rated as village wine and part is rated as Premier Cru. But the entire vineyard, which lies adjacent to Musigny and Clos de Vougeot, has soil similar to that of Musigny. Its exposition, however, is dissimilar, with a northerly facing, and that is the difference. Anne Gros makes a village wine from La Combe d'Orveau that drinks like a Premier Cru but costs like a village wine. And Bruno Clavelier makes a fairly priced Premier Cru that drinks like Musigny!

FRÉDÉRIC MUGNIER

CLOS DE VOUGEOT

Cistercian monks established the Grand Cru vineyard of Clos de Vougeot in 1100. Its fifty hectares, enclosed as the name suggests by a long wall, are now in the hands of around eighty different owners. This is a Grand Cru where the location of the vines within the huge vineyard really matters, as the *terroir* within the vast area varies enormously. Many people find the size of the vineyard and the fact that its entirety bears the Grand Cru designation to be a complete joke (much like entire villages being rated Grand Cru in Champagne). Parts of Clos de Vougeot do indeed deserve Grand Cru classification, but others, especially downslope where the vineyard drops out into water-retaining flats near the road, fall short.

That said, when Clos de Vougeot is good, it is exceptionally so. Its top sections on the north border on Musigny and share a few of the same traits, producing structured and supple wines with wonderful density. The finest producers—those with the best plots—are Domaine Leroy, Domaine Anne Gros, Domaine Gros Frère et Soeur, and Domaine Méo-Camuzet.

BUYER'S TIP

- Many fail to realize that Vougeot has village and Premier Cru vineyards in addition to its Grand Cru vines. The village vineyards are on the flats near the highway and make rarely seen and undistinguished wines. The Premiers Crus sit on the north of the Clos, however, up near the town, and they can yield delicious wines in good hands. Part of Les Petits Vougeots, one of the Premier Cru sites, is owned by Domaine Fourrier of Gevrey-Chambertin, an excellent producer. This Premier Cru is usually fairly inexpensive, yet always expressive and well made.

VOSNE-ROMANÉE

The main competition to Chambolle-Musigny for the world's most ideal rendering of Pinot Noir comes from Vosne-Romanée, its near neighbor to the south. Vosne-Romanée, with its eight Grands Crus (two are technically in the neighboring village of Flagey-Echézeaux), is perhaps the greatest collection of vineyards in one place in France. You can barely take a step out of this village without tripping over some legendary vines that go into making the planet's most prized and expensive wines.

Stylistically, the wines sit between the sturdiness of Gevrey-Chambertin and the delicate perfume and grace of Chambolle-Musigny. They are often described as opulent, radiant, satiny, and silky—quintessential Burgundy. The Grands Crus share a profound depth and sophistication but differ drastically in character, despite being clustered together in a single large patch. They range from the lighter but aromatic Romanée-Saint-Vivant to the rich and deep Richebourg. Other Grands Crus have names that simply inspire awe, such as La Tâche and Romanée-Conti, both owned entirely by the icon of aspirational wine, the Domaine de la Romanée-Conti, which is known, like a celebrity, by an acronym, DRC. But DRC is not the only regal resident of this posh postal code. There is also Domaine Leroy, one of the few outfits that can match or even surpass DRC in price and quality. Other domaines of excellence include Comte Liger-Belair, Anne Gros, Mongeard-Mugneret, Rouget, and Méo-Camuzet. And the town is also still marked by the career of Henri Jayer, not a regal personage, but widely considered one of the greatest winemakers in the history of France. Jayer was hailed as both a vineyardist and a winemaker. As a vineyardist, he revived for modern times the idea—now taken for granted—that great wines begin with intensive vineyard work. As a winemaker, he pioneered techniques like cold maceration of the grapes before fermentation. His wines were known for their purity and intensity and for the grace with which they age. Jayer died in 2006, but left an imprint that will never be forgotten. When I drive by, I always pause to acknowledge the small house in which he lived on the periphery of Vosne-Romanée.

Not *all* of Vosne-Romanée's wines are unobtainable or prohibitively expensive. Rather, a few tricks will allow you to enjoy the charms of Vosne-Romanée wines without draining your bank account. But before you learn those, you need to know the dos and don'ts of the Grand Cru vineyards, as these are some of the most highly requested wines of sommeliers with big lists.

My first piece of advice is to avoid La Grand Rue. Solely owned by Domaine Lamarche, the vineyard only recently achieved Grand Cru status, in 1992. And despite being surrounded by four of the greatest vineyards on earth (Romanée-Conti, La Romanée, Romanée-Saint-Vivant, and La Tâche), it underperforms to a degree that is hard to comprehend.

Echézeaux, which is lumped in as Vosne-Romanée but technically resides in the tiny neighboring commune of Flagey-Echézeaux (the few village and Premier Cru wines from here are sold as Vosne-Romanée) is the largest Grand Cru and has more than a dozen producers putting out its wine. Frankly, it is a minefield, so you have to make sure you are buying a good producer's wine. (Trustworthy sources include DRC, Rouget, Mongeard-Mugneret, and Mugneret-Gibourg.) Contrast this to Grands-Echézeaux, whose name seems to suggest that it is bigger, but actually means it is better than Echézeaux. Grands-Echézeaux is the smaller vineyard, and its wine is more concentrated, layered, and reliable. At its best, it rivals any of the top wines of Vosne-Romanée. Recommended producers include DRC, Mongeard-Mugneret, and Drouhin.

Romanée-Saint-Vivant is a less heralded Grand Cru than La Tâche and Romanée-Conti, but its wines are ethereal and often comparable in quality. The vineyard plays host to an incredible concentration of wine-making talent: DRC, Domaine Leroy, Domaine Dujac, Domaine de l'Arlot, Domaine Robert Arnoux, Domaine Sylvain Cathiard, and Domaine

Jean-Jacques Confuron. Almost every producer is making a top wine, showing some facet of the rose petals, raspberries, and mineral that mark this vineyard, which is right next to Romanée-Conti. It does not have quite the same aromatics as its neighbor, but it is the closest in style at about one-fifth the price.

Richebourg is one of the most powerful and dense wines in Burgundy and is closer in style to Chambertin than it is to neighboring wines in Vosne-Romanée. The wines have enormous fruit, tannin, and spice, which make them easy to identify at a blind tasting. And, like Romanée-Saint-Vivant, an all-star team of producers vinify them, ensuring a great forum to compare their styles: DRC, Leroy, Mongeard-Mugneret, Méo-Camuzet, and Anne Gros.

La Tâche and Romanée-Conti are the last two Grands Crus, both *monopoles* of DRC. Little can be said about them that has not already been said a thousand times. La Tâche is consistently awe-inspiring: powerful, complex, untamed, and regal in its expression and ability to flower over decades and decades. Romanée-Conti is perhaps the ideal Burgundy, always less intense than La Tâche and less colossal than Richebourg, yet sublimely aromatic and spicy.

The most exciting of the Grand Cru vineyards in Vosne-Romanée right now is La Romanée, which sits just up the hill from Romanée-Conti (some say they were once one vineyard). It is owned by Comte Liger-Belair, though this domaine is not yet widely known for it. In fact, no one is known for La Romanée. The wine is exceedingly rare and has been lost in the vast portfolios of various *négociants* for more than sixty years. La Romanée is also the smallest appellation in France, producing but a few hundred cases each year. The wine becomes even more exciting when a little of the history behind the estate is revealed.

La Romanée is the best of the remaining possessions of Comte Liger-Belair, once the owner of the most opulent estate in Burgundy. It is jaw-dropping to know that the Liger-Belair family at one time owned all of the original La Tâche; all of La Grand Rue; one-third of Clos de Vougeot; a large portion of Richebourg, Chambertin, and Echézeaux; and land in the Premiers Crus of Les Saint-Georges, Suchots, Beaux Monts, Reignots, and more. If it was a game of Monopoly, it would be like owning Boardwalk, Park Place, and, well, that whole side of the board. Were those holdings intact, Liger-Belair would stand above DRC. But in the 1930s, after a death in the family, the estate, tangled in a complicated inheritance, was broken up. Some members of the family chose money over vineyards, so in 1933, the property was auctioned off. Juste Liger-Belair, who was a priest, did not want to see the whole estate sold to others and purchased what he could. This included the tiny La Romanée and a few other small pieces, all of which now comprise the estate of Louis-Michel Liger-Belair, a young man in his midthirties and the seventh generation of the family.

From 1946 to 2001, the wines of these vineyards were made under *métayage* agreements (see page 74) by a plethora of different houses. In 2001, La Romanée reverted back to Louis-Michel Liger-Belair, although he continued to share its fruit with Bouchard, a large *négociant* house, until 2005. Today, the small but storied La Romanée is entirely back in Louis-Michel's

184

LOUIS-MICHEL LIGER-BELAIR

hands. And they are turning out to be exceptionally capable hands. Besides a wry sense of humor and a dark charm, Louis-Michel is a wine-making prodigy. His pure, detailed, and fruit-driven style is said to be reminiscent of the great Henri Jayer, who tutored him in wine making. In the few years that he has been vinifying La Romanée, he has been able to present it as the kingly Grand Cru that it is, with wines of haunting, delicate fruit, ethereal structure, and dazzling complexity.

BUYER'S TIPS

- If you want to taste DRC but cannot afford to throw down a grand or two for the pleasure, there is only one wine for you: Cuvée Duvault-Blochet. Its first vintage was 1999, and now it is made every few years. It is a blend of the leftover grapes (lesser quality) of all the Grands Crus. Technically, it is a Vosne-Romanée Premier Cru, because to earn Grand Cru status, a wine must be from a single vineyard. But this bottle is a good way to taste the DRC style of viticulture and wine making and some Grand Cru juice for a price that is about one-tenth of what you pay for the famous wines.

- The vineyard of Les Gaudichots is relatively obscure, but it is on sacred ground, adjacent to La Tâche. In the 1930s, most of what is La Tâche today was Les Gaudichots, so the theory is that Les Gaudichots is equal to and part of La Tâche. DRC owns a portion of Les Gaudichots, which it vinifies and sells in bulk, but it never reveals to whom. So, who bottles it? Mostly *négociants*. That means if you see a Les Gaudichots on a wine list, order it, because it is a good bet you will drinking wine made by DRC. Domaine Regis Forey also makes Les Gaudichots every year.

- The vineyard Aux Malconsorts is adjacent to La Tâche. A portion of it is actually tucked into La Tâche, however. In fact, if you are standing in the vineyard, you would assume that it is part of La Tâche, but this little corner is owned by Domaine de Montille. Étienne de Montille's first vintage was in 2005, and he bottles the wine under the name Aux Malconsorts Cuvée Christiane, in honor of his mother. Although Étienne insists the idea is not to make another La Tâche, but rather an expression of Malconsorts, the wine is similar in style to the DRC *monopole*. It rivals DRC in quality for about one-third the price.

- Daniel Bocquenet is a small, first-rate producer of Echézeaux, making a soft, juicy, delicious wine. It is not terribly serious, but it is always enjoyable and comes at a reasonable price.

186

After the incomparable journey through Vosne-Romanée, Nuits-Saint-Georges, which has no Grands Crus, may seem a letdown. But you will find some good wines here, and a welcome price break, too. Nuits is the longest commune in the Côte d'Or, extending for about three miles, and the small town it takes its name from is bustling with industry—label printers, liqueur distillers, and the like.

The wines here are generally characterized as earthy or rustic, known for notes of leather and game. In fact, the *terroir* changes as you head from north to south, resulting in two distinct styles of Nuits-Saint-Georges. The vineyards adjacent to Vosne-Romanée—Aux Cras, Aux Boudots, and Les Damodes—have the Vosne style and are powerful but silky, with that lovely red fruit of Vosne. Many top Vosne-Romanée producers have vineyards here and tend to make the wines in the style of their home village: a softer, gentler extraction yielding a more subtle wine. The vineyards on the south end of town—Les Saint-Georges and Les Vaucrains are two of the most prominent Crus—show more earthiness, gaminess, and mineral austerity and require long aging to become pleasurable.

The top producers of Nuits-Saint-Georges tend to be old school. Modern techniques have never taken hold. The extractions are often rough, resulting in hard, massive tannins. Less or no new oak is employed to retain the minerality of the wines, leaving them angular and hard in their youth. They can turn into lovely, characterful wines with age, but they take time. The best producers are Robert Chevillon, Henri Gouges, and Domaine de l'Arlot.

BUYER'S TIP

- Domaine Jean-Jacques Confuron, an excellent producer, bottles Les Fleurières, a Nuits-Saint-Georges village wine made from vines with an average age of thirty-five years. This wine is strangely the anti-Nuits: not hard and coarse, but instead soft, light, and delicious, more like Chambolle-Musigny, but with dark fruit and spice. A great wine and a great deal.

CORTON

A massive hill surrounded by three small villages, Corton marks with authority the beginning of the Côte de Beaune. The red wines of Corton are fat and rich—the biggest of the Côte de Beaune—but depending on where on the hill they come from, they may either have a hardness in their youth that requires cellaring or they may be fleshy and fruit-forward and somewhat lacking in structure. The best examples are some of the longest-lived wines in Burgundy.

Corton is the largest Grand Cru in Burgundy, and because of its enormous size, its varied *terroirs*, and the variance in quality among producers, it is not taken too seriously by sommeliers. There is simply lots of bad wine made by uncaring producers who get to price and label their wine with the name of a Grand Cru, even if what they make is inferior. Corton has been like this for a long time. Brilliant wines are also made here, however, so the *terroir* cannot be written off. Rather, it is just a difficult area: top-notch producers can make great wines, though given their austerity, they may not be ready until the next generation. Tollot-Beaut, Louis Jadot, and Bouchard have been the most reliable Corton producers in the past.

The commune may be due for a renaissance. Domaine de Montille, one of the best producers of the Côte de Beaune, started making a Corton in 2005, and it is a great wine. An even bigger development was Domaine de la Romanée-Conti's 2009 announcement that it would commence making wines from three leased Corton Grands Crus: Les Bressandes, Clos du Roi, and Les Renardes.

BEAUNE

The bustling, beautiful town of Beaune is filled with cafés, boutiques, and more than its fair share of wine shops. It is the capital of wine making in Burgundy, and it is the home of all the *négociants* who not only dominate the wine shops and caves underneath the town, but also own most of the Beaune AOC vineyard land around it. Today, a few of the top *négociants* produce some very good wines, though perhaps not at the quality of the finest small domaines. Maison Leroy is the best, followed closely by the exquisite wines of Drouhin and Louis Jadot, and then by Bouchard, Faiveley, and Boisset. Wines from big names like Patriarch and Moillard are subpar.

Beaune vineyards produce a range of wines from dense and jammy to light and fruity. But many of the sites have a higher clay content, which produces heavier wines that are flatter in profile, earthy, and less aromatic than those from more chalky vineyards. Les Grèves, Les Marconnets, and Les Teurons are considered some of the best sites. For the most part, Beaune wines are moderately priced and drink well in their younger years or after medium aging.

BUYER'S TIP

- Domaine de Montille brings its wine-making expertise to a couple of Beaune Premiers Crus that perform at a higher level than their prices warrant. Les Perrières is a classic, earthy Beaune with lovely weight, perfume, and spice. Les Sizies is a little heavier and darker, with red and black fruit and rich, supple texture overlaying a quiet minerality. Both can be found for around fifty dollars, a great price for a producer of this reputation.

Beaune is filled with restaurants, but only a few places—where the lists are good, the food is excellent, and the wine vibe is humming all night—are favored by the wine trade. Ma Cuisine, hidden away on a downtown alley, is the winemakers' hangout of Burgundy. Its food, which is classic bistro with a casual, creative twist, is prepared by the hardworking Fabienne Escoffier and is routinely delicious. Since the restaurant's rise to popularity over the last ten years, its wine list has been well picked over, but you can still find lots of good deals and treats, and the restaurant has wonderful connections to the best producers, who keep its cellar full. Bistro de l'Hôtel is run by Swedish-born Johan Björklund, a great chef and an insatiable wine hound whose upscale bistro has become the hangout for many of the wealthy collectors. The adjacent l'Hôtel de Beaune offers the most luxurious accommodation in the region.

POMMARD

"The sound of the name Pommard corresponds to most people's idea of what Burgundy should be," wrote Anthony Hanson, acutely, in his tome *Burgundy*. "It's not just easy to pronounce, it has a full-bodied generous ring to it. This has been a mixed blessing, for the wine has had an easier sale than other Burgundies, lulling growers into a false sense of security. If a wine will sell on its name, the pressure to make something of interest is diminished."

Pommard has suffered under a well-earned reputation of producing hardy, rough-hewn wines requiring long aging in order to give pleasure. The soil composition includes a good deal of clay mixed with some limestone, yielding wines that are earthy and minerally. In great vintages, they can have an extra dimension of spice and aromatics, especially when mature.

In the absence of any Grands Crus, the best vineyards are Premiers Crus Les Rugiens, Les Epenots, and Les Pézerolles. Producers making excellent wines from Pommard's hard soils are Comte Armand, Domaine Lejeune, and Domaine de Montille.

BUYER'S TIPS

- Benjamin Leroux, the manager and winemaker at Domaine Comte Armand in Pommard, is one of the young wine-making stars of France. In addition to his day job, he has set up his own business as merchant and producer, focused on making characterful wines from more humble vineyards. His Saint-Aubin Les Murgers des Dents de Chien and Savigny-lès-Beaune Hauts Jarrons match the quality of many more famous and expensive wines.

189

- One of the more remarkable producers of the Côte de Beaune is Domaine Lejeune, which is as staunchly traditional a producer as can be found in mainstream Burgundy. Its grapes are not destemmed before they are put into vats, where they are foot-trodden to crush and break the skins. Fermentation and maceration can take up to four weeks, before the grapes are processed in an antique wooden basket press and the wine taken off for aging in old barrels. The wines are a bit dense and tannic, but full of life and quite beautiful. The best is the Pommard Premier Cru Les Argillières.

VOLNAY

Volnay and Pommard are the yin and yang of Pinot Noir in Burgundy. Whereas Pommard is hard, dark, and dense, Volnay is all light, perfume, and satin. Consequently, Volnay makes some of the most charming and delightful red wines of the Côte d'Or. The soils have a higher degree of limestone and much less clay than Pommard's, giving them a firm mineral edge that woks as a support beam for all the lovely fruit. Sommeliers in general are big fans of the ethereal, mineral wines of Volnay, as they are accessible, elegant, and often fruit-forward, pairing well with a wide range of foods.

Although Volnay has no Grands Crus, it does have many excellent vineyards, including Clos des Chênes, Clos des Ducs, Les Santenots, Champans, and Les Caillerets. Wine making here is primarily traditional in style. Modernists, with their long extractions and cellars full of new barrels, would have little to do in Volnay, as the wines are too finesse driven. The grapes lack the extract to make massive wines, so they are easily overwhelmed by new oak. Thus, the style of Volnay is elegant for a reason. The classic producers, among them Domaine de Montille, Lafarge, Pousse d'Or, and Marquis d'Angerville, are excellent.

BUYER'S TIP

- Some of the best Volnays are made by white-wine producers of Meursault. Coche-Dury makes a difficult-to-find Volnay Premier Cru that is well worth seeking out, as it is an excellent expression. Likewise, Dominique Lafon, another white-wine specialist from Meursault, makes an impressive roster of Volnays in the Premiers Crus Santenots, Champans, and Clos des Chênes. Lafon's Volnays are well distributed, but they take a few years of cellaring before they are ready to drink.

190

Chassagne-Montrachet may mark the southern end of the Côte d'Or, but it hardly signals the end of Burgundy. In fact, Burgundy is overflowing with wine throughout the entire, vast region. Visitors rarely have the opportunity to get off the beaten path of famous villages and Grand Cru vineyards to explore the lesser-known appellations. Yet these small towns and out-of-the-way vineyards share similar weather conditions and geography with the greatest of wines of the Côte d'Or. Grapes from these vines often result in fine wines, though rarely are they known outside of their own locales. Generally soft and easy to drink, ready on release and not for the cellar, these wines offer great pleasure and good value for that inimitable taste of Burgundy.

The Côte Chalonnaise continues straight down after the end of the Côte d'Or. Although it has no Grand Cru vineyards, the towns Bouzeron, Rully, Mercurey, Givry, and Montagny all have Premier Cru vineyards, and the wines can be exciting. Indeed, Domaine de Villaine, the private estate of DRC owner and administrator Aubert de Villaine, makes Aligoté, Chardonnay, and Pinot Noir exclusively in the Côte Chalonnaise, using organic viticulture on sloping, limestone-rich hillside vineyards. In Givry, Domaine Joblot makes amazing wine at incredible prices. Joblot's Pinot Noirs are intense, forward, and multidimensional—as good as most village wines from the Côte d'Or. I have been in many blind tastings where people have suggested that Joblot's wines were Premiers Crus from the Côte de Beaune. Try its Premier Cru Clos de la Servoisine to understand why.

The Mâconnais is just to the south of the Côte Chalonnaise. It has gentler slopes, less limestone, richer soils, and less extreme exposures, and grows predominantly Chardonnay. But there are good wines—if not with the depth and intensity of those of the Côte d'Or— and great deals. In the past few years, producers like Dominique Lafon and Domaine Leflaive purchased vineyards in the Mâconnais and are practicing their wine-making skills, which allows them to offer their wares to a much wider audience. Olivier Merlin is also making wonderful wines from this area.

STREET MUSICIAN, PARIS

BEAUJOLAIS

"Beaujolais must be the most inspired invention in the history of wine," wrote Kermit Lynch in *Adventures on the Wine Route*. "What a concept, downing a newborn wine that has barely left the grape. . . . It even serves to remind us of the first time man tasted fermented grape juice and decided it was an accident of nature worth pursuing."

Lynch is, of course, talking about Beaujolais Nouveau, the drinkable, just-out-of-the-fermenter wine of the current vintage that he—and many others—also blame for the downfall of Beaujolais. And that indeed might be true: the liberties taken by growers and winemakers to mass-produce a quick and easy industrial product ended up bringing the wine industry, albeit vibrantly and cheerfully, to its knees. But thankfully for sommeliers—and for the rest of the world—Beaujolais is now bouncing back. These days, there is probably no wine that I am more excited about (well, along with the reds of the northern Rhône) than Beaujolais. I drink it at home, I drink it at restaurants, I push it at RN74. I cannot get enough of it.

Perhaps, as Lynch wrote of Beaujolais Nouveau, "one sees that the nightmare can happen. A recipe, a formula, can take over an entire region." But the formula itself is not the problem. In fact, I drank an incredibly delicious Beaujolais Nouveau in a Paris bistro while working on this book. It was from Marcel Lapierre (one of Lynch's producers, coincidentally), and it was as fresh as the morning dew. Delivered to the restaurant in bulk and served by carafe, the wine was a cloudy, dark cherry color, exuberantly fruity, flush with acidity, and with just enough gentle tannin to be the perfect quaffing companion to my *onglet*. It was nothing like the insipid, strawberry-flavored juice we have come to know. It was real wine.

Everything I have just described about a simple carafe of wine at a Paris café is what is great about Beaujolais. And Lapierre's Nouveau is his most basic wine; it only gets better from there. As you move up the ladder into Beaujolais-Villages and Crus Beaujolais, the wines not only remain delicious, easy to drink, and affordable, but also become complex and age-worthy. Not long ago, Daniel Johnnes served me a 1929 Moulin-à-Vent from his cellar. Yes, a 1929! People who consider Beaujolais insubstantial would need only a sip from this bottle to change their opinion. At that age, the Beaujolais was unmistakable from a great Burgundy.

The quiet revolution now happening in Beaujolais is driven by only a handful of producers, all of whom are going back to old methods to ensure the integrity of the wines of this noble region is preserved. They are fermenting their wines with natural yeasts, instead of the infamous yeast employed in the 1980s and 1990s that made Beaujolais smell like bananas. They insist on mature vines, and they use zero or very little chaptalization. And they don't fine, filter, or add much, if any, sulfur. Given the level of risk taken in making them (a winemaker is courting trouble by removing the safeguards of modern technology) and the level of quality achieved, these wines are also sickly cheap.

The producers to look for are Kermit Lynch's so-called Gang of Four: Jean-Paul Thévenet, Guy Breton, Jean Foillard, and Marcel Lapierre. Other great producers are Yvon Métras, Potel-Aviron, Château des Jacques, Trénel, Clos de la Roilette, Desvignes, and Descombes. The complexity of the wines of the region vary. Some Crus, like Saint-Amour, Fleurie, and Chiroubles, offer light, straightforward wines to drink right away. Other areas, notably Morgon, Moulin-à-Vent, and Chénas, are famous for producing relatively dense, powerful wines that warrant at least a couple years of aging, if not ten or more.

The issue of storage is more complicated for some of the natural producers. Crus Beaujolais, like Morgon from Lapierre or Thévenet, are big, intense wines that will relax and expand nicely with a few years of aging. These wines contain very little or, more likely, no sulfur, however. In other words, nothing has been added to protect them from oxidation or anything else that might destabilize them. That means that you must give the wines as much support as possible when you cellar them. If your cellar is not temperature controlled, store the bottles in the coolest part of it. Make sure the area is dark, and try never to move the wines. If you keep them cool, dark, and static, they should last for ten years, and perhaps longer. (If you do cellar one of these wines, drink it promptly after opening. I have been told by other sommeliers that it can fade quickly once it has been uncorked, though I have not had this problem myself.)

BUYER'S TIP

- A special bottling of Domaine Jean Foillard Morgon, the Cuvée Corcelette comes from sandy soils, not the granitic schist of the more commonly seen Morgon Côte du Py. These soils give the wine a unique grace, a floral character, and a buoyancy without giving up any concentration or intensity. It is a must-buy if you see it on a wine list or in a shop.

NORTHERN RHÔNE

It is only an hour or so drive from Beaujolais down the autoroute and around the metropolis of Lyon to Ampuis, the first important spot in the northern Rhône. But the Rhône could not be a more different place from Beaujolais. You have left pastoral calm for industrial, urban, highway-pierced tension. The vines grow on the steep cliffs and hills overlooking the massive Rhône River, which cuts a tight valley through much of the industrial territory of Lyon and Valence. In several places, vines look out over a multilane highway, and a weird flow of energy surges straight through the valley. But it is hard to keep your eyes on the road as you rocket along, because the tiny, vertiginous terraced vineyards are so precariously stamped into the

194

outsized, towering cliffs. You have left bucolic, gently undulating vine-covered slopes for sheer, soaring precipices studded with thousands of individual vine posts like acupuncture needles in a patient's back. And the wines, well, they are also a world unto themselves.

The best wines in the northern Rhône are made with one grape, Syrah. Yes, some Viognier is found here and there, but for the most part it is Syrah and nothing but. Syrah is popular in Australia, where it is called Shiraz, and in California, where I even make some myself, but this is where it reaches its apex, and nothing else in the world is like it.

The Syrah of the northern Rhône makes a blackish purple wine that, depending on where it is grown, can be one of the most ornery and impenetrable wines in the world or lithe and pretty, with flamboyant aromatics and sweet, luscious tannins. It is a wine that can last for generations, yet can often be enjoyed when young. It is also a wine that can surprise with its versatility, partnering as well with roast chicken as with gamy lamb. But more than anything, it is a wine that, when you develop a taste for it, brings remarkable pleasure. No other grape can marry the joy of bountiful, juicy fruit with the visceral attraction of animal wildness, and then layer the result with the intellectual stimulation of structure and minerality. Great northern Rhône Syrah is like tantric stimulation: it hits all the chakras at once.

There are three great expressions of Syrah and two good ones along the river. Côte-Rôtie, Hermitage, and Cornas are the upper-echelon AOCs, while Crozes-Hermitage and Saint-Joseph tend to produce more ordinary Syrah. The top appellations are all set on enormous hills that bank the river, with the great, singular mounds of Hermitage and Côte-Rôtie especially prominent. Cornas is also set on hills, but the hills form a complex, craggy amphitheater facing the Rhône and are less dramatically visible from the ground. Saint-Joseph has many great vineyards and exposures as well, but the region, hugging the Rhône, has been overexpanded in the last fifty years. Now the AOC is over thirty miles long and thus impossible to talk about as a specific *terroir*. Crozes-Hermitage, the largest appellation of the northern Rhône, was created in 1937 from land previously classified as Côtes du Rhône. For decades it honored its promotion by producing insipid, bland wine, but in the last twenty years, quality has improved considerably.

The style of the wines in the region has changed over the years, as well. Until around 1990, about 20 percent of the producers were new style and 80 percent were traditionalists. Today, the numbers are reversed, with 80 percent of the producers choosing modern methods. In some respects, this is not a terrible thing, as it has resulted in cleaner, more focused, and more consistent wines. For years, the northern Rhône had a reputation for rusticity born out of decades of unclean, *Brettanomyces*-infested wines. Modern methods have eliminated much of this problem. At the same time, other hallmarks of modernity—cultured yeasts, enzymes, and new oak—have changed the profile of much of the wine, homogenizing it, rather than detailing the differences among the *terroirs* and the producers. Naturally, my preference is for traditionally made wines, so long as they are clean and well made.

Côte-Rôtie, or "the roasted slope," produces some of the greatest red wines in the world. The hill of Côte-Rôtie is so steep and so close to the Rhône River that it is difficult to find a good vantage point from which to take in all of it. It is just as difficult for *vignerons* to work the slope, with its sixty-degree inclines, treacherous footing on slick, loose stones, and hard, compact rock soils. The wines are defined by both their power and their finesse. In their youth, they are rustic, spicy, and tannic. But as they age, they become supple, with layers of complex, savory flavors that range from black currant and bacon to coffee and dried herbs—almost Burgundian in their intricacy and grace. Côte-Rôtie has made the biggest gains in reputation of any northern Rhône location in the last generation. Even though Hermitage is historically king, many sommeliers now prefer the aromatics and more graceful structure of Côte-Rôtie.

People think of Côte-Rôtie as one great vineyard, but the soil actually changes dramatically across the hill, resulting in many distinct vineyards, or *climats*, producing wines of distinct character. The names of these vineyards are unknown to most wine drinkers, as the wines are often blended together, but single-vineyard Côte-Rôties are gaining in popularity.

The most famous *climats* of the Côte-Rôtie are the Côte Brune and Côte Blonde, neighboring hillside faces that stand above the town of Ampuis. (The misconception exists that Côte Brune and Côte Blonde are separate hills of Côte-Rôtie, but they are simply nearby plots on the same large hillside.) These two spots generally define the two major soil types of the hill. The northern part of the slope, starting from Côte Brune, is largely composed of iron-rich mica schist, a soil that yields a darker wine with more structure, tannin, and black fruit. The southern end of the slope, heading south from Côte Blonde, has decomposed granite with quartz and white mica, a poor soil that results in lighter-colored wines that are more floral, show red fruit, and have less tannin for long aging. More Viognier is planted on the southern end, where the soil is similar to that of the Viognier appellation Condrieu. The addition of the white grape to the blend contributes to the finesse of the southern-slope wines.

Like Vosne-Romanée, Côte-Rôtie boasts an incredible array of producers, each working in a different style. The best are Jasmin, Ogier, Rostaing, Clusel-Roch, Jamet, and Gangloff.

BUYER'S TIP

- My favorite Côte-Rôtie is from the highly traditionalist producer Domaine Jamet, whose wines are the gutsiest, most intense, and most aromatically complex of the appellation. Jamet does not have a high profile, as neither of the two brothers who run the estate speak much English, nor do they care to travel to promote their wines. This is fine by me. As long as they keep busy producing what is one of the three greatest wines of the northern Rhône, I am happy (the other two: Chave Hermitage and Allemand Cornas).

JEAN-PAUL JAMET

Even if Hermitage were not a famous vineyard, not terraced for agriculture, and not littered with giant signs emblazoned with the names of various commercial wine producers—if it were just a giant, barren hill peering out over the Rhône—it would still be obvious that planting this mass of southern-facing rock with grapevines would almost instantaneously produce some of the most stunning wine in the world. That's because the great hill of Hermitage is an enormous solar panel positioned perfectly due south to collect the sun's rays at their maximum intensity and turn them into something magnificent. The sad part is that the wines rarely live up to the grand promise of the visual spectacle and the long history.

The most renowned wines of the northern Rhône come from 134 hectares of south-facing granite slopes. Legend has it that the vineyards were first planted by Phoenicians in the sixth century BCE. It is known that they date at least to Roman times, when they produced a wine described as "peppery." More savory than fruity, red Hermitage today is an opaque, inky wine offering aromas of blackberry, spice, black pepper, tar, and meat. These wines are long-lived, evolving for two or three decades and shedding some of their girth along the way.

What is left to like about Hermitage? The wines are difficult to define. When they are big, chunky, high in alcohol, and tannic, they threaten to overpower everything with which they come in contact. But if they are not that way, they taste like something has been stripped out of them—like something is lacking. Simply put, it is hard to find balanced Hermitage wines that reflect the true soul of the place.

Unlike Côte-Rôtie, which has a concentration of small artisanal producers, Hermitage is dominated by big *négociants* who not only compromise the beauty of the hill with their gigantic "look at me" signs, but also fail to make compelling wines. Jaboulet has been terrible for some time now, with even La Chapelle, its iconic vineyard, turning out unpalatable wines since 1995. Michel Chapoutier, master marketer, likes to talk more than he likes to craft convincing wine. His wines may be biodynamic and varietally correct, but they taste as if they have no soul. Delas Frères, another *négociant*, owns a great chunk of Hermitage, but makes wines that are devoid of character and personality.

When it comes to producers of Hermitage, there is just Jean-Louis Chave and everyone else. And even Chave's style has changed dramatically, beginning in the early 2000s, when he made a move toward cleaner, fresher wines and away from the murky but incredibly complex wines of old. I do not drink much Hermitage these days, unless its quite old, preferring instead to skip down the road to the next big slope.

198

JEAN-LOUIS CHAVE

• Chave Hermitage Blanc may seem like the obvious choice here, and for many sommeliers it is, but thick, heavy whites are not my style. I like two other wines in the Chave lineup, however, that few people even know are made. The first is the Hermitage Cuvée Cathelin, named for the late painter Bernard Cathelin. According to Jean-Louis Chave, the artist wanted to paint a label for the producer, so Chave created a new wine for the label. It was first made in 1990, and then only in select vintages: 1991, 1995, 1998, 2000, and 2003. The cuvée is a selection of certain barrels of the lots that go into Chave's regular Hermitage, but it has a little more of everything: power, complexity, finesse. It is one of the most stunning Syrahs you will ever drink: dense, jammy, and forceful, yet neither heavy nor hot, and complex with everything savory and succulent. Alas, it is made in very limited quantities and is mind-bogglingly expensive when it can be located. But if someone offers you a glass, jump on it.

• The second wine is Vin de Paille, which is made from grapes (mostly Marsanne) that are air-dried on straw mats (*paille* means "straw"), a process that concentrates the juice by removing water. The intense, reduced liquid is then fermented in old casks, usually for years. I am not a fan of sweet wines, but this is amazing nectar! It carries the essence of peaches and apricots while layering on honey, grass, and pineapple, and has a dazzling acidity that keeps things firm. It is so rich that one sip is enough, and a single half bottle will satisfy a party of twelve.

CORNAS

Cornas, once the barefooted country cousin to suave Côte-Rôtie and regal Hermitage, has been discovered. It was never as rustic and rough-hewn a place as the literature made it out to be, but in a matter of a few years, the prices of its finest wines have caught up with those of some of the top Côte-Rôties. Even at sixty to eighty dollars a bottle, the best wines of Cornas are well worth it.

Cornas means "burnt earth," and, indeed, the wines from this perfect sun-catching bowl are often more inky black than any other wines of the Rhône. Most of the soils are granitic, covering deep, impenetrable rock. But veins of limestone and a more sandy soil that yield (relatively) lighter wines are also here. In general, the wines are dense, with tannins that often seem chewable. In less-ripe vintages, these tannins are not chewable; indeed, they will break your teeth. But in the warmer vintages that seem to be more commonplace these days, these thick, dark tannins give the wine viscosity and carry the flavor lastingly into the back of the throat. Some examples can be wild and gamy, especially as they age, but they also show a purer, sweeter note of blackberry and blueberry than any other northern Rhône appellation.

I drink a lot of Cornas, especially young Cornas, from 2004 through 2006. Infanticide? Not for me. Young Cornas is lusty and visceral, an irresistible conduit to the carnal experience of red wine. I would be remiss not to quote Kermit Lynch once again, as he obviously feels the same way: "In the wine literature, it is repeatedly advised that Cornas must be aged several years before it is worthwhile, but there is something about a brand-new Cornas that should not be missed. . . . A bottle should be uncorked when it appears on the market, in order to experience its youthful extravagance of color and size."

In fact, if you ever find yourself with the opportunity to taste from the barrel a few months before bottling, take it. Cornas seems to hit a sweet spot—a gracefulness, a peace—at this moment in its development that it may not find again until many more years in the bottle. I had a chance to do this when the lovely 2008s were still in barrel at the two best, albeit markedly different, domaines in Cornas: Clape and Thierry Allemand. Clape is the oldest of old school. Not only is there not a new barrel in its dank, moldy cellar, but there are hardly even barrels as most people know them. Rather, you see many big, old wooden *foudres*—massive, tall, oval-shaped containers. These age wine more slowly and with less oxidation than a standard barrel and also introduce the chance of reduction, which can bring Syrah's signature gamy aromas to the fore. Clape's wines are impeccable, wonderfully pure and concentrated with expansive and endless finishes.

Thierry Allemand is a force of nature. He has an intense glint in his eye and an infectious energy that borders on daunting. He has no formal training, is self-made, and is one of the best winemakers in France. Allemand's style is neither traditional nor modern, but a mix. Like a traditionalist, he never destems, he uses minimal sulfur and no new wood, and he does not scientifically analyze his wines. At the same time, he has used some unorthodox methods, such as occasionally employing carbonic maceration, as is typically done in Beaujolais. Also, his wines do not taste old school. They have an amazing purity and exacting cleanliness, and while they are dense with minerality, they favor the fruity side of Syrah over the savory. Inarguably, they are delicious, joyful wines.

Cornas is blessed with other good producers, as well. For such a small town, it takes its wine making seriously and appears to keep it in the family. Be on the lookout for the wines of Alain Voge, Franck Balthazar, Vincent Paris, and Domaine Courbis.

BUYER'S TIP

- Until 1986, Thierry Allemand made wine fairly conventionally. But he noticed that he was suffering from poor digestion and headaches after drinking red wines. After a conversation with Marcel Lapierre (of Beaujolais) and Pierre Overnoy (of Jura), both natural winemakers, he decreased the use of sulfur in his wines to nothing or almost nothing. And, to his surprise, he started feeling better. So, he altered his method to using almost no sulfur in his wines. In fact, he makes one wine called Sans Soufre, literally "Without Sulfur." It is labeled simply Cornas, as opposed to his other two wines, each of which bears the name of its vineyard, Chaillot or Reynard. I tasted the 2004 Sans Soufre next to the 2004 Reynard, which was the same wine except that it contained one part sulfur. Both wines were great, but the Sans Soufre had a level of expansiveness and depth that was not apparent in the Reynard. It was open to my palate with its generous soft fruit in a way that the other wine was not. If you buy the Sans Soufre and wish to age it, be aware that it needs to be kept unmoved and in a cold, dark place until consumed. Sulfur is a protectant for wine, and in its absence, the bottle is exceedingly fragile.

SOUTHERN RHÔNE

With its ancient stone villages and craggy pinnacles, the southern Rhône is more beautiful than the narrow slash of vineyards in the north. Alas, in general, the wines of the southern Rhône are not nearly as captivating as their northern siblings. Without question, the greatest wine of the south is from Châteauneuf-du-Pape, a small but majestic town not far from Avignon. Its Grenache-based bottlings are the longest lived, biggest, and most complex of the region. I have been a steady fan of the wine—two domaines, Château Rayas and Château de Beaucastel, are among my favorites in France—but my loyalty has been in decline since 1998. That vintage, a hot one that produced huge, jammy wines, was a watershed. Highly praised by the dominant critics, it launched Châteauneuf-du-Pape into an era of colossal-sized wines, and the hot vintages of 2000, 2003, and 2007 cemented that style. Today's Châteauneuf-du-Papes are not food friendly. Bottles I have enjoyed from the 1950s, 1960s, and 1970s were all between 13 and 14 percent alcohol and balanced. In a good vintage today, wines are rarely below 15 percent alcohol—a rise due to global warming, attempts to please the critics, or both.

If the cause is global warming, my interest in Châteauneuf-du-Pape will continue to wane. But while I do not like the so-called great vintages, I do like some of the more challenging ones, like 1999, 2004, and 2006. Grenache, the foundation of Châteauneuf-du-Pape, gives the wine its ripeness, alcohol, and heady flavors. The Mourvèdre that appears in some blends is what gives the wines their structure, however. Consequently, the Châteauneuf-du-Papes with a higher percentage of Mourvèdre will often be more balanced in overripe, hot vintages. Château de Beaucastel, Domaine Grand Veneur, and Château La Nerthe are my favorites of this style. (The greatest Châteauneuf-du-Pape, Château Rayas, is made with Grenache only. How that wine, in every vintage, manages to be so graceful, complex, and

THIERRY ALLEMAND

balanced is extraordinary.) The elevated levels of Mourvèdre also mean that the wines will require more years to be ready to drink. For me, this is fine, because a well-aged Châteauneuf-du-Pape can be one of the most compelling wines, expressing pure, vibrant red fruit, mulberry, cranberry, and white pepper.

Gigondas, a gorgeous village at the base of the spectacularly jagged Dentelles de Montmirail mountains, gives its name to a wine that is often known as a baby Châteauneuf-du-Pape, so called because it is a Grenache-based wine with a good solid core of red fruit and an earthy exterior. It is less plush and more rough-hewn than Châteauneuf-du-Pape, due to its primary cultivation on steep, rugged slopes, but it can be delicious, especially with some age. My favorite producers are Château de Saint-Cosme, Domaine Santa Duc, Domaine Brusset, and Domaine Les Pallières.

BUYER'S TIP

- Syrah is the grape of the northern Rhône and, for the most part, does not make compelling wines in the south. A few exceptions exist, however. Not surprisingly, these Syrahs come from the extreme northern end of the southern Rhône. They are not as expansive as, say, Cornas, but they do capture the beautiful tones of the grape: white and black pepper, smoked meat, blackberry, and wild herbs. Although labeled Côtes du Rhône, they offer much more character than the typical, solid but forgettable Côtes du Rhône wines. Look for the bottlings of Domaine Gramenon, Maxime-François Laurent, and Château de Fonsalette.

LOIRE VALLEY

One of the most important tools for sommeliers in food and wine pairing is the Loire Valley. Its great variety of reds and (mostly) whites are some of the world's finest food wines. Anyone studying for the master sommelier exam quickly discovers that the Loire is a devilishly complicated region because of its incredible panoply of appellations. Those of us not studying for the exam, however, can concentrate on the few appellations that rank among the greatest in France: Vouvray, Savennières, Sancerre, Pouilly-Fumé, Chinon, and Muscadet. These hold the true value of the region.

Some of my favorite Loire wines are from Sancerre, especially wines in the appellation near the town of Chavignol. This is the limestone side of Sancerre, whose wines are finer and more mineral than the lower clay fields. The soil here is Kimmeridgian marl, as in Chablis and Champagne, and the soil often trumps the grape. Indeed, it can sometimes be hard in a blind tasting to distinguish Chavignol Sauvignon from Chablisienne Chardonnay. Producers to look for on the Chavignol side are Edmond Vatan and François Cotat. Vatan's name is largely unknown, but he is considered by many (including me) to be the greatest producer of Sancerre. His wine is so wild and mineral that it tastes more like Chablis than Sancerre. Vatan retired in 2007, but his daughter, Anne, continues to make the wine under his guidance. François Cotat is the other great producer here. His wines are impeccably balanced and speak less of the fruit of the grape than of the rocks and minerals in the soil, to yield an absolutely delicious result.

Another of my favorite Sancerre producers is Domaine Vacheron, a small biodynamic estate run by two young *vignerons*, Jean-Laurent and Jean-Dominique. The vineyards are split between limestone soil and flinty *silex* and include some of the best sites in the appellation. Vacheron also makes the best Pinot Noir of the region. Jean-Laurent, the phenom who is the face of the domaine, worked at DRC and consulted in California for Etude and Joseph Phelps. He was also the first winemaker at HdV, the California venture of DRC's Aubert de Villaine.

But whereas Sauvignon Blanc makes celebrated wines all over the world, the Loire's other famous white grape, Chenin Blanc, is more unique to the region (the only other country known for it is South Africa). With their exotic, hard-to-describe flavors, Chenin Blancs are in many ways the Loire's soul: so versatile with food, so interesting to age, and so affordable for the quality they offer. They are go-to wines for sommeliers, and my favorite producers from the various Chenin appellations include Montlouis from Jacky Blot and François Chidaine; Savennières from Jo Pithon, Domaine des Baumard (Clos du Papillon), and Nicolas Joly; and Vouvray from Huet and Chidaine. If you see these wines, buy them, and do not worry about drinking them right away, as they become more incredible with every year they age.

It is easy to forget about red wine in the Loire, but Loire reds play an important role in my wine programs. Cabernet Franc, the major red grape of the Loire, is the delicate, aromatic feminine side of the Cabernet family. What cannot be done with this grape in Bordeaux with all of its new oak is accomplished here with the grape's purer state of violets, cherries, and a telltale hint of green. In Chinon, drink Philippe Alliet and Charles Joguet. In Bourgueil, drink Pierre et Catherine Breton and Jacky Blot. In Saumur-Champigny, look for Clos Rougeard. These are accessible alternatives to the right bank of Bordeaux and much, much cheaper. You can find many for less than twenty dollars. They are all great with mushrooms, veal, and pork, and are light bodied enough to pair with heavier fish (with a red wine sauce) and vegetables.

BUYER'S TIP

- Simple, bright, sharp Mucadet is still one of the greatest white wine deals in France—and not just when you are serving oysters. Always buy Muscadet from the Sèvre et Maine area. Domaine de la Pépière, Pierre Luneau-Papin, and Domaine de l'Ecu all make complex, minerally, deliciously citrusy wine that is as fine as it is inexpensive. And if you want to set some bottles aside, they can age successfully for fifteen to twenty years if well cellared.

BORDEAUX

Bordeaux plays a rather small role in both my wine programs and my personal cellar. You will see lots of aged Bordeaux on my lists, but they are generally bought from old cellars. It's not that there aren't proficient winemakers and some delicious wines in the region. And six of my top ten wines of all time are Bordeaux: 1870 Lafite, 1945 Mouton, 1947 Cheval Blanc, 1947 Lafleur, 1921 Petrus, and 1847 Y'quem. (The others are 1978 DRC Montrachet, 1875 DRC Romanée-Conti, 1945 Roumier Bonnes-Mares, and 1962 Château Rayas.) Do I love great Bordeaux? Yes. Do I drink it all the time? No, and I do not buy new vintages.

As a destination in the French wine country, Bordeaux is less appealing than almost anywhere else. I have been once and felt that was enough. When you go to Bordeaux, you do not taste out of barrel and you are never taken to a vineyard. Instead, you are given an aperitif. The interaction is with businesspeople and technical winemakers, not in-the-field *vignerons*. This formal distance from the vineyards and grapes cannot help but influence my experience of the wines. It is difficult to feel a connection to and an intimacy with wines that are so commoditized and soulless. So, I see no reason why I should go to Bordeaux when I can go to Burgundy and actually learn about wine and experience the true environment of its making— where I can see vineyards, visit cellars, and talk to winemakers.

GERMANY

When I think of German wines, I think of classic, off-dry Riesling, a remarkable wine because although it is somewhat sweet, it is also mineral, racy, and capable of long aging. Germany, with its cold climate, desperately steep slopes, and unique slate soil, is the only place in the world where you can make this brilliant style of wine. Unfortunately, young German wine drinkers have almost given up on the off-dry style, preferring instead wines that are so austere and sharp as to be almost without pleasure, and German producers are striving to make these misguided wines for their home markets. Who is going to save the off-dry style? Sommeliers. For us it is a dream wine: there is no better white-wine value, the quality of the vineyards and wine making throughout the country is astonishingly high, and no wine is more food friendly.

The designations of German wine style, such as Kabinett, Spätlese, and Auslese, are not indications of how sweet the wines taste, as many people believe, but rather of the ripeness of the grapes at the time of picking. A good Auslese will have both more sugar and more acid than a lighter Kabinett. I like a German Riesling of moderate body, so I tend to balance vintages by countering their extremes with my choice in wine style. In very ripe vintages like

2006, I prefer lighter wines like Kabinett. Conversely, in lean vintages like 2007, I buy more Spätlese and even Auslese.

MOSEL-SAAR-RUWER

Of the three rivers from which this central-western area takes its name, the Mosel is the largest and most renowned. The region has a cool climate and is famous for the sheer cliffs on which its vineyards astoundingly perch. It is loaded with great producers; my favorites include Willi Schaefer, Dr. Loosen, Fritz Haag, Selbach-Oster, J.J. Prüm, and J.J. Christoffel.

The Saar and Ruwer are tributaries that flow into the great Mosel. The vineyards overlooking each of these rivers have an even cooler climate than those of the Mosel, which means they have their own style of wines. The Saar is celebrated for the powerful, mineral wines of Egon Müller of Scharzhofberger, some of the most expensive and sought-after bottlings of Germany. The Ruwer, which is cooler and even more austere than the Saar, boasts the crackling, taut wines of Maximin Grünhäuser and Karthäuserhof, both eminent estates.

RHEINGAU

The Rheingau, the premier region of the Rhine River, had its glory days in the past, and today, its biggest names, like Schloss Johannisberg, are not as important as they once were. Often state-run wineries, they have been largely surpassed by an ambitious and committed new generation of small producers. These young wineries are making some unfortunate choices, however. The Rheingau is a relatively warm region (compared to the Mosel), which means it is capable of turning out big, rich Rieslings. This richness allows producers to make drier wines (dry Rieslings seem more balanced when they are richer), however, and today more than 80 percent of the region's output is just that. But two of Germany's finest producers, Johannes Leitz and Robert Weil, still make delicious wines in the more classic mode.

NAHE

The Nahe has a mineral style that falls between the perfumed Mosel and the rotund Rheingau. It is not particularly prominent, probably because of its paucity of famous producers, but its one big name, Dönnhoff, could be the greatest producer in all of Germany. Helmut Dönnhoff's wines are wondrous at every level. His ice wines are incredibly rare and collectible, and his estate Riesling, which costs only twenty dollars retail, is a tremendous value.

AUSTRIA

I am a huge fan of Austrian wines. In the last fifteen years, they have risen from relative obscurity to become important players, and they have a place on all wine lists for three reasons. One, the level of the wines is incredible. Much like Germany, Austria is largely devoted to quality wine growing. A few bad wines are made, of course, but the many good ones far outnumber them. Two, regional identity is strong. Lots of places try to express individual character with only limited success. Austria succeeds at it beautifully. Finally, Austria has stuck with a style: dry wines, most famously with Grüner Veltliner and Riesling. Its Rieslings have benefited in the marketplace from the inconsistency and sweetness currently found in the comparable Rieslings of Alsace, which has traditionally been the only other region known for dry Riesling. Austrian Grüner Veltliner is often not as austere as Riesling. A robust white, it features some of the greenish flavors of Sauvignon Blanc and a hint of legumes, making it the perfect match for green vegetables like peas, asparagus, artichokes, and lettuces.

Wachau, Kremstal, and Kamptal are Austria's three most important wine regions. The Wachau is the biggest player. Its Rieslings and Gruners are the ripest and most powerful, thanks to the higher heat index gained from proximity to the Danube, from which many of the vineyards rise steeply. The soils here are stony and shallow, with a hardpan of gneiss. Because Wachau's producers have the ability to push the ripeness envelope, they are tempted to overdo it, as is happening in Germany's Rheingau. A few well-known producers have fallen into this trap—F.X. Pichler and Hirtzberger to name two—and for the privilege of drinking their unbalanced wines, you pay a costly premium. Stick to the better, more proportional wines of Prager, Altzinger, and Knoll. For the best value, seek out the wines of Domaine Wachau.

Kremstal, with its weathered primary rock, is similar to Wachau. The major point of departure is the lack of the Danube, which means the wines are less fruity and have a pronounced mineral, acidic austerity. The region is short on widely known producers with two exceptions, Nigl and Salomon, who stand among the best makers of white wine in the world.

The soils in the Kamptal are mostly composed of loess, a sandlike clay that gives the wines subtlety and delicate aromatics of peaches and flowers. A slew of top-notch producers, led by Willi Bründlmeyer, Hirsch, Heidler, and Loimer, call this region home.

A plethora of other interesting wines are made in Austria, from different and wonderful grapes like Zweigelt and Blauburger. But two producers must be singled out. Heidi Schröck's dry Muscat is a phenomenal wine with a knack for difficult pairings. The other producer is Kracher, from the Burgenland, who makes some of the world's most acclaimed sweet wines. The wines are labeled by number, indicating relative sweetness levels. For example, the wine called 2 is less sweet than the wine called 9. Alois Kracher passed away in 2007, and now the business is in the capable hands of his son, Gerhard.

ITALY

Italian wine is a vast and endlessly fascinating category. Just when you think you have a handle on most of the appellations and varieties, someone gives you a taste of something completely alien—and mind-blowing. In general, a level of rusticity and warmth permeates many of the wines that I consider to be quintessentially Italian. These wines are first and foremost for the table, a quality I revere. But only one region, Piedmont, has wines that I like across the board. Many of Italy's other regions produce the occasional individual wine of brilliance, but none of them makes consistently genius wines like Piedmont does.

Italy's wine culture is an interesting case study. David Lynch, sommelier of San Francisco's Quince restaurant and coauthor of *Vino Italiano* (the best book on Italian wine), characterized it perfectly by pointing out that it is relatively young. "Most cite that Italy's wine making goes back to the ancient Greeks and before," Lynch said, in conversation, "but if you really look at meaningful Italian wines prior to the 1960s, you can count them on one or two hands. In that way, it has paralleled the evolution of American wine making, with the difference that Italy has both much more established *terroir* and many more wine grapes to work with." I agree with Lynch's assessment, and it also helps to explain how parts of Italy can fall prey to many of the stylistic pitfalls that have plagued American wine. The famed region of Tuscany best illustrates the problem.

Tuscany is the Italian bastion of the international style, and frankly, I have little positive to say about what is going on there. With the exception of Sassicaia, Montevertine, and Soldera, most of the wines coming from the region are comprised of Sangiovese muddled with New World grapes like Cabernet Sauvignon, Merlot, and Syrah, along with a heavy dollop of new oak. All you need to know about Tuscany's supposedly best wine, Brunello di Montalcino, is that in the 1960s, exactly eleven producers were making it, and today, their ranks have swollen to over two hundred. Where did they all come from? Is there really that much acceptable vineyard land? No wonder scandal after scandal about illegal blending of unauthorized grapes have plagued production in recent years.

That said, Italy is a treasure trove of grapes and wines, many of which I am still discovering. Consider Lacrima di Morro d'Alba, an aromatic red from the Marche. It adds a "cool factor" to wine lists, as no one knows it, and it is as versatile a pairing partner as Pinot Noir. The nose is unusual, with rose petal, geranium, and high-toned spiciness, and it is light, inexpensive, low alcohol, and great with food, especially Indian food. Serve it lightly chilled.

I also admire the wines of Mount Etna. This active volcano on the island of Sicily produces wines that do not fit easily alongside their southern Italian neighbors. From pure volcanic soil and grapes most people have never heard of come wines with lightness, freshness, and unusual elegance. The flinty, complex Pietramarina from Benanti, made from the obscure

Carricante grape, is the best white wine in Italy. The reds from the area, made mostly from Nerello Mascalese, are likewise incredible. Some have called them the Barolos of the south. Try Benanti's rustic Rovittello, or legendary importer Marc de Grazia's Tenuta delle Terre Nere, which is light, graceful, and reminiscent of Burgundy. Examples such as these are what make Italy the exciting wine culture that it is today.

PIEDMONT

The people of Piedmont are serious, and so are their wines. The famed vineyards of Barolo and Barbaresco are structured somewhat like Burgundy, with great single vineyards shared by several producers. The well-publicized dispute between traditional and modern style, which has been going on for more than twenty years, is becoming less clear-cut. The middle ground between the two camps has grown to include a majority of producers who employ modern techniques but strive to make balanced, *terroir*-expressive wines. Nevertheless, my favorite Barolo and Barbaresco producers are the ones in the extreme traditionalist camp: Bruno Giacosa, Giacomo Conterno, Vietti, Giacomo Borgogno, Massolino, and Cappellano. And, of course, there is Gaja. Although Angelo Gaja is not a traditional producer—his early use of French *barrique* aging helped usher in the modern age—his wines are always delicious and on point. They are also very expensive.

But for all the glamour of Barolo and Barbaresco, Piedmont has many other wines to offer. White wines like Arneis and Gavi make ideal aperitifs. Barbera is an excellent everyday table wine. Moscato d'Asti is scrumptious and is one of the wines to pair with fresh fruit. Some first-rate obscure wines are found here, too, such as Ruché di Castagnole Monferrato, a DOC that covers only one hundred acres of vineyard. Ruché is a red grape that makes an interesting, highly aromatic, medium-bodied wine with flavors of strawberries, cherries, and white pepper. It tastes less like Nebbiolo than it does like Pinot Noir or ripe Gamay, which is probably why I like it.

BUYER'S TIP

- If you like Barolo and Barbaresco but are put off by the prices, look to the appellation Langhe Nebbiolo, which is the basic regional wine designation of the area that includes the famous B's. Langhe Nebbiolo, a more ordinary expression of the grape but from good producers, has the charm that pure Nebbiolo can offer in an early-drinking, unadorned package. Vietti Perbacco is 100-percent declassified Barolo, and is great juice usually priced at about twenty-five dollars. The well-regarded cooperative Produttori del Barbaresco and the producers Giovanni Manzone and Bruno Rocca are also good sources.

SPAIN

The wine revolution in Spain is perhaps the biggest story in the industry over the last ten to twenty years. In that period, Spain has gone from wine backwater to global force. The problem for me and for most sommeliers is that the red wines show little typicity. The extracted, high-alcohol, oaky, slick blockbuster style has been embraced across Spain, and its practitioners seem to care more about reeling in 95-point scores from folks like Robert Parker than they do about expressing the subtleties of their *terroir* or making wines that can accompany food. The result is that it is difficult to tell a big, rich Rioja from a Toro from a Ribera del Duero.

Most modern Spanish wine does not satisfy the sommelier's goal of finding moderate, earthy wines that perform well at the dinner table. It is surprising that the famous cutting-edge Spanish cuisine—typically light, molecular, and playful—is often fully incompatible with modern Spanish wine. The two worlds seems to exist in isolation from each other. And revolution or not, the best wine in Spain is still the same as it was forty years ago: Vega Sicilia.

Priorat is an example of everything that is wrong with Spanish wine. The first real vintage from this hot, hilly region outside Barcelona was 1992, yet today the wines are hailed as among the best in the world and cost up to four hundred dollars a bottle. Some people like the heavy, dense style that characterizes most Priorats, but I find them undrinkable and a glaring example of wines created for the critics and the trophy collectors and not for people looking to enjoy them regularly and with food. If you want the experience of heavy, dark Priorat-styled wines, drink Montsant (a contiguous appellation) for less oak and less money.

That said, the Spanish revolution offers more than big, modern reds. One of the most interesting developments has been the advancement of white wine in what was traditionally a red-drinking culture. The explosion of Albariño has been significant, as has the growing familiarity of wine drinkers with such esoteric whites as Txakoli, a bracingly taut wine from the Basque region. My favorite whites of the new Spain are not from a specific region, but are almost like anomalies. Naiades, from Bodegas Naia in Rueda, is a lush yet bright wine from prephylloxera Verdejo vines. La Cana Albariño has minerality to go with its opulent citrus and white peach aromas. And the Moscatel from Botani is a genius wine: a dry white made from grapes that had long gone into sweet wines. It shows white flowers, melons, and mineral in a light, refreshing, balanced wine. And at twenty dollars retail, it is a delicious quaffer.

The whites are often as satisfying to me as Spain's modern reds are off-putting. I can find Spanish reds that I enjoy drinking, however. Although it is not really my type—an oaky, new-school red—I cannot help but like Calvario from the Rioja producer Finca Allende. Made mostly from sixty-year-old Tempranillo vines, it is dense, spicy, and dark. But its exceedingly generous dose of new French oak is brilliantly integrated, making for a plush, pillowy drinking experience. Guimaro B1P is an amazing wine from the Ribeira Sacra, a whole-cluster-fermented red from the rare Mencía grape. With its delicate, lacy texture, the wine reminds me of a Burgundy, though the flavors are peppery and smoky with a hint of blackberries and meat. When it comes to Rioja, I like the classic, old-school styles of Muga and Remelluri.

One of the greatest and most seriously traditional wines in the world is also one of the most neglected: sherry. The resistance that people have to this unique and ancient class of wines from Andalusia is a mystery. At Rubicon, Larry Stone used to offer a complimentary glass of Manzanilla sherry to guests who ordered raw oysters, because he thought the pairing was so perfect. Amazingly, he rarely found any takers. But in fact, sherry in all styles makes not only a wonderful aperitif, but also pairs beautifully with a variety of foods from sushi to stews (obviously pour the lighter styles of fino and Manzanilla with the fish and the heavier olorosos with the meat). I like the wines of Lustau, Hidalgo, and Barbadillo.

GREECE

Greece is a region to watch. The reds are a work in progress, but a couple of whites are already among my favorite wines. The producer Sigalas from the island of Santorini makes a wine from the Assyrtiko grape that is estimable. It has body and weight, yet it is as taut as a tightrope and sharp on the tongue with flavors of lemon zest and dried herbs—perfect alongside Mediterranean fish and olives. Likewise with the Moschofilero from Skouras, which shares qualities of vibrancy and acidity with the Assyrtiko, but is lighter and more perfumed. These two wines deserve to be on all top wine lists.

NEW ZEALAND

Ten years ago, the rage was New Zealand Sauvignon Blanc, and it still is. The quality is high and the wines are refreshing and food friendly. Sauvignon Blancs—easy to grow and to produce in quantity—make sense for New Zealand, a country whose small population does not supply it with a large vineyard workforce. Machine harvested, high yielding, and topped with a screw cap, the wines have stayed affordable. My favorites are Dog Point Section 94, which breaks the mold of stainless-steel New Zealand in favor of old oak barrels; Craggy Range Te Muna; and Clos Henri, which was begun by Sancerre producer Henri Bourgeois.

Pinot Noir, New Zealand's other focus, is a more difficult case. The grape is widely planted, and a lot of energy and enthusiasm bolsters the variety. The problem is that Pinot is labor-intensive and thus costly to grow, and the wine is priced accordingly. At the low end, New Zealand Pinots do not compete well on price with their American counterparts. At the high end, New Zealand is forced to battle against Burgundy, which is a losing proposition. For my money, the best Pinot Noir from the islands is not coming from the highly fashionable Otago district, but from a district just outside the South Island region of Waipara. Two producers there, Bell Hill and Pyramid Valley, have discovered big limestone deposits and are beginning to release truly original and interesting Pinot Noir and Chardonnay that are bright, delicate, and mineral. These are wines to track.

OREGON

In 2010, the part of my wine lists that experienced the largest growth was the Oregon section. That's because I was able to purchase a cellar of old wines from Portland. These Pinot Noirs from the mid-1980s and the 1990s are wonderful, having aged not just gracefully but also spectacularly, growing mellow and complex without losing their energy.

Oregon is perhaps the best place in America to produce wines in the style of Burgundy. That Burgundian stars like Véronique Drouhin (Domaine Drouhin Oregon) and Dominique Lafon (Evening Land) have come to make wine there supports that statement. The wines do not have all the nuances of Burgundy, but they can have the same lightness and texture. The weather is similar, but, crucially, the soil is much richer in Oregon than it is in Burgundy, and it lacks any trace of *calcaire*, the limestone that exists in various concentrations throughout France's Pinot Noir country. After only thirty years of intensive wine production, Oregon has come a long way. Within the Willamette Valley, all of the subappellations have been defined, and now differences in the typicity of the wines are starting to become evident. Oregon's challenge is the same as that faced by other young regions: modern farming and modern wine making have allowed producers to push the envelope, and many give in to the temptation to make clunky, over-the-top wines, rather than balanced, *terroir*-driven wines of restraint.

The finest examples of Oregon Pinot Noir are the most restrained. They are also among the greatest Pinot Noirs in the New World: Brick House, Domaine Drouhin, Ponzi, Scott Paul, Cristom, Evening Land, Soter, Eyrie, and J.K. Carriere.

CALIFORNIA

I love living in California and expect it to be my home for the rest of my life. That said, I have a rather uneasy relationship with the wine industry here. I visit Europe more than I do Napa, which is just fifty miles north of my home. The number of French wines on my wine lists dwarfs the number of California wines. But this is less a commentary on the potential of California wine than it is an indication of my feelings about the current wine-making attitudes and tendencies in the state.

NAPA

Until around 1990, the top wines from Napa were important, relevant to the world of wine. Pioneers like Robert Mondavi, André Tchelistcheff, Joseph Phelps, and Warren Winiarski made balanced, complex, age-worthy Cabernets. Twenty years on, however, the tradition they built has been appropriated and commercialized to death. The economic boom of the 1990s brought a wave of investment in the valley, and the focus shifted from crafting wines of integrity to marketing a luxury brand. The typical Napa Cab of today is oaky, superripe, overextracted, and high alcohol—and almost completely incompatible with food. The world of decadent wineries and high-end restaurants that flog the product feels more like a theme park than a home for serious, *terroir*-driven wine.

That said, there is a lot of wine-making talent in Napa, and some of my favorite people live and work there, including Larry Stone, the general manager of Rubicon Estate, and Randy Lewis of Lewis Cellars. Napa today still has the same soils and climate that produced the great wines of the past. Knowing this, I am happy to taste any new Napa wine put before me. But I am still waiting for a greater part of the region to get serious and start making wines of balance and originality—the kind of wines I find from estates such as Araujo, Diamond Creek, Harlan Estate, Grace Family, Dalla Valle, Spottswoode, Corison, and Rubicon Estate.

THE COAST

Today, the most exciting wine in California is being produced on its coast, from the northern Sonoma Coast down through Santa Cruz and as far south as Santa Barbara. The most interesting wines from these places are being made from Pinot Noir and Syrah. The Sonoma Coast gets a lot of press, some of which is deserved. I have respect for the producers who work there, since the climate is even more marginal than it is in Burgundy. A whole crop can be ruined at any time of year by rain, wind, or extreme heat. But in a good vintage, the Pinots are both fruity and earthy, the Chardonnays have real tang, and the Syrahs are deeply savory and exotically complex. I am a big supporter of brilliant wineries like Hirsch, Whetstone, and Littorai, as well as exciting new producers like Ceritas, Soliste, and Cobb. Peay Vineyards, a favorite, has a vineyard in the remote coastal hills and makes exceptional wines from Pinot Noir, Chardonnay, Syrah, and white Rhône varieties. Copain, the label of Wells Guthrie, is notable for making a huge change in style in 2006, from big, blowsy wines to a low-alcohol, delicate style. Guthrie, who was a darling of critics and enthusiasts alike, risked alienating both camps to make Pinots and Syrahs that he could be proud to drink himself. It is this kind of courage and conviction that I wish pervaded all of California wine making.

THE SANTA CRUZ MOUNTAINS

This area, which lies about forty-five miles south of San Francisco in the high hills that separate Silicon Valley from the coast, does not boast many producers, but three of them are among my all-time favorites. First, there is the unparalleled Ridge Vineyards, whose Monte Bello is the greatest Cabernet-based wine outside of France. Winemaker Paul Draper, a gentleman and philosopher of wine, has always kept Ridge on the same path, despite the numerous trends in the marketplace that have swayed so many of his peers. His wines are consistently balanced and honest and never pander.

Mount Eden Vineyards, now owned by winemaker Jeff Patterson, is an almost forgotten treasure. One of the most historical wine places in California, it was planted in the late nineteenth century and became one of the best-known vineyards in the United States for outstanding varietal wines from grapes like Chardonnay and Pinot Noir, at a time when most American wines were field blends. Today, without ever reaching for the spotlight, Patterson still crafts wonderful wines in a classic style and prices them far lower than what comparable wines from other regions bring. I have drunk forty-year-old Pinot Noirs from this property that were positively extraordinary, and the Cabernets are even better.

Finally, in the vicinity, though not in the actual Santa Cruz Mountains, is Calera, the celebrated estate of Pinot fanatic Josh Jensen. A true pioneer, Jensen famously searched the length of the West Coast in the 1970s for limestone soil where he could realize his Burgundian dream. The spot he found, Mount Harlan, is an outpost, far removed from the wine-making mainstream. Yet Jensen made it work, no matter the challenges thrown him by drought and a fickle marketplace. His whole-cluster Pinots are among the best in the New World. The harvest I worked here crucially gave me my first hands-on experience in wine making.

This is where I make Parr Wines, under the guidance of Sashi Moorman. There aren't many examples from this region on my wine lists, however, as I require balanced wines of moderate alcohol levels. With few exceptions, such wines are still difficult to find in this vast area. There is a lot of potential, but the region is dominated by producers who rely on power, alcohol, and oak to make wines that will impress critics.

The exceptions are Au Bon Climat and Qupé, the iconic, cohabitating wineries run by, respectively, my friends and mentors Jim Clendenen and Bob Lindquist. Tireless advocates for wines of balance and restraint, Lindquist and, especially, Clendenen (the more vocal of the pair) have continuously practiced what they have preached for over twenty years. Their wines are still among California's best and age better than any other in their categories.

JIM CLENDENEN

ACKNOWLEDGMENTS

RAJAT PARR: It is incredibly gratifying to see this book realized, as I feel it is not just for me, but for all the sommeliers who have taught me, worked with me, and eaten and drunk with me over the years. Being a sommelier is a way of life, and all of us have been in it together.

None of this would have been possible without my parents, to whom I am extremely grateful for trusting me and letting me live my dream, even though it took me far from home. I must thank Michael Mina, a remarkable chef and partner. He has believed in me and given me everything I have asked for, enabling me to follow my vision. Jim Clendenen has been one of the most important figures in my life. He has helped me understand the grape in its purest form and been a true friend. And, finally, no one has impacted my life more than Larry Stone, who has been the kind of mentor and friend I wish everyone were lucky enough to have. It has been his guiding light that has illuminated my path as a sommelier and a teacher.

JORDAN MACKAY: Sommeliers are unique creatures. Although I am not one of them, I have been fortunate to spend most of my last few years surrounded by them, observing and absorbing their passion for work and life. Thanks to them all for welcoming me so warmly into their circle. Among them, a few stand out: First, there is Rajat, who has shared so much with me, including this book project. It has been a pleasure and an honor to spend time with such a busy guy. Larry Stone allowed me to learn from him when I didn't even work at his restaurant and then practically made me part of the family. And, finally, thanks to the greatest sommelier of them all, Christie Dufault, my wife, my love, and my inspiration. She was a huge part of this book, well beyond the printed word.

I would be remiss not to thank my mother, Leslie Geballe, who looked over the text at an early stage; my father, who has been a rock of support throughout; and my sister, Eden, and my niece, Clementine, who continuously bring joy to my life, a necessity during long hours of writing.

R.P. & J.M.: We are grateful to all the sommeliers, winemakers, and chefs who helped us with this book. They all took time out of their crowded schedules to talk and taste with us, making the experience of writing as much pleasure as work.

We would also like to acknowledge Carole Bidnick, who helped get the book deal done. And the team at Ten Speed has been phenomenal. Sharon Silva, our copyeditor, is a whiz. She contributed far more to the text than her title suggests. Thanks also to Clancy Drake for top-notch proofreading.

One thing that kept us going during the intense effort of producing this book was the occasional peek at the visuals created by our photographer and designer, Ed Anderson. We traveled with him in France and found him to be a fine road companion. But his photography has often left us speechless. By lending this book his remarkable eye, he has made it more beautiful than we ever could have hoped.

Finally, we acknowledge our editor, Aaron Wehner. Aaron spent countless hours and many late nights editing and proofing what proved to be a challenging project. He went far beyond the call of duty in improving the text, and this book is as much his as it is ours.

NORTHERN RHÔNE

INDEX

228

Published in the United States by Ten Speed Press, an imprint of
the Crown Publishing Group, a division of Random House, Inc.,
New York.
www.crownpublishing.com
www.tenspeed.com

Ten Speed Press and the Ten Speed Press colophon are registered
trademarks of Random House, Inc.

Library of Congress Cataloging-in-Publication Data

Parr, Rajat.
   Secrets of the sommeliers : how to think and drink like the
world's top wine professionals / Rajat Parr & Jordan Mackay ;
photography by Ed Anderson.
      p. cm.
   Includes index.
   1. Sommeliers. 2. Sommeliers—United States—Biography.
I. Mackay, Jordan. II. Anderson, Ed. III. Title.
TX925.P35 2010
641.2'2—dc22
                                                          2010022017

ISBN 978-1-58008-298-3

Printed in China

Design by Ed Anderson

11 10 9 8 7 6 5

First Edition